D0915700

GENDER AND CLASS CONSCIOUSNESS

GENDER AND CLASS CONSCIOUSNESS)

Pauline Hunt

HOLMES & MEIER PUBLISHERS, INC.
New York

First published in the United States of America by
HOLMES & MEIER PUBLISHERS, INC.
30 Irving Place, New York, N.Y. 10003

Library of Congress Cataloging in Publication Data

Hunt, Pauline.
  Gender and class consciousness
  Bibliography: p.
  Includes index.
  1. Sex role—Case studies.
  2. Labor and laboring classes—United States—
  Case studies.
  3. Housewives—United States—Case studies.
  4. Wives—Employment—United States—Case
  studies.
  5. Married people—Employment—United States—
  Case studies.
  I. Title.

HQ1075.H86   301.41   79-22107

ISBN 0-8419-0580-0

Printed in Hong Kong

Contents

Acknowledgements   vi

Introduction   I

1 Family and Ideology   7

2 This busy worker goes to market, and this
   busy worker stays home   37

3 Workers Side by Side   102

4 Conclusion   180

Appendix I Methodological Points   187

Appendix II Group 1, biographical data and
frequency of quotation in Chapter 1   193

Appendix III Group 2, biographical data and
frequency of quotation in Chapter 2   194

Appendix IV Group 3, biographical data and
frequency of quotation in Chapter 3   196

Bibliography   198

Index   203

Acknowledgements

I warmly thank the people of Silverdale who participated in this research, and who appear here with fictitious names. Their help was indispensable, as was the help of the SSRC who financed this research. I am grateful to Betty Matthews who provided the initial encouragement, to John Howell who willingly shared his knowledge of Silverdale people, and to Liz Brown for her interest and help when fieldwork was in progress. I would also like to thank Frank Bechhofer, Harry Christian and Jaap Van Velsen, who read the first draft of the manuscript and who made many helpful suggestions and criticisms. I am particularly indebted to Ron Frankenberg who accompanied me to Silverdale clubs and pubs, to some of the homes, turned his hand to photography, who, for a brief period, took up residence in Silverdale, read and discussed each draft almost while the ink was still wet, and whose suggestions concerning theory and methodology have qualitatively improved the work.

Finally, the publishers and I are grateful to the following who have kindly given permission for the use of copyright material: Labour Research for the table from *Labour Research*, 1978; National Labour Women's Advisory Committee for the table in 'Obstacles' from *Women in Politics* folder; and Punch Publications Ltd for the extract from the poem 'The Proper Study' by W. S. Slater.

Introduction

Those who approach history from a feminist standpoint have stressed that patriarchy, in a variety of forms, has characterised human society for thousands of years. What marks out Capitalism is not the subjection of women as such, since this pre-dates Capitalism, but the privatisation of domestic labour and the exclusion of women from social labour, which serves to reproduce the subjection of women in a specifically capitalist form.

Thus as Angela Weir points out:

> In other historical epochs the family was more or less co-determinous with the unit of production, although women were still subjugated within it. Under capitalism the family ceased to have a direct relationship with production and women and children were gradually excluded from the factories, mines and workshops . . . Women began to labour in the home to reproduce male labour power for the market. (Weir, 1974, p. 218)

As a result the domestic worker became totally dependent on incoming wages (Gardiner, 1974, p. 246). Even when the domestic worker also worked in industry, the separation between women's work in the family and work for wages created a situation in which women never quite came to see themselves as wage earners (Rowbotham, 1973, p. 33), and the belief took root that men's wages ought to be enough to support the entire family (Oren, 1974, p. 227).

Awareness of women's confinement to a narrow domestic sphere, and her consequent dependency, forms a backcloth to many feminist studies of the broad cultural ramifications of woman's position within capitalist society. Mary Wollstonecraft, writing in 1792, relates shallow, vain aspects of 'feminine' psychology to women's confinement to a lap-dog existence. Betty Friedan (1963) provides a similar explanation for the apparent vacuousness of the modern American housewife, although, as one might expect in a more consumer-oriented era, Friedan has much to say about mass-media manipulation of the feminine psyche. Shulamith Firestone (1971) explores in vivid terms the development of capitalism and the nuclear family, the new dependency of women on men and children on adults, and the resulting sexual, cultural and aesthetic distortions which characterise modern social relationships.

The scope of this work is less grand. I share the view that, in order to understand the position of women in Capitalist Society, it is necessary to take the physical separation of the family unit from social production as its central feature. In this work, however, a theme of equal importance is the underlying integration of the family unit and social production, in the sense that each sphere constitutes the condition of existence of the other. In fact the contradiction between the apparent separation, but actual integration, of the domestic and industrial arena provides the theoretical framework for the study of gender and class consciousness presented here.

Rather surprisingly such a study has not been conducted in any detail previously. On the contrary, as Sheila Rowbotham has observed, 'As the separation of production-work and reproduction-childbearing and the family have become physically separated in space . . . there has been a tendency in sociology to study these areas in isolation' (Rowbotham, 1972, p. 70).

One example, noted by Richard Brown (1976), of the failure to approach industrial studies in the context of the division between home and work, and the related division between men and women in industry, is the tendency to treat employees as 'unisex'. Not only may this lead the research worker unwisely to assume that conclusions based on the study of one sex are applicable to the other, but it may also severely limit the usefulness of the industrial study undertaken.

Of the latter failing I can speak from personal experience. Between 1970 and 1972 I was engaged in a study of the Upper Clyde Shipbuilding Workers' work-in. Despite being female I had been so well socialised into the male ethos of industrial sociology that I did not pause to consider if it was relevant that the overwhelming majority of the workers involved were male, or what consequences could follow from the social and domestic position of male shipyard workers, and the ideology which shaped their position. Blissfully unaware of the relevance of the workers' family situation I focused almost exclusively on social relationships within the shipyard and thought that in so doing I was conducting an adequate study of class consciousness. Looking back I can see that the shipyard workers self-definition and position as family breadwinners was intimately related to their demand for the right to work, their experience of the work-in, and to the relative success their campaign scored in the Clyde community.

Some industrial studies avoid an over narrow focus on the industrial workplace by considering the domestic commitments of the workers concerned. Generally, emphasis is given to the problems women workers encounter as a result of their double job burden as houseworkers and wageworkers. This problem of a double workload has been explored from both the employers' and the employees' viewpoint in a whole series of studies from the comprehensive study by Myrdal and Klein (1956), through many successors listed by Brown (1976, pp. 27-8), culminating in the study of problems and options confronting working couples edited by Rhona Rapoport and Robert N. Rapoport (1978). These studies frequently recommend proposals, directed at governments, trade unions and employers, aimed at easing the double work burden which weighs most heavily on women workers.

However factually informative, such studies are often theoretically unsatisfactory. As Richard Brown says:

> this category of research . . . contributes very little to an under-standing of the sociological problems raised by the employment of women in societies like our own . . . These problems can be stated as: in what ways do sexual divisions in society affect the social consciousness of workers who otherwise have in common that they sell their labour power in the market; and how far can comparisons between men and women increase our understand-ing of the nature and determinants of workers' orientations towards and actions in the work situation? (Brown, 1976, pp. 29-30)

Feminist writers have made some impact on this situation. For example Ross Davies (1975), Adams and Laurikietis (1976) and Machie and Pattullo (1977) explore the obstacles confronting women in the labour market in the form of deadend, monotonous, poorly paid jobs, which result from socialisation into conventional gender roles, inadequate training and education of females, family and household responsibilities, discrimination against women by employers and trade unions and inadequate state-provided facilities for the care of children and reduction of housework. Such studies do not, however, fully meet Richard Brown's criticism since they do not address themselves to an investigation of the ramification gender-related experiences and ideologies have on the development of class consciousness and practice.

In this study I make an attempt to fill this gap by exploring the integration of domestic and industrial production, and how the two sexes are differently related to this double production process, both in general structural terms and at different stages of the life-cycle of the family. I am equally concerned with ideological conceptions which obscure the interdependence of industrial and domestic production, notably by emphasising gender differences between men serving as breadwinners and women serving as homemakers. I then discuss different tendencies which characterise male and female workers in the light of their different relationship to the double production process, and the way in which conventional ideology reinforces or conflicts with their practical experience.

Although I regard this work as an attempt to theorise an as yet largely unexplored terrain, the initial ground-clearing has been done for me by the Women's Liberation Movement. Sheila Rowbotham has pointed this out. Until recent times, workers' consciousness was seen as developing primarily at the industrial point of production. If a wider field of view is embraced which includes the social relations of reproduction in the family, the theory of consciousness is off to a new start, made possible by the Women's Liberation Movement, which 'directs attention to precisely these areas which have remained in theoretical obscurity within Marxist theory' (Rowbotham, 1972, p. 70).

The research has been structured round long conversations with three types of households:

GROUP 1 Married couples, no children, both wage earners.
GROUP 2 Married couples one of whom is a fulltime house worker, children.
GROUP 3 Married couples, both wage earners, children.

Although these groups have been studied synchronically, general experience suggests that most couples move through these three situations chronologically, and return to the situation of group one as retirement approaches.

The three situations lend themselves to different questions which have a bearing on the connection between home and work. A discussion of the methodology used in this research will be found in the appendix I, together with an explanation of the codes used for references. Here I want to preview the questions to be addressed in the following pages.

In Chapter 1 I explore the following questions: How does socialisation into gender and work-roles develop in the family of origin? What effect does the anticipation of future gender roles have on the socialisation process? In the case of couples without children the burden of domestic work is at a minimum; in this less pressurised situation are household chores shared to a greater extent than in the other type of households? How does family ideology influence behaviour at home and in the market place?

In Chapter 2 the questions are focused on Group 2 families, that is families in which one spouse, usually the woman, works full time in the home. I refer to such workers as houseworkers rather than housewives in order to include the minority of households where the man is the houseworker. In this chapter I consider the following questions: What production processes take place within the family? What is the sexual division of labour within the family? Do couples in this group regard the industrial wage as joint payment for work done in the home as well as in industry, or does the wage earner have more control of the wage than the houseworker? Is the relationship between husband and wife less egalitarian in group two households compared to group one and group three household? If so, is such inequality reinforced by state agencies? To what extent are houseworkers isolated from the world of organised labour?

In Chapter 3, which is concerned with group three households, a new set of questions is considered: What, if any, adjustments are occasioned in the domestic division of labour when both parents go out to work? Are housework standards redefined where there is less time available for domestic tasks? Of the woman's two jobs which is regarded as basic by the husband?—by the wife? What are the implications of the choice? Are relationships between the spouses more equal in group three households in comparison to group two households? If so does this greater equality extend to control of the households' money? How deeply involved do women become in the world of work? What is the relationship, if any, between the oppositional class consciousness of men and women outside the home and their domestic attitudes and behaviour?

I hope that by exploring these sets of questions it will be possible to arrive at a more comprehensive picture of the connections between family structure and the economic, social and political structure of capitalist society.

In capitalist society the division between industrial production and domestic production is the foundation of the gender division between men, primarily seen and acting as breadwinners, and women, primarily seen and acting as homemakers.

In this work the family is treated as a production unit in contrast to the work of most sociologists, for example, J. H. Goldthorpe *et al* (1968, 1969) and M. Young and P. Willmott (1973), who talk about the family almost exclusively in terms of consumption, thereby neglecting both the fact that nearly all goods brought into the home require some additional work before they become consumable, as well as the domestic production and servicing of labour-power.

The division between industrial production and domestic production has a marked impact on gender behaviour, in the form of orientation towards work, in the privatisation of the plans and goals made by family members, in the domestic division of labour, in the control of money and in the exercise of power and authority in family life. Conversely, gender divisions have an impact on the industrial sector; in the development of a male and female labour market, in the definition and limitation of workers' industrial goals and struggles, in the development of class consciousness, and in the formation of trade-union policy objectives.

1 Family and Ideology

Long before a woman has children and fully experiences the socially imposed responsibilities of motherhood and domesticity she has embraced the characteristics of womanhood which are rooted in the domestic functions reserved for her sex. Long before a man assumes the task of supporting a family he has defined himself as a future wage earner. The socialisation of men into workers and women into life-long assistants to men begins with the infant's first social contacts and continues for a lifetime.

Men also, of course, form personal attachments, and women work for a lifetime inside and outside the house. However, it remains true that the man's foothold in the work-a-day world is basic to his concept of masculine selfhood, and the woman's intimate relations with others are basic to her concept of feminine selfhood. The work-a-day world seems to offer broader scope for the validation of masculinity than does the arena of intimate relations for the validation of femininity.

The social relationships children encounter equip them to seek out selfhood primarily in one or other of these arenas, depending on their adoption of male or female gender. I use the term 'adoption' to avoid the idea of socialisation as a process imposed upon a passive recipient. Rather, I think Kohlberg (1974) is correct to argue that once gender identity stabilises, at about the same age as the child acquires language, the child henceforth structures experience in accordance with his or her gender identity. Kohlberg contrasts his theoretical position with that held by social learning theorists:

> The social learning syllogism is 'I want rewards, I am rewarded for doing boy things, therefore I want to be a boy'. In contrast, a cognitive theory assumes this sequence: 'I am a boy, therefore I want to do boy things, therefore the opportunity to do boy things (and to gain approval for doing them) is rewarding'. (Kohlberg, 1974, p. 139)

7

Once stabilised, gender identity becomes a basic means by which lived experiences are defined and recollected. It is, therefore, extremely difficult to change sex role assignment once gender identity has been established. This statement presupposes that important social differences are linked with gender distinctions. It is only the existence of socially reproduced distinctions between male and female practice which invests gender identity with this comprehensive cognitive significance. The fact that gender is a significant distinction in a large number of situations is a social rather than a biological fact.

I want briefly to document some masculine/feminine distinctions and relate these to men and women's places within the family, and to the family's place within society. Although my discussion is confined to modern capitalist society, a more general distinction between the active and assertive male and the domesticated woman straddles history. As E. Sullerot has observed:

> Woman was confined indoors, turned into a recluse and often hidden, like the Chinese behind screens and the Moslem behind veils, while man alone had the freedom of the outside world. Socrates claimed that it was thus that the gods had decreed. But this territorial division quickly became a moral one—'the house is for the good woman, the street for the wicked one' said Menander, repeating a popular cliché. Consequently activities within the home are feminine, those which take place outside— business, politics, war—are masculine. (Sullerot, 1971, p. 23)

Sociologists have often made similar ahistorical assumptions about gender differences. Durkheim is an extreme case. We are told that man's aspirations and humour have in large part a collective origin 'while his companion's are more directly influenced by her organism'. This distinction encourages Durkheim to suggest that social activities should correspond with gender related capacities— 'Why for instance, should not aesthetic functions become woman's as man, more and more absorbed by functions of utility, has to renounce them?' (1972, p. 385) Parsons's distinction between expressive and instrumental roles is, of course, a direct continuation of this line of thought.

The socialisation of children occurs initially in the family; a family which has a specific relation to society, the function of which has been clearly spelt out by Judith and Alan Hunt:

The general function of the family is the reproduction of the social relations of production. It needs to be insisted that 'reproduction' is only minimally biological. Procreation is therefore only one aspect of the family's function. Of much greater importance is the process of socialisation including learning gender that goes on within the family, and the servicing of the labour force.

Individuals are born into social classes, but they are socialised into their class position. Thus working class boys learn to accept as natural a lifetime as wage earners; their sisters learn to accept as natural a lifetime as adjuncts to the male. (Hunt and Hunt, 1974, p. 59)

It is to this socialising process that we now turn.

ADULTS AND CHILDREN

Most adults who have had personal experience of male and female children assert that there are marked differences. From their accounts it seems that girls are quieter, more obedient, and less assertive than boys. Thus Mrs Munden comments: 'Girls are girls and boys are boys. I think boys are rougher. We've got a nephew, he's three now, and he likes a rough roll around.' (B1, p. 17)

Mr and Mrs Arnold make a similar point:

PETER ARNOLD: There's a vast difference between boys and girls. I think a girl's still a girl.
MARY ARNOLD: My Kate's still a girl. Our Lawrence would sit here and let our Kate wait on him wouldn't he? He'd love it, and my other son did.
PETER: Boys are boys. We've got two grandsons now. If you were to pick them up they don't like it. But start playing rough with them and they like it.
Would you play rough with your granddaughters?
MARY: No. We don't do that with our granddaughters do we? We treat them like little ladies.
PETER: Oh they are different. My son's little girl, Pat, she sits by her mum all day doesn't she? And when Linda brings her girls they've got the crayoning books out and they'll draw all the time. But when the other daughter's boys come down they run round and play up the field don't they?

MARY: Oh yes. As soon as they get here they want their boots on. (D1, pp. 32-3)

In most cases those who report such differences between males and females also approve of the differences. Jeff and Wendy James, on the other hand, are amongst the minority of adults who criticise an over-emphasis on differences associated with gender.

If you had a child would you bring it up in the same way whether it was a boy or girl?
WENDY: Oh yes. I wouldn't for example stop a boy baking.
JEFF: Definitely not! There was a boy in my class who was incredibly good at cookery. He got a real kick out of that, and I certainly would not have insisted that he did metalwork or anything. I've known girls to be very good at what are generally considered to be masculine things. (A1, pp. 42-3)

Joyce Atkin, who will be discussed in the next chapter, and Sarah, who appears in the third chapter, have both attempted with their own children to break down traditional gender specialisation. The majority of parents, however, seem to accept traditional gender differences, and it seems to me to be largely true that:

> With sons, socialisation seems to be focused primarily on directing and constraining the boy's impact on the environment. With daughters the aim is rather to protect the girl from the impact of environment. The boy is being prepared to mould his world, the girl to be moulded by it. (Bronfenbrenner, quoted by Freeman, 1974)

Fathers seem to be marginally more concerned than mothers with 'correct' gender training, and both parents seem to be more concerned with the adequacy of a son's masculinity than a daughter's feminity. These two factors are closely related. Fathers seem to feel a special need to introduce their sons into the masculine world and mothers may well sense that, by implication, femininity is being slighted. For example, Janet Austin observes:

> I don't think there would be any difference between boys and girls if it wasn't for the parents. There's a little girl next door but one, the same age as him (her three year old). She was playing

with him on Saturday. The father came and knocked on the door and said, 'Do you mind, only he's playing with dolls and prams?' I said, 'He loves dolls and prams', 'cos he *does*. In fact he pretends he can visualise a baby in his arms sometimes and there's nothing there. And he'll go like that (Janet performs a rocking motion). He'll carry it sometimes for half a day, and suddenly he forgets and it's dropped sort of thing. But I think if it wasn't for parents— like my husband. If the older one (six years) comes in crying, 'Don't be such a sissie! You're just like a girl.' I said, 'He's every right to cry if he wants to! What's wrong with being like a girl anyway?' (G2, pp. 39–40)

Andrew Austin says proudly that he is trying to 'toughen up' the six year old. Since young boys, like young girls, do by and large grow up in a woman's world, the masculine socialisation of the boy is more problematic than the feminine socialisation of the girl. As Firestone (1971) has pointed out, a boy's tie with his mother and sister has to be severed before he can take up in full his place in the man's world. If the transition is successful he will be motivated to masculine goals, like these described by Andrew Austin:

If I had money I'd have a job where I was walking about in a suit and tie, driving a big car. I'd have a business and be the boss, and I'd have a big house built in the middle of a golf course. (H2, p. 22)

The need to toughen a boy so that he is equal to life's trials is taken very seriously by many parents. In the daughter's case the aim is to equip her with feminine desirability which, one can only suppose, is intended to enable her to win a protector rather than to protect herself. Even parents who are unconventional in some respects take gender training seriously. Gill and Mark Carter, for example, are unconventional in that they have changed places; Gill goes out to work and Mark stays home to care for their baby son. Their attitude to gender roles, however, is very traditional:

MARK: If he'd been a girl I'd have thought twice about staying home.
Why is that?
MARK: Well, a lad can sort of—I mean, there's a sort of boundary between a male and a female. If a young girl's with her mother she'll

act like her mother, you know, be more feminine. But if she was with her father all the time it wouldn't work, she'd develop big muscles and things like that. So if it had been a girl it would have been a lot different.

But usually mothers bring up little boys.

MARK: Oh yes, but I would feel different about it myself. I feel much better with him being a lad.

So you can show him how to be a man?

MARK: That's it, yes.

How do you do that with such a young child?

MARK: I think more things creative, building models and things for him. I look forward to when he's got more understanding and I can teach him things I know.

Things you wouldn't teach a little girl?

MARK: I couldn't teach a little girl to go fishing or tie a knot.

Why not?

MARK: I could do, but I wouldn't feel it was right. I like a girl to be feminine.

Do you feel like that?

GILL: I understand Mark's point. He's a boy and he means to bring him up as a little boy, and show him all the things he used to do—football, and up the woods playing, that sort of thing. I think that's the point he's trying to stress. He's not going to be crying at every little thing. If he cries he'll just push him on one side.

Couldn't you behave like that with a girl?

GILL: I don't think he'd have the patience with a girl, you know, playing with little dollies. He's sort of roughing him up a lot. He's hardening him, even though he's so young. You wouldn't believe it he's so hard with him. He buys him things which are for the future sort of thing. His father lives for the future and what he's going to teach him when he gets older.

You wouldn't roughen up a little girl like that?

MARK: No. As I said, I like to make a boy a boy and a girl a girl. Do you see what I mean? Dress her in pretty dresses and things like that. I wouldn't be able to teach her how to become a lady.

You could go fishing with her.

MARK: Yes, but I wouldn't want that. I wouldn't want a girl wandering round with a shot gun and that.

Did you play with dolls when you were little Gill?

GILL: No I was rougher, up trees and in the woods. I wasn't keen on dolls and prams.

Do you think Gill is feminine?

MARK: No!

Is that good or bad?

MARK: The situation we've got is very good. It's a funny thing actually. I'm not running down Women's Liberation. I agree with equal rights and that sort of thing. But I like women to keep on their own side of the fence. I don't like women to act like fellows, climbing trees with dresses on.

What if she wore jeans?

MARK: That's the same sort of thing. I prefer a young girl to play with young girls and dress nice, and lads to be lads. I don't mind women having their own opinion.

GILL: Well I don't know. I really enjoyed myself playing with boys, I mean, there were girls there as well. If I had a girl and she wanted to go climbing with the boys it wouldn't bother me. If she wanted to she wanted to. (K2, pp. 20–2)

I have included this interview exchange at some length because I think it illustrates a number of tendencies. Although Mark Carter's concern with the trappings of femininity is somewhat unusual, the Carters' concern with masculinity, defined in terms of activity, toughness and non-emotionalism, seems to be typical of the majority of parents. Furthermore I think it is evident that Mark sees his son as an extension of his own life project, which he defines in masculine terms. Again I think this is a general feature of father-son relationships.

Self-realisation through one's offspring is not likely to be this clear cut in the case of mother-daughter relationships. If we assume that the mother structures her life in feminine terms she is nevertheless less likely to impose such feminine conceptions dogmatically upon her daughter. This is not merely because of the possibility that, like Gill, she may remember her own youthful flirtations with masculine conduct. The main reason is that activities associated with men are indeed more challenging, interesting, and carry more prestige than activities associated with feminine conduct. Most parents, and particularly mothers, indulge their 'tomboy' daughters, who seek to enjoy the excitement of boy-type activities. This female divergence from gender norms is more socially acceptable, even laudable, than male deviation from gender norms. As Sue Sharpe has observed: 'Being called a "sissie", with its feminine connotations, has a negative value. Being a "tomboy" is much more positive, and is a label that can be taken with pride.' (1976, p. 83)

It is not therefore surprising that over a third of the women I talked with announced spontaneously that they had been tomboys in their youth, whereas not one man let it be known that he had been a sissie.

SOCIALISATION INTO ADULT WORK

Indulgence towards gender deviations, whether in the case of boys or girls has a time limit. As school days draw to a close it is felt to be time that adult-gender was embraced. Janet Austin expresses a general attitude when she says:

> When I was young I always had guns and cars. I can't see that it hurts at all. I let them play with anything, whatever they like. I think it does them good; if he wants to play with dolls, alright. But perhaps if he was about fifteen and wanted to play with dolls I'd worry, you know. (G2, p. 41)

It is, of course, not just parents who wish to steer their children towards appropriate adult-gender objectives. Olive Braman (1977), in her analysis of comics, identifies the under ten–over ten age division as an important transition period for girls:

> *Mandy* . . . is full of splendid girls like Fay Fearless, Secret Agent, Baby-faced Bobbie, a policewoman, and the Amazing Valda, who dives into the depths of the ocean to rescue a trapped diver . . .
>   Unfortunately at the age of ten-plus *Mandy* gives way to *Jackie*, *Diana*, *Pink*, *Valentine*, and then what happens to our heroines? . . . all their talents evaporate and the sole focus of their attention is boys and how to get them.

If we think about the different tasks men and women are expected to perform in our society, and the capacities associated with those tasks, we are able to appreciate why certain practices are regarded as masculine and others as feminine. It is expected that men will work in industry for all of their active years, and that during part of this time they will support a non-employed wife and children. In the case of women it is expected that although part of their adult years will be spent in industry, for a period they will occupy themselves on a full-time basis with caring for the needs of their husband and children. The fact that most men cannot adequately support a family financially without the addition of female earnings, and the fact that women spend a far greater proportion of their lives in industry than in full-time maternity, has not invalidated the distinction between man the breadwinner and woman the wife and mother. The fact that the breadwinning aspect of the man's life and the domestic and maternal aspect of the woman's life are singled out as typifying their situation is rooted in ideology, but such ideology produces effects which have their own potency at the economic and political level of social practice.

The capacities which facilitate breadwinning are different from the capacities associated with homemaking. In capitalist society the labour market is a harshly competitive and insecure place, and those destined to be life-long contestants in the market place require some 'toughening up'. On the other hand those who will require support during a period of non-earning maternity will need to acquire attractive and accommodating characteristics in order to win and retain such support.

It is not my intention here to document how these different gender capacities are built in and fostered by the educational system, the mass media and the labour market context within which children mature. This has been well done by others. I am primarily concerned with how anticipation of adult-gender roles influences behaviour in the family. Socialisation within the family is likely to be very effective because, particularly for the young child, the family serves as a shield against the non-familiar world. Such protection, however, enhances the influence of the protectors, as Morgan has noted in his discussion of the work of Laing and Esterson: '. . . at one and the same time a parent may be creating a particularly binding form of relationship to the child (that of protector) and also defining the nature of the outside world for the child' (Morgan, 1975, p. 111).

The family itself, of course, not only differs according to social class but is also subject to social change. There is a marked difference in the childhood experiences of those who grew up in working class homes in the 1920s and 1930s, compared with those whose working class childhoods occurred in the 1940s and 1950s.

The older age groups spent a lot of their childhood working. In the case of boys, gardening was a common occupation. The boy worked on the family allotment side by side with his father. Such labour was required to supplement the family diet. Other forms of occupation,—errand boy, milk boy, paper boy—supplemented the family income.

Although girls' work was by and large home based, where the mother took in work, notably washing, the children, male or female, were drawn into the domestic toil. In the case of Peter Arnold, his mother's laundry work represented a vital component of the family income, and everyone, including his father, was involved:

PETER ARNOLD: We used to take laundry in from different people. It was a full-time job. Me mother used to go up Hanley to fetch washing. My sisters and I used to go out on a Monday morning to fetch washing from different houses. We used to have it tied round us, two or three different bundles at a time. It had to be tied on because we weren't very big, otherwise we should have had to have made several journeys. We used to bring it in. My mother would be washing all day Monday and Tuesday. It was very hard. We never had much time for pleasure. We had to take it back again when my mother had washed and ironed it. We took it back in a big basket.

Did she get much for doing it?

PETER: Oh, no. She'd only get a penny in those days, for doing a sheet or a shirt. They were all master potters, and people like that, because in those days it was only people like that who could afford to have their washing sent out.

It must have been very hard work.

PETER: Really hard work, very hard. Me mother's tub was the old dolly tub, and it was solid iron. That used to heat on the gas stove. And of course it was the old fashioned mangle in those days.

Did any of the children do ironing?

PETER: Oh yes we did, I did, we were all involved.

MARY ARNOLD: They never saw a fire because there was always washing round. They were on from morning 'till night.

PETER: The laundry stood round on clothes pegs. Even in the depths of winter we never saw a fire, only on a Sunday when everything was cleared away.

Was your father down the pit in the daytime?

PETER: He was down the pit, but even when he came in from work the laundry wasn't got out of the way. Even in the summer it was risky drying the washing outside, because there was a lot of smoke about in those days and it could get dirty while it was drying on the line.

Did your father do any ironing?

PETER: My father used to iron as well as my mother. It was a way of life then. We had to do, because it was a way of getting a few coppers. (D1, pp. 3-5)

The fact that children and boys in particular, had a certain earning capacity in pre-war times, did nothing to alter their subordinate position within the home. Not only were part-time earnings handed over to the parent, usually the mother, but full-time earnings were also relinquished in return for which the son or daughter was paid pocket money. Thus the material dependency of childhood continued well into adult life. Usually the pocket money arrangement continued up to marriage, and where the newly weds lived in the parental home this arrangement could continue after marriage.

In pre-war days the parents' word was taken to be law. Both men and women report that right up to the day of their marriage when they went out for an evening a deadline was fixed for their return. Usually they had to be back by nine or ten o'clock at night. Failure to meet the deadline could be harshly punished, as Bill Ross reports:

BILL: We had to be in by half past nine to ten o'clock at night, and the trouble was you couldn't rely on 'buses in our area, and while we were courting Pam lived about two miles away, and with it being country you had to run through fields if you missed the last 'bus. My father would be standing by the back door, and when I was being hit I couldn't put a fist up, nothing like that.

Did he hit you with anything?

BILL: With a big buckle and a belt. (C1, p. 19)

This harshness may well seem shocking by modern standards. Most people who report such sternness, however, defend the old regime on the grounds that it taught the young to respect their elders. Mr Peter Arnold without doubt respected his mother:

PETER: I never answered my mother back, not till the day she died.

MARY: And she was 89 then.

PETER: Yes, I never answered my mother back, even when I knew she was wrong I never answered her back. (D1, p. 36)

Peter Arnold's attitude towards his first and second wife make it clear that he respected his mother because she was older, not because she was female:

PETER: Even when I was married I still turned my wages up to my mother, not to my wife, because after I was married I lived with my mother for seven years.
Was your wife going out to work?
PETER: No she was at home with my mother.
Did your mother pay her housekeeping money?
PETER: No because my mother used to keep us, we lived with my mother.
Did your mother give you pocket money?
PETER: She gave me pocket money yes.
Did she give your wife pocket money?
PETER: Not to my knowledge, no. I suppose what she gave me she thought that was for both of us. (D1, p. 37)

Peter Arnold's present wife is less financially dependent on him than his first wife. She has a part-time cleaning job and Peter is retired. Despite this greater financial equality, however, Peter makes it clear that he is the boss:

Would you say one of you has more say about things than the other?
PETER: We both share responsibility, but what I say has *got* to go.
What kind of things do you have in mind?
PETER: If I said a thing I should mean it.
Say you were wondering about buying something.
PETER: If I said 'no' it would be no!
What if you didn't agree?
MARY: I accept it.
PETER: Because I should know if we could afford it.
Wouldn't you both know that?
PETER: Yes but she'd be more inclined to go into debt than I would.
So you think you're the boss?
PETER: As regards that end, I should say yes. (D1, pp. 34–5)

The post-war generation has had different childhood experiences. Poverty has, perhaps only temporarily, lost its biting hold, and the extra pennies child labour can bring in are not coveted. Children are indulged. They receive gifts and pocket money. Part-time earnings are regarded as the child's property. When young people leave school and go out to work they retain the best part of their wages.

Parents are not merely more relaxed about money; there has been a general relaxation of parental discipline. This partly expresses itself in children's release from chores, both inside and outside the home. While it remains true that girls do more domestic work than boys, in most families girls seem required to do relatively little domestic work, unless they choose to do it. On this point, however, the real test comes when mother either isn't around, or when she cannot cope single handed. In these situations it is still the women folk rather than the men folk who fill-in for the mother.

Jean Spencer, for example, needs help fairly regularly because she has a family of nine children to cater for. Jean recognises that her eldest daughter Jane is her main helper:

JEAN: She helps me more than any of them, being the eldest girl. She's always done it. The boy who's seventeen, he'll go outside and clean windows, which saves 35p a week . . . I've never let Jane climb a ladder, I think that's a lad's job. She does everything else. She's pretty good at everything really, washing, cleaning, ironing. (C2, pp. 80–1)

George, Jean's seventeen year old son, takes it for granted that Jean and Jane are interchangeable:

My snap-in is always done by mum or Jane.

Although there are occasions when George is the only adult at home, he sees his duties in terms of masculine supervision:

When mum and dad are out who cares for baby?
GEORGE: If Jane was in, she would. But if I was in I would. I won't leave little ones.
Do you feel confident changing nappies?
GEORGE: Well Judy or Debbie are usually in. I leave it to them. I make sure they do it properly. I don't think I've changed one yet.

You make sure they do it properly.

GEORGE: Yes. I don't think I could do one. (E1, p. 3)

It is far from unusual for daughters to be drawn into housework and childcare to a greater extent than sons, and for most girls, domestic science lessons in school are backed up with practical experience in the home.

However, the main processes through which children are socialised into adult roles operate less directly than this. The general pattern of relationships which surrounds children teaches its own implicit lessons. For example, George's father, Paul Spencer, works in a Silverdale factory for a full seven days each week. His two year old daughter Sally is used to his daily exits and entrances. Recently Paul was away from work through sickness. It was the first time Sally had known him to be home in the day time. She enjoyed his company at home but each evening she would position herself at the door to meet him on his return from work. Sally has understood that fathers regularly go out to work before she is old enough to understand that you can't be in two places at once.

Sally's whole family operates with a 'taken-for-granted' conception of the breadwinner's role. Jean Spencer, for example, says of her eldest son:

Richard goes to work all week in the pit, so I don't expect him to do anything. (C2, p. 82)

George is not slow to take advantage of this attitude:

Are there any jobs in the house you do regularly?

GEORGE: Well I used to do a lot of tidying up. But now I've started work I just don't do it.

Because you work?

GEORGE: Well I pay board and I think I've got a right not to.

Since in Jean's view a good husband is defined in terms of a steady wage earner and little else, it is perhaps not surprising that George sees his new earning capacity as a passport to a new status within the family. When George thinks about his own family of the future he bases it on his present family:

If you ever had a child, do you think you may stay home with your child while your wife goes out to work?
GEORGE: No. Well later she would have the choice of going out to work, but I want to go as well.

Suppose you both wanted to go out to work, rather than stay home with the child.
GEORGE: Well, I'd see who was earning most money in their job, and whoever it was that would be the person who would go out to work.

How would you share money as a couple?
GEORGE: Well I'd hand it over and take pocket money. Me Dad hands his over and has pocket money.

If you were at home full-time, do you think your wife should hand her wage to you and you pay her pocket money?
GEORGE: No. If I wasn't at work she could just give me pocket money and keep her wages.

Why is that best?
GEORGE: Well she would probably know more about running the house than I would, shopping and that.

So she would need the wages to buy groceries.
GEORGE: Yes.

Why do you think she would do more in the house than you?
GEORGE: Well women do most of the shopping. You very rarely see a husband going down the street for a pound of potatoes. Round here you don't anyway. (E1, pp. 14–15)

Although George is blunt I think he represents most young men in the sense that the home-making side of marriage is given little thought, and it certainly does not influence their attitude to employment. Matters are quite different with girls. Sue Sharpe, in her investigation of Ealing School pupils, has shown the narrowness of the range of job preferences sought by female school leavers. The most popular job was office work, followed by teacher, nurse, shop assistant, bank clerk, followed by receptionist, telephonist, air hostess, hairdresser, children's nurse or nanny. This narrow range of preference accounted for three quarters of all jobs sought.

As Sue Sharpe points out, these jobs represent a continuation of the feminine role, since they involve a large component of caring and looking after others (see also Stacey, 1960, p. 136).

Having stated their preferences, the girls were then asked what job they would have chosen had they been a boy. Most girls selected skilled work which was often the hoped for career choices of their boyfriends or boys in their forms. If the job chosen was different from their previous job choice they were asked why they did not choose it as a girl. The replies mainly demonstrated that school leavers are well aware of what is or is not women's work:

> It's a man's job. I'd look silly in a pair of dirty overalls under a car. (Mechanic)
> Girls are not interested in engineering. (Engineer)
> You do not hear of any female executives. (Executive) (Sharpe, 1976, p. 173)

And so on. Some girls did at least show some awareness of the social processes which conditioned their choices:

> They never want a girl mechanic. (Mechanic)
> This job is wanted by men mostly and they have more chance of getting it because a lot of people like men driving instructors better than women. (Driving Instructor)
> People would say it's not done for a girl to do this. But if I had guts I would. (Electrician) (Sharpe, 1976, p. 174)

The girls' job choices reflect the real employment prospects open to them as well as traditional ideas about male and female work. Furthermore the popular job choices relate to woman's other role as wife and mother. Of these London girls, 75 per cent would have preferred to have been born girls had they been given the choice. Looking at the attitudes of these pro-female girls it was found that traditional feminine activities were central to their concerns. They were anticipating the 'joys and satisfactions of becoming wives and mothers and caring for homes and children'. (Sharpe, 1976, p. 206)

In the light of this it is not surprising to learn that in an unpublished survey by Anna Coote and Laura King (1973) '97 per cent of the girls between the ages of fifteen and eighteen years who were asked about their working plans said they would work after marriage, (43 per cent part-time and 54 per cent full-time), and although 91 per cent said they would not work before their children went to school, 93 per cent said they would work while they were at school . . .' (Sharpe, 1976, p. 197)

It is worthy of note that 46 per cent of these girls once married would, before starting a family, either not go out to work at all or only on a part-time basis. In other words 46 per cent of the girls surveyed imply that breadwinning is primarily a male responsibility.

Small though my interview groups are they offer some evidence of this outlook in practice. Two women out of the seven interviewed in group two, where one spouse was employed full-time in the home, said that they had or were about to take on part-time work before the birth of their child, and a third altered her job to fit in with her husband's wishes.

This was Joyce Atkin. Joyce gave up her hairdressing job because her husband objected to the long hours of work involved. Thus Joyce put her then childless home before career considerations.

Ann Tate did not feel she had a career to sacrifice. Ann was tired of office work and welcomed the 'escape' her marriage offered.

ANN: I had been thinking about taking a part-time job for a while before I knew I was pregnant. In fact I'd applied for a part-time job. Then the day after I heard I'd got the job the doctor told me I was expecting so I didn't take it.

Why did you want to go part-time?

ANN: Well I felt I wanted to be at home more. I'd been working full-time for a long time, and I felt I'd like to be at home more so I could do more at home. (A2, p. 24)

Maureen Clark gave up both her career and full-time work when she got married. This is somewhat surprising in Maureen's case because she acknowledges that her work had made her very independent. Maureen left home as soon as she left school to take up a residential post in a children's home. She married in her late twenties and continued to work for six years, but mainly on a part-time basis. Although Maureen's job ceased to be residential after her marriage her husband found that it intruded into their 'private' life:

MAUREEN: My last job was in fact in a flower shop in Newcastle.

Did you prefer that to working with children?

MAUREEN: No I prefer to work with children but my husband—you see, when you work with children you have to bring a certain amount of work home with you, and he was not prepared for me to work at home.

What kind of work did you bring home?

MAUREEN: Well, you've got to bring a certain amount home. You might have to do case histories at home.

Does your husband bring work home?

MAUREEN: Not much no. And his boss comes here on a Wednesday but they don't talk about work. He never mentions it.

So your husband thinks work should be kept separate from home.

MAUREEN: Exactly yes.

And that was your view?

MAUREEN: Well, I didn't do that, no. You see, with not living at home I could do my work whenever I wanted. It didn't matter really you see. And you tend to carry on that way. You tend to forget you've got something else to take note of as well.

So you gave up the children's job.

MAUREEN: Yes. Clive didn't want it brought home.

Before baby came you both went out to work. At that time did you mainly do the household jobs we've just discussed?

MAUREEN: Yes it was still mainly me who did the jobs. I didn't work full-time, at least only for the first six months after getting married. After that I didn't work full-time. I used to do twenty hours and that left time for the jobs (at home). Clive didn't do much, not even cleaning the windows. I do inside *and* outside. (J2, pp. 57–8)

In Silverdale men usually clean the outside, women the inside of windows, a highly symbolic division of labour!

The view that wage earning is primarily the husband's job goes hand in hand with the view that housekeeping is more the woman's job. If a married but childless woman gives up full-time work she is almost certainly doing so in order to devote more time to housework.

Of course, as Sue Sharpe, amongst others, has noted, for working class girls the available jobs are not particularly enticing, and the opportunity of avoiding work in industry is often seen as one of the advantages of being a woman. This outlook is supplemented by the tendency for the marriage objective to obliterate other objectives, particularly during teenage years. Teenage magazines for girls focus exclusively on romantic encounters with males. The general media, from school books through the popular press to television is packed with women-serving-men images. Carolyn Faulder (1977) is no doubt correct when she suggests that the stereotype images of women projected in advertising are the product of the advertisers need to communicate instantly. Put together these cultural strands add up to a strong ideological influence which characterises—and helps to create—women without any interests beyond the walls of their home and the man within it.

The results of socialisation can be tragic, as in the case of schoolgirl Debra Anne Groves, described in a *Guardian* report, who has failed to attend school since her marriage. Her husband commented, 'She doesn't want to know about the Battle of Hastings. She wants a quiet life at home looking after me!' Debra agrees with this, 'My life is now looking after Alan and our home. I have a job to do, and that is looking after him. I spend my days cleaning the flat, washing and making meals—that takes up all my time.' Not only does Alan want the housework taken out of his hands but out of sight too. 'He didn't want her coming home at four o'clock and having to start the housework. "I won't have her cleaning round my feet in the evenings. She knows how to look after me!"' (*Guardian*, 30 December 1976.)

Debra has been beaten down to a greater extent than most women, but her case serves to show which way the wind is blowing. As Carol Adams and Rae Laurikietis note, although both sexes give certain reasons for marriage—pregnancy, love, company etc.—the view of marriage as a career applies mainly to girls. They comment:

> So many girls when asked what they expect to be doing in several years time automatically reply, 'Oh, I'll be married', as if that answered the question—as if with marriage all their problems would be solved, and as though the answer to life were to rely on a man rather than yourself. (1976, pp. 74–5)

Girls who do not see marriage as a career, and who have employment aspirations, nevertheless confront a different situation from boys when it comes to the question of starting a family. Caroline's outlook illustrates this difference. Caroline is seventeen and has just commenced training to become a State Registered Nurse. Although at the time of the interview Caroline was full of enthusiasm about her career, she did not want to miss out on the experiences of motherhood:

Would you like to marry ever?
CAROLINE: I hope so yes, when I'm about twenty-five.
Would you like to have children then?
CAROLINE: Yes.

You may well be a sister or matron by then. Do you think you will give that up while you start a family?

CAROLINE: Well I shouldn't let my career spoil my life outside. I'd be prepared to stop nursing. Some wouldn't, would they? Women's Liberation wouldn't. But I would.

Despite the fact that you are very enthusiastic about nursing?

CAROLINE: Yes.

If you were a man in that situation would you interrupt your career?

CAROLINE: Well he wouldn't have to would he?

Well suppose you decided together that your husband should stay home with the child while you carried on nursing?

CAROLINE: Well I don't think—some men might—but I think the majority wouldn't, 'cos the majority of men like to feel they're the breadwinners don't they? I think its more the woman's place to bring up children rather than the man stay at home. (F1, pp. 15–16)

As Caroline recognises, the choice between a career or a family is not one most men will ever have to confront, and it is not therefore an issue they are likely to anticipate at the start of their career. The reality of prevailing social practice reinforces the ideology of which it is the product.

SOME IMPLICATIONS OF THE BREADWINNER ROLE

In this section I am interested in the effect the man's role as breadwinner has on family life where children are not involved. The first of the four childless couples I want to discuss is the Arnolds. Both Peter and Mary Arnold have raised children in previous marriages; but they now live together as a childless couple. Mr Arnold is retired and Mrs Arnold works part-time.

Mary Arnold not only makes a financial contribution in her present marriage; in her first marriage she was the family bread-winner because her first husband was disabled. These experiences, however, have not undermined the Arnolds' view that the man of the house should have the final word on expenditure. In the course of the interview it also became apparent that Peter Arnold was the household authority on all questions to do with industry and politics. Mary Arnold's eloquence was confined to her convent childhood and family matters, and on both of these topics her husband found a lot to say. On the question of controlling children it was clear that in days gone by he had had most say:

PETER: I think that people, boys and girls, look up to men, and I still think that's the case.
Do you think that?
MARY: I think so yes.
PETER: They take more notice of what a man says to them than what a woman says.

Peter Arnold relates men's authority in general to their position within industry:

> In industry I think you get more men who go through a practical experience, as well as a theoretical experience in their work. You don't get women doing the same. Because to get the practical experience you've got to go into a job from A to Z haven't you? The same as me, when I learnt the trade (in the pottery industry) there were one thousand and one things that seemed insignificant in that job, but they all amounted into one big thing. You were there straight away and knew what you were doing. I think a man more so than a woman. (D1, pp. 18–19)

Work, as well as enabling some men to gain status through their technical competence, also enhances men's standing, through a process of association with the political and economic importance of the industrial world. When Peter Arnold spoke about politics his active subject was the working *man*, the ordinary *man* in the street. This is not simply a matter of syntax. Mary Arnold's silence and Peter Arnold's sound on the topic of the working *man* and *his* industrial, trade union and political activities point to the popular acceptance of the idea that women's position in industrial society is very subordinate. The male breadwinner ideology provides men with an authority which transcends individual circumstances and limitations.

The second couple, Bill and Pam Ross have had occasion to realise that the male breadwinner ideology can conflict with reality. Mrs Ross is fifty and her husband is one year older. They have never had children. Pam Ross has endured one miscarriage followed by three still-births, owing to the incompatibility between her blood group and that of their children. She was too old to benefit personally from the medical development which has provided the solution to such incompatibility.

Mr Ross has mainly worked as a miner. His health has been seriously impaired by an accident which occurred a few years ago in the pit involving gas. The compensation he has recently received for this misfortune has enabled Mrs Ross to retire from her work in a local factory, and shortly after the interview Mr Ross also retired on the advice of his doctor.

After the accident Bill Ross was moved to a surface job in an office. Since this change involved a considerable drop in pay Pam Ross changed from her cleaning job to more lucrative factory work. This meant that she was earning more than Bill. For a couple who oppose equal pay for women because they think it would degrade men, this pay differential between Pam and Bill was hard to accept:

PAM: I didn't agree with equal pay for women. It's degrading for a man. Some jobs women can't do.

Are there some jobs men can't do?

PAM: Yes, there is, because men haven't got nimble hands like women.

So if there are jobs women can do but not men, inability to do a job is not in itself an argument against equal pay.

PAM: Yes but I don't believe in equal pay for women. It's degrading to a man.

BILL: I can see the wife's point of view. I don't know about factory work, but in stores where a man's on an hourly rate, after stoppages he will only take home about £35 a week, whereas a woman on these production jobs, granted she works hard but so does the storeman, and she's going home with £38.

PAM: Some men earn less than their wives.

Does that matter?

PAM: Well I thought it did. For instance, when Bill went in the office and I worked at Rist's I was bringing more in the house than what Bill was bringing in.

Did you mind that?

BILL: Well you see, the point is, I'm supposed to be the breadwinner.

PAM: A man thinks he's the breadwinner.

But is that right?

PAM: I think he should be.

BILL: Well a lot of people have got the idea that the man is the breadwinner. As the wife says, I thought it was degrading for a woman to make more than a man.

PAM: You see, when I put my pay packet on the table and Bill put his down I'd brought in more than him.

Did you put the money together?

PAM: Oh yes.

BILL: It didn't matter to us combined, no, but I can see what the wife means, it's degrading for a woman to make more than a man.

In the Ross's case the ideology is a bit difficult to live up to. The reflected glory from the realm of industry which illuminated Mr Arnold's superiority exposes Mr Ross to a harsh light.

As with all ideologies, the ideology of man seen as breadwinner chimes in with social practice. This does not mean that ideology is merely a summary of prevailing social practice, because at the individual level ideology exerts an independent influence. This can be seen in the case of Mr and Mrs Ross where personal practice contradicted prevailing ideology without seriously weakening the hold of that ideology. The couple endorsed the ideology that men should earn more than women, which in turn arises from the belief that men should be breadwinners, although in their own situation Mrs Ross earned more than her husband. This contradiction resulted in them condemning their own situation rather than the ideology.

The third couple, Mr Charles and Mrs Evelyn Munden aged forty and thirty-six respectively have not had children. For a number of years they occupied a tied cottage, and they felt their insecure circumstances prohibited them from adopting a child. Now they say they are too old to adopt children.

Despite the availability of parents and kin in the locality the Mundens seem to be a very self-contained couple. Mr Munden has been on sick leave from his job as a local authority gardener for a year. He describes his trouble as 'nerves'. Mrs Munden is and has been a nursery nurse for twenty years. They share domestic chores, and combine their incomes. Any major item of expenditure is decided after a joint discussion. Charles Munden says, I think correctly, that his wife is the boss. She would, however, prefer that this were otherwise:

Do you think women are treated equally to men at work?

EVELYN: Well they are in nursing, I don't know about anything else.

But I think women should be women, not acting as men.

Could you give an example of women acting as men?

EVELYN: Well all this business about equal rights and Women's Liberation, it's ridiculous. Women are supposed to be women. And I don't think married women should have to go out to work. I don't. I think they should double men's wages and make married women stay at home. Then there would be more jobs for young people.

Would you prefer to be at home?

EVELYN: Yes. I like being at home don't I.

CHARLES: Yes. Mind you, when we're eventually settled I might open my own shop up, and it might be possible then.

Do you think other women in your situation would choose to stay home?

EVELYN: No, not today. They're too indoctrinated, too keen on having their rights. They don't think of themselves as women. But I only go to work for the money. When we got married he only got £18 a fortnight.

Supposing you were able to be at home, would you do more of the household chores?

EVELYN: Oh yes. I don't think men should have to do housework.

So you share the household jobs because you go out to work.

EVELYN: Yes. When it's my day off and he's working he doesn't come in and get the tea ready, do you? It's all done.

So if you had your choice you would stay home and do the housework?

EVELYN: Yes.

Do you think you would get to feel enclosed?

EVELYN: No I don't. There's plenty to do and I wouldn't get lonely.

CHARLES: Oh yes there's plenty to do. You'd be surprised how much there is to do in a house.

Do you think equal pay for women is a good thing?

EVELYN: No. I think the man should be the breadwinner. (B1, pp. 15–16)

Evelyn Munden's father owned a small grocery shop which enabled her mother to give her undivided attention to caring for the needs of her husband and three children. This 'ideal' arrangement seems to cast Evelyn's present situation (and her husband's?) in a dim light. Given the absence of children whose presence would have given her desire to stay home the seal of social approval, Mrs

Munden feels threatened by the ideas of the women's movement which question the validity of her traditional choice. In the modern world where women represent 38 per cent of the workforce it is increasingly normative for women without children to go out to work. In this context Mrs Munden may well feel out of step, and hit out at what she sees as the most open source of opposition—the Women's Liberation Movement.

Mr and Mrs James, our last couple, are exceptional both in their rejection of conventional roles and in their educational background. Mrs Wendy James is twenty-seven and has a degree and postgraduate research experience in Biology. Mr Jeff James is twenty-eight, he also has a first degree and postgraduate experience, in English Literature. He is currently unemployed, but he is thinking about the possibility of doing research with a view to gaining a Ph.D. degree.

Wendy James has a well paid teaching job in a private school. They are not very keen to start a family; Wendy seems to be even less keen than her husband. The main reason given as to why they may decide not to have children is their desire to safeguard their freedom of movement geographically and occupationally:

Neither of you seems committed to either a particular place or job indefinitely.

JEFF: Yes and we would probably want to preserve that. Wendy likes teaching but she wouldn't want to do it for more than about five years.

WENDY: I think after that time there's too much repetition.

Most people stay in a particular occupation for longer than that.

WENDY: Because most people have children and they are forced into a routine by their children . . . I think many people have children without thinking how they are committing themselves; they have *got* to provide security for those children. Therefore they are stuck in their job and in their area. We would hope to have sufficient money and flexibility not to be tied. We would plan for them, and decide whether we had the time and facilities for children. They would be thoroughly planned. I had this argument at the family planning clinic. The doctor said, 'You've been taking the pill for a long time you must come off for three months' . . . I said, 'why' . . . She said, 'To make sure the ovaries are working'. I said, 'Well if that's the only reason, there's no health reason, I'm not'. And she was most uppity about it, and wouldn't accept that I was prepared to face infertility . . . If we were desperate for children we would adopt. (A1, pp. 57–8)

Like the majority of childless couples studied by J. E. Veevers, Jeff and Wendy James are keeping their options open, and in all probability will postpone childbearing until it no longer seems desirable at all. (1974, p. 503)

The Jameses have a very egalitarian relationship. They do not keep money separately and they discuss all major purchases. Both of them clean up in the kitchen and house, and both of them wash clothes. Wendy James does the cooking because she is better at it, in fact:

JEFF: Whoever is good at a job does it.
WENDY: And he's good at making really mucky pots and pans come clean. I haven't got the patience to stand half an hour and do it, whereas he has.
JEFF: Wendy's better at putting up shelves than I am so she does it. (A1, p. 53)

Although the first three couples considered here have very conventional marriages, if the four childless couples as a whole are compared with the couples in the next and final chapter it is apparent that in the homes of childless couples more tasks are shared, and there is in general more discussion and more companionship.

If we look at the general structure of domestic life, however, it becomes clear that there are important similarities between these four couples and the two-generation families to be considered shortly. In modern capitalist society the world of industrial production is distinct from the world of domestic production. This distinction is the site of the separation between public and private domains. Each domain is not absolutely public or private, for each is the condition of existence of the other.

The goods produced in industry are consumed by family members, buying them with money earned in industry. The yield of collective production is privately appropriated in the form of profit and wages. The worker works in industry in order to benefit outside industry. The family's contribution to the reproduction and maintenance of the worker is its 'export' to industry which cancels out the value of the goods 'imported' in the form of purchases.

The private sphere of the family remains the prime motivating factor in the worker's life. You work so that you and your family may live a better life. The Jameses have chosen to invest more on labour saving purchases than any other couple. They own two large freezers which enable them to reduce shopping to one trip each six months. They have a dishwasher and automatic washing machine and all the more usual household devices. The Jameses, like other families, provide capitalism with a market for privatised goods; one oven to cater for one household, a washing machine to serve one unit, etc. In this they differ from other families only in the extent of their purchases.

More important perhaps, the Jameses are concerned with maintaining their 'life-style'. They don't want to be tied down. The idea of being self-employed appeals to them. Their dream or objective is to open a handicrafts shop plus cafe, where they could sell their own produce. They would like to be self-sufficient and avoid the employee's experience of subordination, which is built into the employer-employee relationship.

This specific form of individualism is common no doubt in particular social groups. Nevertheless if the form of their individualism sets them apart from the broad mass of people, the family based, private nature of their ambition does not. To some extent all families have exclusive objectives which influence the way family members interact with 'outsiders'. Most families make short and long-term private plans—Where 'we' will go on holiday, whether 'we' should buy a car, the educational and occupational chances of 'our' children, 'our' retirement etc. The family through its exclusiveness manufactures individualism, and individualism inhibits collective identity and collective action.

Class divided society lives out its contradictions in the form of collective struggle. As Perry Anderson (1967) has noted, trade union struggle is an unavoidable and integral part of capitalist society. One factor which serves to limit trade union struggle, and which serves to confine all struggle to the narrow trade union sphere, is the contradiction between individuals who are motivated in terms of family projects, and collective action which is needed both to redefine and realise family projects.

Previously we have looked at the ideology of gender roles—man the breadwinner, woman the homemaker. These ideological conceptions express and reinforce a process within which men on the whole assume the main financial support for their family, and women on the whole assume the main responsibility for servicing their family. These different male/female experiences, and the socialisation process that leads up to them, serve to divide men from women, and thereby inhibit prospects of united working class action.

At a different level, however, this gender division can be seen as being rooted in the division between privatised domestic production and socialised industrial production. The fact that women rather than men are allocated to the domestic sphere must be understood in terms of the ideology which specifies the place which men and women occupy in society; an ideological divide which has, in different forms, been operative for thousands of years. In capitalist society this gender division is rooted in the division between industrial production and domestic production.

The privatising influence of family life remains intact where the woman rather than the man takes on the breadwinner role, as in the case of Wendy James and Gill Carter. The family structure remains exclusive whether or not it is the man rather than the woman who works full-time in the home.

Because gender division is related to the social division between industrial production and domestic production the ideology which specifies gender roles will be influenced by this social structure. This is illustrated quite well if we look at the ideology of romance.

Throughout her long interview Carol Parker spoke in a tired, dull voice. She seemed drained of energy. At one point, however, she revived. This was when she was describing her courtship. This episode she described with considerable glee. Her account is too long and detailed to include here, but one extract may indicate how the story rolled off her tongue. Carol had for months walked to work past a building site on which Alan, her future husband, worked. Alan eventually introduced himself, and they arranged to meet after the August industrial holiday:

> When I was getting ready I thought, 'What if I don't know him?' 'Cos I'd only seen him in overalls. Suppose I couldn't tell him? Anyway he was waiting for me.
>
> He took me to Chester Zoo. He said, 'Where do you want to go?' I says, 'I don't know'. He said, 'Have you been to Chester Zoo?' I said, 'I haven't'. I thought, 'Fancy going there!' He says, 'Well we'll go'.
>
> When we come out he says, 'I'll take you a run round'.

Somewhere in Wales it was. And I thought 'Suppose he leaves me! I can't get back home myself!' When we got home he said, 'I'm taking my Mum and Dad out tomorrow, would you like to come?' I says, 'Oh I don't know'. I'd never met them or nothing. He said, 'It'll be quite alright'. So I went. He dropped me off outside our house, he wouldn't come in. And I went in and said to me mother, 'I'm going with Alan tomorrow, to meet his Mum and Dad and we're going out for the day'. And me father says, 'Where are you meeting him?' I said, 'He's not coming up here, in Longton'. So he says, 'Well I'll walk down with you and see what sort of person he is'. Then when he went he came back to my mother and said, 'I think he's a nice lad'. (E2, pp. 35–6)

After Carol had reached the point where she was safely installed in her new home, my questions continued, but her interest did not. As in the popular romance story the end is reached when they got married. Full stop. Carol can gain some pleasure from reliving her own story, or from reading about other people's romances. The number of people, overwhelmingly women, who gain solace from the latter activity is huge. Worldwide sales for Mills and Boon romance books were seventy million in 1976 (*The Sunday Times Magazine*, 12 February 1977).

The glorification of a personal encounter, which is the heart of these stories, terminates abruptly when the couple marry. The male waits on the female until they marry, then she waits on him, although the latter sequence isn't part of the story as told.

David Morgan, stimulated by Firestone's analysis of love in relation to the privatisation of women, puts his finger on a crucial aspect of what is involved here:

Sexually, women are treated as interchangeable. A girl is a 'date', a 'good screw', a set of statistics under her picture in the middle of a Sunday newspaper. At the same time in the love encounter she is treated as if she were the only one that mattered. (Morgan, 1975, p. 147)

The contradiction between a woman's general predicament and her privatised self in a particular relationship takes on a new form after marriage when she takes over more than her share of domestic drudgery. The isolation of her own four walls obscures the similarity between her oppression and that of other women. It has the same privatising effect as her romance, that is it leaves the common oppression unnoticed and intact. But unlike the individual love encounter, domestic privatisation is dreary. She is shut in with her identity as a houseworker which she tries to embellish with romantic memories and themes.

Such embellishment is not an escape from her predicament. Escape would require both recognition of the social processes which reproduce housework and child rearing as a privatised occupation, and a readiness to engage in collective struggle aimed at the socialisation of that occupation. A diet of romanticism, on the other hand, serves to reconcile the individual houseworker to her situation; a situation I now intend to examine in more detail.

2 This Busy Worker Goes to Market, and This Busy Worker Stays Home

With the arrival of baby a drastic change frequently occurs in the life of the mother. She gives up outside employment and takes on the arduous round of domestic duties. Her labour now is less supervised and regulated, but far more isolated and continuous. Whereas previously she contributed directly to the financial strength of the household she now becomes financially dependent. These changes and the repercussions which follow from them clearly mark off this chapter of her life from her life preceding motherhood, and from the life her male partner continues to lead.

FINANCIAL DEPENDENCY

With the cessation of outside employment the domestic worker becomes excessively dependent on the breadwinner. This dependency takes several forms, the most obvious of which is financial dependency.

Direct questions concerning money will only shed a little light on the situation. It is primarily over questions of money that, in their dealings with welfare agencies, working class people have been subject to arrogant inquiry. As a humble sociologist I did not have, fortunately, the power to allocate or withhold benefit, and the people I talked with were more forthcoming than by their own acknowledgement they would have been in an official situation. Even so, money seems to impinge on a sphere of life people regard as private, more private perhaps than their love life. Partly this is because the *way* a family handles money tells us a considerable

37

amount about the nature of the relationships prevailing in that household. Nearly everyone questioned said they were satisfied with the monetary arrangements made in their home. This is not surprising since family loyalty is a deeprooted ideology. D. H. Lawrence expresses its impact admirably:

> Outside the family, what was there for them but danger and insult and ignominy? Had not the rector experienced it in his marriage? So now, caution! Caution and loyalty, fronting the world! Let there be as much hate and friction *inside* the family as you like. To the outer world, a stubborn fence of unison. (quoted by Morgan, 1975, p. 133)

Sociologists are part of the outer world the family confronts. As Lee Comer has observed:

> If any sociologist . . . had inquired into the financial arrangements in my marriage I would have lain my hand on my heart and sworn that we shared money equally. And in theory I would have been telling the truth. In fact, it would no more have occurred to me to spend money on anything but housekeeping as it would for him not to . . . a reality in which the husband can spend the money howsoever he wishes but a reality . . . in which she makes do because to do otherwise is to encroach too far into the man's rights. The only money she spends guiltlessly is on food for the family and clothes for the children. (1974, p. 124)

This contradiction between theory and practice is sometimes perceived by houseworkers. Maureen Clark manages the family finances. The Clarks have a joint bank account, and it is Maureen who counts up the cash and decides the order in which bills will be paid. But the fact that Maureen has free access to their money in theory, does not mean that this freedom is exercised in practice:

> When I was working I bought a lot of clothes, shoes, handbags and hats. Of course I don't have the same amount of money now. Funnily enough I was talking to my friend only the other day on the telephone, and she was saying her husband had been out and bought a sports jacket and something or other that he desperately needed. He spent a lot of money, and she said, 'I don't mind about this, and Bob doesn't bother about me spending money,

but it's funny when I go out, I find myself looking for the cheapest shop for myself!' Yet when she buys the boys things she buys the best things, and the best things for her husband. And I find myself doing the same. I think nothing of going out and spending £7.50 on a shirt for my husband if I like it, but I would think, 'I should have to buy myself two jumpers and two blouses for that money'. (J2, pp. 25–6)

Maureen's self-restraint, however, is not as self-imposed as her reply to direct questions indicated. Liz Brown, a sociology student, was present during the interview. As we left, Maureen helped Liz on with her sheepskin coat, and remarked that she had asked her husband if he would agree to her purchasing a sheepskin coat, on the grounds that it would last a lifetime. He replied that she did not need a new coat, quite in the style of the husbands described by Arnold Bennett in the Potteries of old (Bennett, 1975).

Times have changed though; Maureen knows how much her husband earns, and since they have a joint bank account, in theory she has equal access to the money. Such openness is typical today; in her mother's day it was not. Maureen's mother receives housekeeping money, and to this day she remains ignorant of the surplus retained by her husband. As Andrew Austin observed:

My father was the old type, you know, so long as he'd got a pound in his pocket for a pint he was alright. It was the same with tons of blokes in Silverdale in those days. If a bloke had got a pound in his pocket, and if he was on nights, there was no chance of getting it from him. Things have changed since then. (H2, p. 16)

But they haven't changed out of all recognition, as Andrew Austin's wife, Janet, is able to testify:

Me mum gets a good wage now, with me saying how much I have for myself, because I don't have housekeeping, well I call it housekeeping, but it's just food money. I let my husband pay all the mortgage, and all the big things. I won't have it—there's so much, and you've got to manage out of that. That money is for my use, though there isn't a lot left really. I mean, I can go many a time Monday to Friday and run out. But if I said to Andrew I want some money he'd turn round and give me some. He'd most probably say, 'What have you done with it' sort of thing. But I don't have to worry about the mortgage, the gas bill and that. Whereas me mum, he'd give her £8 a week and that was it. And when I got married, that was six years ago, he was giving her £10 a week, and she'd got to pay everything out of that. I was getting £10 six years ago just for food . . .

But I'd love to go and buy things on my own. This jumper I just went and bought, but say I wanted a dress or coat or anything. I've got to say, 'Look I want some money'. It isn't that he'd say no, but then again he'd say, 'Don't you think we've got enough? We've got such and such a thing to pay this week.' I'd love to just go. I suppose this is really why I want to work. Although we'd pool the money together, I wouldn't keep mine like my mum, what's hers is hers, but you can understand me mum for that. But I do miss that. It's your independence in a way. If I was working I'd say, 'I want £10 this week', it's going sort of thing. (G2, pp. 28–31)

Janet asserts explicitly that which Maureen senses, namely, that it is the breadwinner's right to spend the cash, or more often in these inflationary times, the breadwinner has the right to decide *not* to spend the cash.

Carol Parker was able to 'dip into a tin' when she ran short. The only apparent difference between Carol and her husband, Alan, concerned the availability of this stand-by:

CAROL: I have me housekeeping. Then we put the mortgage up, and the electric, and all the bills we put on one side. What's over we save a bit. He has to see his car's alright, so he puts so much up for the maintenance of the car like. Then he only has his petrol money to go to work with. If he wants anything we've always got money in a tin in the house.

When we first got married we used to have about £7 to live on. It was enough for us two. But as things were going up, and when I had Leon I said, 'I want more money now'. So we had £10 just for the food. But since then it's gone up and up and up. So now we need £15, that's just for the food. If we want anything else I dip in my tin. I have to do. Alan says, 'Take it down and put it in the bank'. I say, 'No, not all of it'. That's in case I need anything, 'cos once it goes in he doesn't like to draw it out again you see. I would, but he wouldn't, not unless he wants something really desperate and couldn't afford it. (E2, p. 49)

Alan, a building worker, felt it was necessary to prepare for the inevitable breaks in employment that non-managerial workers suffer in that trade. On the face of it their different attitude towards ready cash reflected their different functions—his that of providing for the security of the future, and hers that of maintaining the standards of the present. Alan did, however, have the final say on questions concerning any major purchase:

ALAN: If we were buying something big for the house we'd talk about it and see how the money situation was. If we thought we could aford it we'd have it; if we didn't think we could afford it we wouldn't have it.

Do you think you have an equal say over things like this?
ALAN: Oh yes. If we can't afford it we're *definitely* not having it. (F2, p. 17)

With one exception, in these families where one partner is the breadwinner that partner has the final say on major purchases. Ann and Michael Tate are typical. Ann, like the other financially dependent women, is ready to make do:

When you're home you tend not to want to spend as much on yourself as when you are out working. When you're at home you make do with old lipstick, if you've got ladders in your tights you wear trousers. (A2, p. 32)

Although on most matters Ann thinks decisions should be arrived at jointly, she also says:

I think 'We'll do that', and I say to him, 'We'll do that—do you think we ought to?' You know, I want his opinion, I prefer him to make decisions really about buying things, if it's something big that's going to cost a lot of money. (A2, p. 35)

The exceptional couple, Gill and Mark Carter, seem in reality to pool their money. Both feel able to take money for their own needs. This relaxed attitude is assisted by the fact that they are relatively well off; it is also perhaps assisted by another factor, Mark stays home to care for their baby son while Gill goes out to work.

On the whole, however, it is the man of the house who controls the purse strings. This represents a basic inequality between men and women. On woman, Jean Spencer, recognises this inequality. With a husband, seven dependent children and two out working to cater for, Jean confronts daily the problem of making the money go round. It is likely that this struggle has made her more sensitive to financial relationships than most women:

> Husbands come in and give you your wages. They either give you the packet, or give you so much out of it, or they pool it, you know, say after the bills we'll have what's left. I've always been given so much. I've never had pocket money. I've gone out with my husband either because I've got no choice, you know, I've gone out with him for a night out because I've got no money to go anywhere so I've got to go where *he* wants to go, or I've suggested somewhere and he's come with me, but he's had to pay like. But if you had a man, say he earned £40 a week, and said, 'Here's £20 housekeeping, that's £20 left, let's halve it', how many men do that? How many men tell you what they've got left? How many men show you their wage packet? (C2, p. 55)
>
> I know how much Paul earns, I've always known. I always think, well if you know what he earns, you know what you're getting, you know what's left, you know where it's going. I have my housekeeping. If I run short of money and I need £1 or £2 I know where Paul keeps it and I go and help myself. I always put it back. We've never hid anything between us. He knows where the money goes. I don't have to write it down in a book, you know, like you hear some women do. They have to write down every half penny. He knows where the money goes, and that's why he'd never take the money over. He'd never go shopping because he said he wouldn't be able to cope. (C2, p. 62)

Some men do indeed closely scrutinise their wife's expenditure. A recent indication of this came from a survey (quoted in *The Sunday Times Business News*, 9 January 1977), 'The Shopping Expedition', prepared for *Marketing Magazine* by Business Decisions:

> The survey found that nearly all the women interviewed complained bitterly about the lack of help from their husbands, but with resignation. They tended to accept that the husband had certain other household duties, especially decorating. They did, however, protest that their husbands were out of touch with prices:

'He hasn't been shopping since the Festival of Britain. I seriously think he believes the prices aren't much different to then . . .'

As other surveys have shown, it is remarkable how tight a financial stranglehold many men keep over their womenfolk: 'I get given £12 each week. If I spend £13 I have to find the extra money myself. There's no point going to my husband—he'd just say I wasn't shopping very well.'

It is dispiriting how many women meekly accept this. 'I haven't had a (housekeeping) rise in two years', says one young non-working wife. 'I drop hints every so often when the going gets tough, but there's no point asking him for more.' Should the right to a joint bank account be in the marriage vows? (9 January 1977)

(It is difficult to evaluate the accuracy of such surveys since the reader is given little idea-of the way in which the survey is conducted. Where survey material from newspapers and magazines is reported in this work, it should be regarded as an indication of a possible tendency, rather than be taken at face value.)

The idea that stipulations concerning the housewife's pay and working conditions should feature in courtship and marriage is not new, judging from a street-song from the 1880s.

> Young women then take my advice,
> When courting your young man:
> Tell him when the knot is tied
> That this will be your plan—
> Eight hours for work, eight hours for sleep,
> And then eight hours for play;
> Sundays must be all your own,
> And 'night work' double pay.
> (quoted by Suzie Fleming and Esther Ronay, n.d.)

Lack of familiarity with current prices does not, it seems, deter some husbands from insisting that their wives adhere to a tight shopping budget fixed by themselves. Jean is satisfied with her own position in comparison with these unfortunate women. Jean would, however, like to have pocket money of her own, though this is largely an idle wish. It does not matter too much whether the woman is paid food money like Janet, or whether she pays all the bills like Jean, or even whether like Maureen she has access to a joint bank account. A decisive issue is whether it is the woman who purchases the family's regular goods, particularly food products, and whether the woman sees as her main work the maintenance of the family's standard of life. If so her domestic function, and the ideology associated with it, will make it difficult for her to distinguish her money from that of the family fund. If her sense of self-hood is lost in her family, her pocket money will get lost also. This has been well stated by the Women's Studies Group:

> The wages are paid to the wage labourer and as such they are seen to be the individual property of that individual. So that where men can often separate two areas of expenditure (personal and family), women, for ideological reasons, tend to merge their interests with those of the family and hence we can see that the division of wages within the family very often works against women in favour of men. (1976, p. 106)

Gill and Mark Carter are illustrative here because they are different. Gill has always been very independent. She hated school discipline and, at the age of sixteen when her mother died, her father, who worked as a long-distance lorry driver, had his work cut out controlling his daughter:

GILL: I was sixteen when I left home, it was for staying out all night. I used to come to the Potteries you see, and from the Potteries I used to go to a dance hall in Talke, and from Talke we used to go to another place that stayed open all night. To do this I had to tell my father I was staying at someone else's house, otherwise he would never have let me stay out all night. I did it quite a few times and my brother found out, and he told my father. And I said to him, 'I won't do it again', and then I did. And, er, he kept threatening me and threatening me, until he told me, you know, to get out. It was a good thing really—for me I suppose, I'd got all the freedom I wanted then. My friend said I could live with them. So that's what I did, I went to live at Cobridge with a friend.

Your Father's thinking seems odd; he wanted more control of you, so he tells you to go and ends up with no control at all.

GILL: Yes. I think he was a bit sick of it, you know. He always used to say, 'Be in for a certain time', but I never used to come in at that time. (K2, pp. 9–10)

It seems to me that Gill's independence remains intact. She could, I think, walk out of her family of procreation as abruptly as she walked out of her family of origin. Although Gill does far more work in the house than any other breadwinner in this group, she is less bound by the ideology that the woman is the homemaker. As far as parenthood is concerned Gill thinks Mark is better suited to be the full-time parent.

Since Mark's assumption of this role is atypical, the conventional ideology which defines this role is weakened. Mark feels as free as Gill to spend their money on his own needs. If Mark, like other houseworkers, had to ask for spending money, he would refuse to stay home. Such refusal would be much easier for him than for his female counterparts not only because public opinion would be on his side, but because he could earn enough to keep a family, which most women cannot.

Gill's freedom to spend their money is enhanced by the fact that she is the family breadwinner. Jean Spencer's acceptance of her lot is, by contrast, conditioned by the fact that she is not the outside wage-earner:

I look at it like this, if I don't work here, if I didn't bother to cook, and if I got poor wages I should understand why I got poor wages. I don't get a great amount but I'm satisfied with what I get. I know what he's getting, and I know that I'm getting the biggest part of it. If he was a man that just gave me food money, like stacking money as we call it, and he was going to pay the bills and he didn't pay them, and if it had got to fall back on me—I would rather have the money for the bills like I'm having, and pay my way out. Because I think a man going out to work has got a bigger responsibility. He's got to have his wits about him; he's working for somebody else. I'm more or less self-employed here you know. I can do my job when I feel like it. Same as I said the other day, if I don't feel like ironing this afternoon I'll do it another day. But if he goes to work he can't sit down all afternoon and say, 'Well I don't feel like it', he's *got* to do it. I think a man has got that bit more responsibility, as far as going out to work is concerned. (C2, p. 75)

Paul Spencer does indeed have a hard life. He works seven days a week as a factory maintenance worker. In the summer he goes directly from work to his allotment, where he puts in two or three hours further work, which serves to reduce the family food bill. How this ceaseless round of work is experienced is best conveyed in his own words:

> It's no life really. It's just one drag. It's just existence, you know. I mean, we've got to clock on and we've got to clock off. We get up with the sun. It's just a drag. There's no freedom. I couldn't express my life at all, to anyone. I've never had the chance to do anything. We were just part of the generation that made the population up. That was enough. Do you know what I mean? We couldn't decide anything. (D2, pp. 15–16)

Few people reading these words will have thought of themselves as part of the nameless mass in quite this way. This expression of endurance reflects not merely present day trials, but a past in which Paul grew up in a family of fifteen who lived in abject poverty.

If, however, Paul's situation is unenviable, so is Jean's. She also works a seven day week, and varied though her timetable may be, the domestic chores have to be done. Her work is as unavoidable as his work and, if their burden in this respect is similar, their remuneration is not. If Jean on occasions seems to accept this inequality, on other occasions she does not:

> If the kiddies are bad you've got to get up in the night because you know he's got to go to work the next morning. You've *also* got to get up, but *you're not equal*. Not equal in pay. How many men have gone home to the wife and said, 'Now I give you £30 out of my £50. I've got £20 left. That's £10 for you and £10 for me.' How many will do it? *None of them will*, will they. But *a woman is working for nothing*. The only thing you're working for are your children, your home which you live in. You're *blocked in* seven days a week. (C2, p. 96)

There is not a great deal of spare cash in the Spencer household. It emerged in my discussion with Paul that whereas he previously kept for himself the equivalent of his week-end earnings, Jean's inability adequately to feed the family on five days pay made it necessary to give her the wages for six days. If Paul misses one day's work a week that week's pocket money is gone. It therefore seems to Paul that all his personal money is made on the seventh day, so that he did not take kindly to my suggestion that if he worked six days instead of seven the family would be entitled to Family Income Supplement:

> Jean would collect that money, but she doesn't give it to me. She hasn't got enough to feed the kids on as it is. It would hit my pocket; my pocket money would be gone and I like to have a pound or two . . . Why should the wife have it all? If I got £100 a week she could spend it. She'd spend it. So I've got to keep it down a bit, I can't afford to give her all the money. I mean, I work Saturday and Sunday, *that* should be mine, but I give her Saturday's. I've got to do. (D2, p. 26)

That 'pound or two' is important to Paul. It enables him to go for a drink once or twice a week, and this is about his only break in an otherwise monotonous week. However, this leaves Jean with no wherewithal to break the monotony of her week. Occasionally, housekeeping money permitting, Jean and her neighbour Caroline will go for a drink. The money spent on these occasions Jean has kept back from the general fund. She can't count on a regular sum, however small, to call her own.

We may conclude that in this respect Jean is Mrs Average. However a couple may handle their money it is usually more difficult for the woman to earmark part of their money for her own use. This is due to ideological and practical reasons.

The ideology which associates women with homemaking and men with breadwinning is linked with the notion that women save money whereas men make money. In the full-time houseworker group the division of labour between the spouses chimes in with this ideology. In this group the woman *is* employed as a homemaker who *is* indeed trying to make her husband's pay stretch further. It is hard for her to spend money freely on her own needs when she is professionally employed in making the family cash go round and in serving the family on a full-time basis.

Another way of putting this point is to say that the work identity of housewife and mother becomes all embracing. Most women in this situation do not think of themselves as people separate from their family role; it is therefore difficult for them to spend money on themselves guiltlessly. This tendency is directly reinforced by the prevailing division of labour between the sexes. Since most male wage earners do not go shopping for the family, the money they spend is more easily disassociated from family requirements. The money in his pocket is likely to be for his use alone, whereas the money in her pocket is likely to be a family resource.

Another ideological influence is related to the wage system. The industrial wage is regarded as being payment received for work performed at the place of employment. The full-time houseworker's claim in this money is seen not as the claim of a co-worker but merely as a member of the family consumption collective. The wage earner is able to spend money more freely partly because the money is thought of as payment for 'his' individual effort at work, rather than as being payment for this effort *and* for the domestic contribution towards the maintenance and reproduction of the workforce. The ideology of the wage system influences the outlook of the domestic worker as well. Her claim on the industrial wage does not seem quite legitimate. She regards it as unearned income, whereas in fact in purchasing the labour of the industrial worker the employer reaps the benefit of the work she has performed in the home.

ADJUSTMENT TO THE BREADWINNERS TIME-TABLE

Gill and Mark Carter aside, the rhythm of family life is adjusted to the routine of the breadwinner. As one might expect where the husband is self-employed, as in the case of Joyce Atkin, domestic co-operation reaches a maximum. In addition to keeping house for a family of six Joyce lends a hand with her husband's mobile grocery service. Joyce also feels that her domestic labour indirectly assists the family business, although she admits that her husband does not see it that way:

> My husband will say, it doesn't matter if this is done or not, if the house is done or not, it doesn't matter. What does matter is whether you make your weekly income. That matters, 'cos you've got to eat, you've got to be warm. That's his attitude. But I think—well unless his tea was ready he couldn't go out so quick at night and carry on making money. I think it's essential that this end should run smooth, so the other end can run smooth. See, I can be called up at any time to fetch groceries and take groceries. Drop this and go. And I've always been like that; I will fit my work here in with that work. (I2, pp. 46–7)

All the women in the group make some adjustment to their husband's work. The preparation and serving of meals is planned to correspond to the wage earner's hours of work, and leisure is also tailored to fit in with his movements:

JANET AUSTIN: We don't go out when he's on afternoons, but when he's on days we can get a babysitter and go out in the week. We'll perhaps go down Newcastle for a drink. If there's anything on at the pictures we go, it's not often, but if there's anything on that everybody's to go and see, like 'Jaws', that was a laugh. I want to go and see 'Earthquake' as well. And when he's off on Sunday we make up for it. On Sunday—he gets one day off in fourteen—yesterday we went to Southport. We were off at half past seven. We took piles of sandwiches, and we were back about half past eight. We were just going to have a relaxing evening and the 'phone rang. He'd got to go to work. I was just going to do a curry as well. I went to bed early. (G2, p. 17)

Whether couples tend to spend their leisure together, as in this case, or apart the content of the wife's leisure is often related to her husband's work. When, for example, the Clarks go out for an evening it is to play darts with his work associates, and on Wednesday evening:

MAUREEN CLARK: My friend, my husband's boss's wife, comes on a Wednesday. We don't watch telly on a Wednesday. My husband and his boss are learning French in the other room, and Anna his wife and I sit in here and chat. If his Lordship (a child of eighteen months) doesn't get up it's quite nice. (J2, p. 15)

Most women spend a lot of their leisure knitting, reading, watching television or sewing. These home pursuits indicate that a woman's leisure as well as her work is home based. For the husband an evening at home may be a comfortable change of scene after a tiring day. For the wife it is more likely to be a tiring continuation of the working day. As Carol Parker reports:

Alan doesn't come in 'till twenty past or half past six at night. Last night it was quarter to seven. So by the time we've had tea we haven't got time to go out very far. We don't go out much. We watch the television and I do a bit of reading, *Woman* and

Woman's Own, and I knit in between when I feel like it. Quarter past nine I feel that tired, I go that tired, I always have an hour, and then I have my Ovaltine and go bed. (E2, p. 12)

Alan Parker spends his evening watching television or reading magazines, particularly *Week End*. It seems, however, that these homely pastimes fit in with Alan's preferences:

CAROL: Me husband used to like dancing, but he won't go to any club, and he doesn't like drinking. *He won't go out for dinner anywhere.* We haven't been for—he's two—(the baby) I bet it's two and a half years since we've been out. In the summer we go for a ride round, or a walk round, you know. But we used to go to the cinema. We used to go once a week. Occasionally Alan would have a meal out then, but he won't now. I don't know why. It's not babysitters; Alan's aunty would have him you know. But he says there's no good pictures on, so . . . (E2, p. 17)

Carol has organised herself one night out a fortnight when she attends a 'Young Wives' meeting. It appears that Alan's duties on these occasions are not strenuous:

Alan has him when I go 'Young Wives', but that's the only time he has him. I undress him before I go, he's all ready. Alan doesn't put him to bed, he lets him sleep here on the settee 'till I come back. Dad won't put him to bed, he wants him where he can see him . . .

And when Carol returns:

And when I come here after 'Young Wives', Alan's been playing with him. He has all his toys out, everything. He doesn't pick them up, he leaves them *everywhere*. He says, 'Well you can soon pick them up'. When I play with him he just has one or two things to play with. Alan will look round and say 'What's wrong with in here? This is home.' (E2, pp. 52 and 62)

It seems that in order to have an evening to herself Carol has to make fairly elaborate arrangements so that Alan will not be over-inconvenienced by her absence. Furthermore, Alan clearly has a consumer rather than a producer attitude towards home comforts.

By way of contrast it is worth looking at the leisure life of Gill and Mark Carter, who share a house with Mark's elderly Aunt Lilly, and have a baby son, Matthew, aged one. Their activities are far more varied and outward going than the activities of the other families:

GILL: We haven't been in much this last month because it's been nice. But before that I'd say we're usually in four or five nights. We'd go out about two or three nights.

MARK: Sometimes at night I'll go and have a game of darts up the miners' club. But at half past three in the morning I like to go shooting. I went yesterday morning.

What do you shoot?

MARK: Pigeons, rabbits, things like that in the woodland area round here.

Do you go?

GILL: No thank you! I'll stay in bed. Riding's my hobby. I do a lot of riding in my spare time. I used to work with horses, and I went to riding school when I was younger. Every spare minute I had I used to go riding. But now I usually go Tuesday. Tuesday is my day off, and we usually have a show on at night, and I take part in that . . .

Last Tuesday I went out with my friend Bridget and listened to some records. Then we came back here and had a game of cards. Mark joined in. We played cards 'till about four o'clock in the morning—well it was holiday week.

Even when it isn't holiday week the Carters keep fairly late hours. For example, when I arrived to talk to them at 8 p.m. as arranged, they were out buying a ferret. They returned at 9.45 p.m., and we didn't conclude our discussion until after twelve. Gill does not have to be at work until mid-morning, so that it is not necessary to go to bed early.

Have you gone out less since having baby?

GILL: It's a lot easier for us because of Aunt Lil. If we fancy going out she'll look after him any time we want her. Any night at all. He hasn't really made a difference. If we go Trentham we take him Trentham. And we even go swimming with him. On Sunday we generally swim in the morning and go out in the afternoon. I go out every Sunday afternoon, even if Mark doesn't. I go up Mark's brothers; I go up their house and we usually find something to do from then on. (K2, pp. 5–6)

The Carters are a working class couple in their early twenties. Mark's father was a miner, and Mark himself became an electrician in the pit before staying home to look after their young son. Gill's father was a long-distance lorry driver, and she had a variety of semi-skilled jobs—waitress, factory worker, stable-maid—before acquiring her present skilled employment. It is unusual for a working class woman to acquire training for a skilled occupation, which in terms of hours is almost part-time work. It is also unusual for a working class woman to achieve the high level of pay Gill receives. This favourable employment situation, together with Mark's willingness to stay home with the child, and Lil's availability to babysit at any time, gives this couple unusual scope for leisure, which, I think, they use to the full.

For most houseworkers leisure is far less full and stimulating. Maureen Clark is trapped by her dependency into accepting cloistered and dull evenings, and in this respect Maureen's life is typical:

> I spend a lot of time on my own. I say to him sometimes when he goes to sleep, 'I'm on my own here all day talking to myself, and when you come home I'm still talking to myself'. But I suppose you've got to learn to accept these things, and I just accept it now. It used to annoy me at one time, a bit. But *one* of us has got to go out to work and that's it. And I can't go out and earn as much as he does, so he has to do it. (J2, p. 36)

The measure of the breadwinner's hegemony is therefore not to be seen solely in terms of explicit control, but rather in terms of the many adjustments the houseworker is prepared to make in order to fit in with the personal implications of the wage earner's social obligations to sell his labour power.

HOME COMFORTS

Dependent wives tend to accept solitude and confinement to the home as a necessary evil. Husbands, however, are accommodated in more active ways. Wives try to provide their husbands with good service. They take upon themselves most of the changes entailed in the arrival of children. The biggest change for women is their temporary renunciation of outside employment and their restriction to the home in the course of their work and their leisure. Both parents spend more time indoors, but the father tends to be less tied than the mother, with the exception of the Tates who have a completely joint pattern of leisure, and Alan Parker who, as we have seen, has no desire to go out at all.

The husband will sometimes recognise his wife's confinement as a problem; Andrew Austin for example:

'Having children makes a great difference. When we were first married we lived in a terraced house, and we'd both be working on the house 'til about nine or half past nine at night. Then we'd wash our hands and go and have a pint. When we got back we'd perhaps do some more. When Len came along, of course things altered. I know there was one occasion when I put my suit on to go out and Janet started crying. So I had to take my suit off. I was only going to the same pub—but on my own.' (H2, p. 15)

The fact that Andrew is aware of the problem does not mean that the problem ceases to exist. On the contrary, as Janet notes:

One day after I'd just passed my driving test he'd got a day off. It was just before Easter, and me mum had got a day off as well. I said, 'I'm going to Hanley with me mum', and he stayed here with the children. And I was gone all day. I didn't think I'd be that long, and when I got back he was a bit funny, a bit sarcastic about leaving him with the children, you know. It was the first time I'd ever been shopping on my own without the children. I said, 'Well I'll do your lunch in a minute'. He said, 'Too late, too late, I've done it. Chips are on!' (Janet laughs)—You know, he wouldn't starve! But he just felt it was not—he was a bit quiet, 'cos it was raining on his day off as well, and I'd gone and left him.

But that's the only thing that gets me. If he wants to go anywhere he just gets himself ready and says, 'I'm going such and such a place!' He won't say to me, 'Will you look after the children 'til I get back?' Whereas I used to say, 'Look, I've cleaned up, I'll be back such and such a time, will you be alright with the children? Is it alright if I go?' If he said no, that would be it, I'd have to take the children with me. I've got to ask, I've got to say, 'Will you be prepared to look after the children?' (G2, pp. 53–4)

While Janet recognises this double standard she is also aware that some mothers have a worse deal. Whereas Andrew had been willing to help change dirty nappies, her friend:

> . . . went out to work at night, and one night her little boy dirtied his nappy, and her husband just dropped it there. He left it there 'till the next morning, 'cos he wouldn't move it. (G2, p. 56)

This latter level of paternal non-involvement is exceptional. But the fact remains that the arrival of children represents for most women a total commitment; the overall responsibility for the child's welfare is hers, not her husband's. If the mother is to have time away from her children, in almost every case she has to make the arrangements which permit her absence; and the very act of arranging this transfer of responsibility is in itself an acknowledgement that the primary responsibility is her own. It is the continuous and inescapable nature of her duty which becomes oppressive:

> MAUREEN CLARK: It's not being able to please yourself. Having *always* to think about *someone else*; never being able to think about yourself. You can't say, 'I'll just please myself today', not ever. Not 'til they go to school, you can to a certain extent then . . . I could strangle my son on occasions, *I could.* And I can quite see why babies get battered. I'm not saying I would, but I can quite see what got them going. (J2, p. 54)

In talking to the mums, one very noticeable factor was that the mothers with one child seemed to be more wearied and weighed down by responsibility than Jean Spencer who has had nine children. Apart from the obvious explanation—that practice makes perfect—Jean has at least two daughters who seem willing to step in and take over from her. The eldest daughter is, in fact, a second 'mother', so that although Jean's load is heavy, others share the responsibility. This is not to say that Jean never feels put-upon, particularly in the daytime when her daughters are at school:

> You'll get a morning when she—well she's never miserable, but half way through the day she may get a bit tired and play up. She

knows the more row she makes, she'll disturb baby, and then he starts. And by the time tea time comes you're just at the level where you're ready to squeal. There's nobody can do anything for you. If you complain they don't want to listen to you. They say, 'Well don't keep on', but if you don't tell somebody—if you've got somebody who understands you and will just listen for five minutes you can get it off your chest. I very often sit some days and I could have a good cry. I think to myself, 'I've been on all week and I've done this and that, and it seems as if its all got turned upside down'. I think every woman has this. It's a depression women go through more so than men. I'm not saying men don't think about children, but not in the sense that a woman does. A woman's carrying them for nine months. A woman's looking after them and rearing them—a mother. They would never dream of going to father with their troubles, it's always mother. (C2, pp. 91–2)

Even so, the contrast remains valid. Maureen Clark could only secure sufficient peace for our conversation by timing it with baby's daily nap. Ann Tate's comments were constantly interspersed with baby quietening procedures. Carol Parker's little boy kept her on tenterhooks throughout our talk. With Jean Spencer matters were very different. Because Jean was recovering from 'flu her eldest daughter was home from school, and the younger children were also present. Jean's neighbour came over to join in, and various visitors came and went. The general background, for me at least, was confusing and noisy, but Jean talked on, uninterrupted for hours. Her eldest daughter, and some of the other children, dealt with interruptions and made tea, leaving Jean relaxed and free to talk with me. There is freedom it seems, as well as security, in numbers.

The fathers' involvement with their children is heavily weighted towards recreation rather than physical care. Michael Tate, with the exception of Mark Carter, does more work in the home than any other father. Even so, his relationship with his young daughter, as described by his wife Ann, emerges as representative of the general pattern of behaviour:

Who baths baby?
ANN: I do now. When she was tiny we used to do it together. But I usually try to get her bathed before her Dad comes home at night.
What about feeding her?

ANN: Well I do now. My husband used to feed her when she was very, very tiny. And sometimes if she's not finished a meal when he gets home from work he'll finish her off for me while I go and get the tea. So you could say I feed her.

Who changes her nappies?

ANN: Mostly I do. He will do sometimes, like about a fortnight ago I was ill and had to be in bed all day. He did it then. He made a very good job of it actually, so he can do it.

What about playing with her?

ANN: Well I tend to just stick her in a chair when she's been fed so I can get my work done. But her Dad plays with her when he gets home from work for a bit. And he plays with her at weekends. (A2, pp. 49–50)

The most helpful and the least helpful of husbands, namely Michael Tate and Alan Parker respectively, are willing to take their child out for walks, and they are willing to play with their child. Carol appreciates this assistance:

Alan will play with him at weekends, when he's in. At night time he likes his Dad to play with him, and he doesn't bother about me then. He likes me to play with him in the day, but he doesn't bother so much about me at night. So long as I'm here. But he likes Alan to play with. He hasn't seen him all day you see. He goes to meet him at the door.

It is clear that the main reason Carol likes Alan to take baby off her hands is so that she can get on with her housework:

How do you feel about ironing?

CAROL: I don't mind doing it if I've got a lot of time to do it, and nobody's bothering me, like him. You see, he will pull on the iron, on the flex, and he'll sit under the ironing board, you know. I do a few each time 'cos of him, 'cos you've got to keep watching him to see where he is. Or I try and do it when he's asleep. I do a few and have to put it up . . .

Sunday morning Alan takes him out. I'm on my own every Sunday morning. It's like heaven; just getting the dinner, just straightening up, and doing his nappies. You don't have to keep seeing where he is and that, you know. (E2, pp. 56–62)

It seems to be clear that a mother's relationship with her child is influenced by her domestic duties. As Carol's experiences serve to illustrate, housework is an up-hill struggle in the company of a boisterous child. In her attempt to control the housework side of her work situation a mother may well tend to leave the entertainment of the child to her husband. It is very probable that this is the only form of child-care husbands are willing to take on, for as Ann Oakley (1974) notes, playing with children and taking them out is the kind of involvement husbands prefer. This is a poor bargain from the woman's point of view, for as Oakley concludes:

> This kind of enlargement of the father's role is an unfortunate development for the woman, who stands to gain little from it but temporary peace to do household chores . . . At the same time, they lose some of the rewards parenthood offers. Satisfaction with housework may be increased, but only at the expense of satisfaction with child-care. (Oakley, 1974, p. 108)

The two exceptions to this tendency are in any case exceptional. Mark Carter, as full-time houseworker, has a very casual attitude towards housework, and Jean Spencer, who regards her seven children as her main companions, is not prepared to sacrifice that companionship to household chores:

> Now I don't have a weekend because he works seven days, so every day's the same to me, it's a work day or a play day. And I've got to work with these. As long as I can get cleaned up, and get the washing out of the way, and fit the dishes and meals in, these children are more important to me. These are my company when he's at work. They are my company, so you've got to fit them in, not with my work, that will be here tomorrow. If you're cleaning you can't turn round to a child and say, 'Well I'm doing the bedrooms, you must wait!' You can't. So as I say, work's here today, but it will also be here tomorrow. (C2, pp. 28–9)

Although a lot of a mother's time tends to be absorbed in the extra commitments children entail, she often tries to maintain her service to her husband. This service is, however, sometimes shaken by the arrival of children. Joyce Atkin describes how she let her looks deteriorate as she became more concerned with her four children:

I think a lot of women don't bother about their appearance, and I think it's a pity because you can't see what's happening at the time, 'cos a lot of men are funny like that. Especially if you are a very motherly person and you take over your children, you tend to. After fussing your husband you fuss the children and he feels left out. It sounds ridiculous in grown-up people, but this does happen. And then you go all slovenly, and it becomes less companionship. You're getting closer with the children. I didn't know at the time, but I can see it now, when I look back at old photographs. (I2, p. 61)

Aside from looking presentable, women may try to please their husbands by taking account of their preferences:

JANET: All his life he always said he was brought up on tins: tinned potatoes, tinned vegetables, tinned meat. And he said if he ever saw them in this house he'd go mad. I've got tinned peas in now, but I don't stress it. I don't say, 'We're having tinned peas', I just put it down, you know, and that's it. But I know he does appreciate—he likes to think I've gone to a bit of effort for his meal. (G2, p. 60)

This statement comes from Janet Austin. She is not alone in conforming to her husband's tastes. Wives tactfully drop from the menu those items which don't suit their husbands, although if the women like these items themselves, they often reappear during their lunch time snack when their husbands are absent. Most wives do not cook a meal for themselves during the day, for their cooking skills are oriented towards their mate. Sometimes, as in the case of Carol Parker, cooking practices are almost dictated by the 'mate'.

Do you use packet puddings, like 'Instant Whip'?
CAROL: No, he doesn't like it. No. We do have rice pudding—tinned rice. Alan likes custard. These Heinz fruit and sponge puddings, he will have them with custard.
  Trifle mixes?
CAROL: He doesn't like it. He doesn't like cream, Alan doesn't.
  What about frozen chips?
CAROL: He doesn't like them. I do, I've tried them, but I make my own chips.
  You can buy whole meals in a packet or tin.

CAROL: No. I tried them once when I was working. He didn't like them, so we've never bothered since.

What about you, did you like them?

CAROL: I don't think they're bad, you know, if you want something quick. Just once in a while when you haven't got the time I think they're alright. (E2, p. 44)

Alan's preferences make no allowance for production considerations, but this is not surprising since the production of meals is decidedly Carol's work:

ALAN: When I come in, I sit down and wait for my tea. (F2, p. 17)

Alan is very dependent on the service Carol provides. His dependency was highlighted when Carol was in hospital for several weeks:

CAROL: When I was in hospital he used to go different places for his meals. He used to go to his step-mother's one night, my mother's another, his auntie's, 'cos he can't cook anything. He can't cook. All he can do is boil an egg, and do toasted cheese. So I had to work out where he could go. And his step-mother did shirts, and anything like that, but my mother used to do all the other washing.

He would never do his own washing?

CAROL: He wouldn't know which way to start; I've told him that.

And you worked out his meals rota.

CAROL: Yes. When people came to visit me while I was in I used to say, 'Is it alright if Alan comes for his tea such and such a day? And I had to tell them what he likes, and what he doesn't like. I had to do all this. (E2, p. 44)

It seems that Alan did not relish this experience:

ALAN: When Carol was in hospital, with having a lot of relatives around I used to go different ones for my meals. It was terrible, it was. (F2, p. 20)

But not sufficiently terrible apparently:

Wouldn't it be worth teaching Alan to cook?

CAROL: He doesn't want to learn. I tried to teach him once. He wouldn't. He says, 'So that's what you do—right, do it.' (E2, p. 59)

All the husbands in this group—except Mark—are far less involved in domestic work than their wives. Their non-involvement often seems, as in the case of Alan, to contain a large element of preference. It seems to be difficult for the woman to involve her husband beyond the point up to which he wishes to be involved. This is partly because housework is a personal service, and it is precisely in the performance of this service that a woman expresses her regard for her husband and family. Thus in the light of earlier comments, it must be noted that the physical care a mother bestows on her child is a mark of affection. This attitude, however, makes it difficult for women to disassociate resentment towards housework from resentment towards the recipients of domestic service. This predicament has been well expressed by Wally Secombe:

> The entire character of this labour is one of personal service—literally a labour so that others may live. This creates the standard attitude of a 'good' housewife—self-denial for the sake of her family . . . In the absence of a pay cheque to justify her toil the housewife must account for her work in non-economic terms. Hers is a 'labour of love performed out of devotion to her family'. A housewife who admits that she hates her work is not a 'good' mother. Often therefore, her alienation from work must be repressed from consciousness, less she implode with guilt and feelings of personal inadequacy. (1973, pp. 19–20)

It is difficult for most women to press their husband into taking on a share of the necessary chores without feeling, on occasions at least, that she is being ungenerous and unloving. This does not mean service is given with a smile; on the contrary:

CAROL: When Alan comes in, he'll throw his overalls here and his shoes there, and he'll leave them, he won't move them. And when Alan comes in, he'll come right through with his muddy showes. So I've got to get the sludge up, every day. He isn't going to take them off outside he says. (E2, p. 61)

Carol occasionally 'has a go' at Alan, about tidying up his belongings, although these strictures seem hardly to register with him:

Is there anything to do with the house or child that Carol is particularly fussy about?

ALAN: There is something, but I can't think what it is now. (He shouts to Carol who is in the kitchen.) 'What do you get on to me about sometimes?'

CAROL: 'Shifting your things.'

ALAN: 'Ah, yes.' (F2, p. 16)

Janet Austin also resents going round picking up after her husband and, in comparison with Carol, Janet adopts more militant tactics:

JANET: When we were both working, before we had children, if he was home first he'd always start the meal. Then when we'd got the child, and I got that part-time job, he'd wait 'til I got in before he'd start.

Was that because he had got used to you doing it?

JANET: Yes he had. He must have got used to me doing it, because his mum never done anything for him at home. He'd always lived with his grandmother, and he always used to wash his own shirts and everything. Now if things are thrown on the floor they'd be there for a week. I rebel sometimes, and say, 'What are these socks doing under the bed? They've been here all week.' And sometimes on purpose I leave them lying around. I think, 'Why the hell should I pick them up? Why should I?' I mean, I pick my own things up, so can he. (G2, pp. 57–8)

STANDARDS

Such rebellion is constricted by the fact that women are trained and conditioned to accept responsibility for household order and cleanliness. All the women in the group have higher housework standards than their husbands. This applies to Gill Carter, for all that she has adopted the breadwinner role:

People sometimes say if the dishes are waiting to be washed they can't relax.

GILL: Oh no. I can sit down and let the dishes stand quite easily. I can sit down and read the *Mirror* all night. It annoys me more if I come in at night time and the dishes are strewn everywhere. I mean, when I stayed at home and looked after the baby, I can honestly say I worked all through the day, doing everything, making sure the house was clean.

MARK: And I would come in and say 'Haven't you done that?' (He laughs.)

GILL: I can honestly say I did more in the house; I was more of a housewife than Mark is now. When I come in from work at night, I come in quite often and say, 'Leaving the housework again? Haven't you done anything in the house today?' And he would say, 'I haven't had time'.

MARK: Down the club, you know.

GILL: But I think I made a better job of cleaning the house than Mark does. (K2, p. 34)

Not only did Gill do more cleaning, she always had the meals ready, whereas nowadays more often than not Gill cooks the evening meal after she comes in from work.

The extent of Gill's involvement in the home, despite being breadwinner, is perhaps not entirely voluntary. She is very conscious that she is only able to go out to work because Mark has agreed to stay home, whereas most male breadwinners in Gill's situation simply take it for granted that their wives will stay home. Because Mark's conduct does not conform with prevailing social practice, Gill is aware of her good fortune in finding a man who will be 'mother'.

This goes a long way in explaining, I think, why the money earned in this household is regarded as a common resource, and why Gill is prepared to do more in the home than other breadwinners. If Gill retained control of the money and refused, when at home, to take an equal share of the domestic work, Mark would, in my view, no longer be prepared to be 'mother'.

Similarly Mark is free from anxiety about maintaining domestic standards and keeping busy because these standards lack ideological force in his case. As his aunt said: 'You can't expect a man to keep house properly—that's her job'. Only when women are just as likely to be the family breadwinner as men will such sharing of household jobs and remuneration reflect genuine choice, rather than the power relationships of the market place.

Joyce Atkin is far less relaxed than Gill about housework:

I don't like the work. I don't like housework really. I don't like housework and yet I've got to have everything just right. It's almost like a sickness, isn't it? (I2, p. 59)

Since all the women have higher domestic standards than their husbands it is not surprising that when husbands lend a hand friction may result. Joyce Atkin, Maureen Clark and Carol Parker get the very minimum of help from their husbands, so the issue does not arise for them, but when Janet Austin's husband lends her a hand:

It's a coal fire, who sees to it?
JANET: Well I have to clean it. He tried to clean it once, but he made such a mess of it, it took me ages to undo what he'd done, you know. I prefer him to keep away from it really. I mean, if he did it *right* I'd like him to do it, but he won't, he'll just do it the quickest way . . .
What about washing up after a meal?
JANET: If there's someone here nine times out of ten after a meal he's straight up and does the dishes. But if we're on our own he'll sit down. And I always say, 'Just look, he's got to show you he can do the dishes for me!' If I say, 'Do the dishes 'cos I've got a lot to do tonight', he'll do them then, but I've got to ask. Then some other times we've eaten and I've gone and had a bath and when I come back the dishes are still there. I like them washed, dried and put away, all in one go, 'cos I made a New Year's resolution two years ago that I would never leave dishes on the sink, 'cos I was that fed up with me draining board being full up with dishes all the time. So whenever I wash them I dry them and put them away. But he won't do that you see. (G2, pp. 52–5)

As these comments serve to indicate, ideas about gender roles are embedded in practices. Previous socialisation and the breadwinner's attitude will have a bearing on whether the domestic worker becomes obsessive about the job. Furthermore, social pressure and domestic isolation can exacerbate the process.

In a mining village like that described in *Coal is Our Life* (1969) the norms of good housekeeping—when the husband returns a meal should be ready on the table, the washing should be out of sight, the house should be in order and welcoming, with a roaring fire in the grate—these norms were held by men and women alike, and were so much the accepted practice that one would be brave indeed to defy them.

In a more urbanised situation like Silverdale, where mothers with even young children take up outside employment for short periods, there is much more scope open to individuals to set their own domestic standards. The variety of such standards was very great. Leaving aside differences related to the material quality of the furniture and the accommodation, differences in the degree of spick and spanness were considerable. Smartness varied on a range from Joyce Atkin's show piece home to Ann Tate's friendly clutter (which nevertheless achieves more spruceness than my own domestic chaos). Undoubtedly some of this difference is based on individual taste. People do make choices about the amount of time they are prepared to devote to housework. These choices are not simply a matter of personal preference. Not only will upbringing play a part, but also other people's expectations, however ill defined these may be.

In some cases the husband's relatives, notably female relatives, may serve the houseworker as a telling reference group. Not only may she feel that she has to provide her husband with the standard of service to which he has become accustomed, she may also sense that her service is being evaluated by his kin who may be somewhat jealous of her position as their relation's helpmate. Certainly Janet Austin is aware that although Andrew may be dependent on the work she performs it does not necessarily follow that he is dependent on her person:

JANET: If I wasn't here he'd get someone in he would. He wouldn't finish his job. Does that sound a bit cold? But he wouldn't. He's got a lot of his family, you see, who would be willing to jump in. (G2, p. 55)

The influence of the husband's kin is likely to be more pronounced if the houseworker is employed in the home on a full-time basis. The houseworker may feel that it is necessary to demonstrate that a full day's work has been put in. Janet Austin is, once again, sensitive to the situation:

When you had a part-time job, did you and Andrew share more jobs in the home?
JANET: I would say less things got done. When I'm at home now I

feel obliged to do things sometimes, because I'm at home. The cooker, I regularly clean it, whereas if I was at work I'd say, 'That can go another week before it gets done'. It's the same with the stairs, you know. When you're at home people come, and they look round and think, 'Well, they're at home, they don't do much, do they like.'

Did it worry you doing less in the house when you went out to work?

JANET: I think I was happier then. I like something to do though, that's the trouble. Sometimes I do jobs just for the sake of doing them, you know, to keep yourself going. If I haven't got anything to read, or it's winter, I just can't sit there doing nothing. I'll perhaps get up and empty a drawer out that doesn't need emptying. Whereas if I was working those drawers would be left for twelve months without being looked at—but it wouldn't bother me. (G2, p. 57)

Janet's experience gives expression to one aspect of the isolation entailed in working full-time in the home:

JANET: One direct consequence of being confined within four walls is that the woman becomes abnormally sensitive about those four walls . . . Her response to confinement is to become obsessive about it . . . cleanliness probably comes top of the list. (Comer, 1974, p. 91)

If you are obsessive about housework then, of course, childcare will be experienced as an interference with that work:

JOYCE: I fed them all myself, and I found with the fourth it was hard to sit and relax. I don't know why I've always had these standards . . . I'd think about things that had to be done. I, say the beds had got to be made, I'd think about this sitting here feeding him. (I2, pp. 42–3)

Joyce here is clearly trying to maintain self-imposed standards, for bedmaking is not a job that has to be done. Obsession with housework can spill over into the houseworker's attitude to leisure. Studs Terkel's study of diverse occupations provides an example of this:

During lunch time I'll look through a magazine because I can put it down and forget about it. But real enjoyable reading I do at night.

I'd feel guilty reading during the day. (She laughs) In your own home. There are so many things you should be doing. (1974, p. 302)

A less direct impact of isolation is that the husband's opinion carries undue authority. This is not to say that women's contact with their kin is negligible; on the contrary most see their relatives frequently, particularly their mothers. Ann Tate has daily contact with her mother. They do the week's wash together, 'for company's sake', and when Ann was employed, her mother did the wash for both households. This degree of mother-daughter involvement is exceptional, although face-to-face contact once or twice a week is very general.

This contact cannot, however, mitigate the isolation which is built in to the houseworker's occupation. The proximity of kin is a boon, particularly for a mother with young children. But the housework rota a wife adopts will fit in with the timetable of her family. She performs the daily chores in isolation, within her own four walls. The money she manages is obtained from her husband's pay packet, and her evenings, in all probability will be spent in his company, quietly at home. This definition of the isolation of the nuclear family would seem to be similar to that used by Parsons, at least Parsons portrayed by Arlene Skolnick:

Parsons was not talking about 'isolation' in the sense of no interaction whatever, but rather about such issues as living in separate households, in a different community from one's parents, about being economically as well as ideologically more focused on one's spouse and children than on one's parents and blood relatives. (1973, p. 117)

In Silverdale one's family of origin and one's family of marriage will, in all probability, inhabit the same local community. The majority of families studied come from Silverdale itself or towns within a forty mile radius, and this is true of all the families in this particular group. Despite the absence of geographical mobility, however, the families in Silverdale remain, as far as the wife's work is concerned, independent enterprises.

In contrast to the women who go out to work—who will be discussed in the next chapter—these domestic workers tend to be dependent on their husband's view of the world. I think there is more than a grain of truth in Bell and Newby's observation that from the superordinate perspective:

> Tension-management will be most effective and most complete when based on face to face contact (as between husband and wife) and where the superordinate (male) interpretation of her situation is the only one available. (1976)

Even so, in Silverdale the husband's interpretation of her situation is never the *only* one available, as the critical tone of the wives' comments, reproduced here, serve to indicate.

THE BASIC DIVISION OF LABOUR

Since her husband goes out and earns their joint income, the houseworker feels it is right that she should perform the bulk of the work that needs to be done in the home. Of course, the husband's *capacity* to earn money is partly the product of the woman's past and present labour, as mother previously and wife now. The cooking and the job of cleaning up afterwards, washing clothes and people (children), maintaining relatively hygienic surroundings; all this is necessary labour, without which industrial production could not take place. The bulk of this necessary 'production of workers' could be performed on a social basis, through the use of nurseries, laundries, canteens, etc. As Jean Gardiner has pointed out, the postwar marketing of convenience foods represents a socialisation of food preparation previously performed individually in people's homes, and which continues to be so performed whenever the housewife is forced to try and make the wage stretch further (Gardiner, 1975, p. 57).

In our society necessary domestic production is performed primarily by women usually for specific people within nuclear families, thereby freeing some of those people for work in industry, unless the industrial worker in question happens to be the domestic worker herself, in which case she has in reality two jobs. Women sometimes feel they could not cope with this double burden:

JOYCE: I don't think I could cope with paid work, not with what I've got here. It would be too much—having to start on time as well. (I2, p. 52)

Joyce knows she could not cope because in her home there would not be a redistribution of domestic tasks that would serve to lighten her load. What can she do about it as an individual? In my view very little, because she is dependent. The fact of dependency goes a long way to explain—Gill and Mark apart—why the best of husbands in this group merely, and as a concession, help their wives on occasions.

Of course, husbands are also dependent on the work women perform. It is, however, difficult for men and women to recognise fully that their dependence is in fact mutual, because for both of them outside work seems to be more vital than domestic work. The latter emerges as a loving service which compensates the wage-worker for the trials withstood in the market place. The wage form of remuneration on the basis of hours worked or output achieved in industry is the main mechanism by which domestic work is pushed into the background in this way. As Secombe says:

> The basis of the wages deception is that, in appearing to be a payment for work done on the industrial job site, it provokes a conceptual substitution of this labour for labour power. Rather than paying for industrial labour, the wage in reality pays for an entirely different labour—the labour that reproduces the labour power of the entire family. This conceptual substitution occurs because the industrial worker stands alone before capital as an independent agent, and the labour that reproduces his labour power is nowhere in sight. The exclusion of the housewife from labour's exchange with capital is thus a critical factor in establishing the wages deceptive appearance. (Secombe, 1973)

The 'wage's deceptive appearance' makes it possible for some men to feel that whereas they do the real job their wives get off lightly. It offers a justification for their lack of involvement in the daily routine of homework. The jobs which emerge in some homes as men's work—cleaning the cooker, gardening, decorating and household repairs—are spasmodic rather than regular duties. In the case of child-care many husbands make a point of maintaining their distance:

CAROL PARKER: I may say to Alan, 'Oh he's been off all day, you have him a bit at night'. He'll say, 'You wanted him so you look after him'. And I say, 'Well I have him twenty-four hours a day'. He only has him when he's in because he's out all day.

Did you both decide to have him?

CAROL: Oh yes. Alan wanted him like, you know. But when he starts crying at night you see, when Alan's disturbed he's tired when he gets up in the morning. He says, 'You can have a rest in the day'; but you don't have a rest in the day, because you have to keep an eye on him. But I like Leon, I like having him and that. (E2, p. 67–8)

Alan is able not to see Carol's point of view by holding an ideology which specifies that such work in the home constitutes her proper place:

What do you think are the best things about being able to stop home with children?

ALAN: Well these women that go out to work and have got kids, they don't know what the kids are doing half the time do they? They get in trouble. A lot of this vandalism is caused because the parents are not interested. I think it's best if the mother doesn't go to work; it's best if she stays home.

Or the father stays home.

ALAN: Well a mother I should think would be the best.

What do you think are the worst things about being home full-time?

ALAN: I can't think of any worst things really. Carol is home all the time; she's not unhappy. She goes down the shops and meets people, her friends. She meets people in different places. (F2, p. 22)

Carol and the other women in the group, with the exception of Jean Spencer and Gill Carter, share the view that their work in the home is secondary. This leads Carol to underestimate her capacities:

Do you think women in general work as hard as men, less hard or more hard?

CAROL: I should say equally, in all but the building trade, 'cos when I said about equal rights Alan says, 'I can't see you going up a ladder to be a bricklayer's labourer, with some cement.'

Can you see Alan managing on a 'bus with a pushchair?

CAROL: Er—I'd like to see that! I never thought about that! I think he could manage, but I'd like to see him.

Andrew Austin, like Alan Parker, expects his wife to be more responsive than himself to the children's needs, particularly during the night:

JANET: The other night we woke up while he was having a nightmare. I must have been really well away in my sleep, and I knocked my husband and said, 'Get up there quick!' And he just got up and he went up there, you know, and it wasn't 'til he was up there he realised that he'd gone up. And he said, 'What the hell am I doing up here for, why didn't you go up?'
Can you catch up on lost sleep in the daytime?
JANET: Oh no. Many times I've tried to get down and have half an hour, but it just isn't possible. (G2, p. 43)

The woman's domestic work is so indirectly appropriated by capital that she appears almost to be self-employed. Her time seems to be her own, even if, as we see here, she is unable to snatch half an hour for a nap. Jean Gardiner has described the relation of industrial and domestic work to capital:

The labour of the worker and his wife is appropriated, the one directly the other indirectly, by capital whilst only that proportion of their labour time is paid (via the man) which is required to maintain them and perpetuate their labouring power at the customary standard of living established in the process of class struggle. (quoted by Rowbotham, 1974, p. 69)

Thus women's domestic work seems on the face of things to be outside the contract between worker and employer, and thereby outside this venue of class struggle. Small wonder that the women as well as the men fail to recognise the social relevance of their work. Most see housework as a personal service. Ann Tate is typical in this respect:

Do you think your work is useful?
ANN: My housework—it's useful to me, useful to my husband. It's only valued by him really isn't it? (A2, p. 37)

It is certainly valued by him:

MICHAEL: My job outside brings in finance, but there's a lot of work in the home that has to be done, that Ann has to do. And I would certainly rather go out to work and earn the money, than stay home and do all the housework and look after baby. (B2, p. 25)

Michael Tate sees that domestic work has to be done, but this compulsion is seen in terms of their own relations within the family unit, not in terms of the relation of that unit to industrial production. Yet the latter relationship is compulsory, in the sense that the division of labour between industrial and domestic production is built in to the prevailing social order.

This division of labour is the bedrock on which gender divisions are based. Some mothers in the group, Joyce Atkin and Janet Austin in particular, try in their upbringing practices to break down traditional gender roles. Yet their verbal exhortations co-exist with a daily practice in which sex roles within their home remain traditional. Because the wife is home full-time it seems fair to both parents that she should take on the bulk of domestic work since the other parent does a day's work elsewhere. The situation itself breeds traditionalism, and where daily practice is at odds with verbal policy, in my view, it is the lived experience which is likely to be the more telling.

There are, however, enough convinced traditionalists around for ideology to reinforce rather than conflict with prevailing practice. Andrew Austin for one recognises through personal practice what Jessie Barnard has demonstrated statistically; namely that marriage is good for men:

Do you think marriage benefits men more than women?
ANDREW: Yes.
Why is that?
ANDREW: You're anchored then aren't you?
Is that a benefit?
ANDREW: Well it is to me. It's nice to come home—like you see on the advertisements; you come home, your wife's got a cup of coffee ready, the fire's roaring away, it's great!
Why do you think women marry?
ANDREW: 'Cos they love you I suppose. (H2, pp. 21–2)

And for a traditional female view:

JEAN: You'd never see him push a pram. Some men are gifted that way. You can't have it all roads. You might have a man that will come in, bake, wash and iron. Now to me—I'd rather have a man go out to work, and come in knowing he's had a good day. (C2, p. 83)

THE EXPERIENCE OF DOMESTIC WORK

When asked to say what were the advantages of working full-time in the home, all the women mentioned their ability to determine their own work routine. Ann Tate is again typical:

The worst thing about going out to work is not being allowed to do what you want. You could up to a point, but you had to toe the line. If it was a nice summer's day you had to be stuck in an office. Now I would say, 'Oh bother the work' and go out. You can't do that working in an office. (A2, p. 58)

Janet Austin kept a diary for me in July 1976. Her diary expresses this flexibility very well. Janet describes the four days leading up to her holiday which, as one would expect, was an unusually varied time because of holiday preparations:

TUESDAY
Up at 8 a.m. Finished reading *The World is Full of Married Men*. Got breakfast ready.
Had a bath.
Went shopping.
Got lunch ready.
Bikini on sunbathing.
3 p.m. Made a cherry pie.
Returned to sunbathing.
Went to Audley to visit an aunt.
We went strawberry picking, and called at the pub. Came home and put children to bed.
Watched television and waited for Andrew to come home. Made chicken curry for supper, and went to bed.

WEDNESDAY

Got up at 9 a.m.

Went to doctors for prescription.

Cleaned through the house.

Got lunch at 1 p.m. Andrew goes to work. The children went out to play. I sunbathe.

3 p.m.—took brother-in-law to Crewe to fetch his car. Stay at Madeley for a while with Linda.

Went to clean Mum's house before she returns from holiday. Came home and put children to bed.

Watched television. Andrew comes home, and we had supper and went to bed.

THURSDAY

Up at 7 a.m.

Light fire and make breakfast.

I'm going to the hairdressers for the first time in five years. Meet mum from her holiday.

I cleaned through the house completely. Changed all the beds. Clothes ready for holiday.

Went shopping.

Visitors all night—trying to pack clothes.

Put children to bed, and watch television.

Robin is crying all the time with eczema.

FRIDAY

Up at 8 a.m.

Down to doctors to fetch prescription.

Tidy house. Ready to pack everything now.

Afternoon—took Robin to hospital to see specialist at 2.15 p.m.

Arrived back at 4.20 p.m.

7 p.m. Set off for Torquay. Travel until 1 o'clock when we reach Torquay.

Spent night on car park, $1\frac{1}{2}$ hours sleep—shattered.

Janet has two children aged six and three. Clearly, as the number of children increase so does the work load. Jean Spencer's baking, for example, is a mammoth task:

Do you buy ready-made pastries and cakes?

JEAN: Well, you pay 22p for a sponge in the shop, and it's no good to us; there's eleven of us. If you buy your bag of flour, $\frac{1}{2}$ lb. of butter,

½ dozen eggs, you've already got sugar in, brown sugar, it will make cake two or three times. This morning for 2 lb. of flour, eight eggs, ¼ cheese, and a spanish onion, and 1 lb. sausages—how many sausage rolls have I made?—I've made custard tart with two pints of milk in a tin like that (Jean demonstrates the large size of the tin), I've made a twelve inch cheese and onion pie, and I've made sausage rolls. (C2, p. 87)

Jean's diary, kept for a week in February 1976, indicates that housework can indeed be hard labour:

MONDAY

Got up 7.30. Had a wash. Put the kettle on for tea.
Got the children up for school. Put porridge on for breakfast.
Made baby his bottle, washed and dressed him.
Washed and dressed Sally.
Took Robert to school.
Came home washed the dishes and tidied up.
Went upstairs to make beds.
Came down hoovered up in the front room.
Went to the shop. Came back and a visitor called.
12.15. Started to get dinner for the children that won't stay to school dinners.
Washed up and watched a film until 3.30.
Fetched Robert from school.
4 o'clock—started to get tea.
After tea had a wash, and went out up to the club. Came home 10.45 p.m.
Cut food for husband and son to carry out to work.
Went to bed 11.45.

TUESDAY

Got up 7.30. Washed. Got breakfast. Got children ready. Took Robert to school.
Went to Post Office to draw family allowance.
Did some shopping.
Got back home 11.30. Got dinner, and prepared tea.
1.30 p.m. went to launderette to do washing.
3.15 went to fetch Robert from school.
Made beds.
Washed up after tea.

Ironed for two hours.

Got baby ready for bed.

Watched TV.

Cut food for work.

Went to bed 11 p.m.

WEDNESDAY

Got up and did usual things.

Two of the children are off school with colds.

Baby offside with his teeth.

Couldn't do much today, apart from cooking dinner.

Did lobby for tea. (Lobby is a Staffordshire term for stew.)

Did some sewing—buttons on shirts, put some zips in.

More ironing. Washed baby's nappies, left them to dry overnight.

Went to bed 12.30.

THURSDAY

Got up 8 o'clock. Did usual things. Had a letter from my mother. They are moving to Sneyd Green.

Did usual jobs.

1.45 started to bake. Made sausage rolls, coconut cakes, fruit cake, to help out 'till weekend. But they didn't last long, they never do.

3.30 I made myself a cup of coffee and made baby his orange drink. He slept while I did my baking, and Sally helped in her own little way.

Changed baby and put him in his pram while I got tea ready. After tea the girls washed up, and put the dishes away.

Watched TV.

8.30 Got the children washed and ready for bed. We went to bed early because Peter is on early turns this week and has to be up by five in the morning.

FRIDAY

Got up 8 o'clock. I don't feel too good. One of my bad heads. I took my tablets and sat for a while. The girls help such a lot when I'm offside. I don't know where I would be without them.

SATURDAY

Always a busy day. After breakfast the children like to watch TV, and I can get on with what I have to do.

I paid the milkman and the postman.

Got the kitchen done, and made the beds.

Sorted the washing out for the launderette. The girls will take it up for me.
Went to the shop. Took two children with me to help carry the bags.
Started to get dinner for us all.
Did some ironing.
Made jelly and trifle for Sunday tea. Put it in the fridge to finish Sunday morning.
Then it's tea time. There doesn't seem to be an end to eating and cooking in this house.
After tea we all watch TV. It's like a cinema, all viewing at once.
After TV. Bed.

Whether one is catering for eleven people or only for two or three the main feature of housework remains the same; it is a continuous job. One may take the afternoon off to sunbathe, but this only involves an alteration in the timing of jobs, the jobs still have to be done. Furthermore while she is sunbathing the mother remains on call so to speak. It is hard for her to map out any completely free time. If junior has to be taken off her hands for a while, she carries on with the never ending planning; what to buy, what to cook for the next meal, etc. And when the next meal has been eaten and the dishes washed and put away, the stage is set for a repeat performance. As it has been noted:

The appropriate symbol for housework . . . is not the interminable conveyor belt but a compulsive circle like a pet mouse in its cage spinning round on its exercise wheel, unable to get off . . . But the routine is never quite routine, so the vacuum in one's mind is never vacuous enough to be filled—'Housework is a worm eating away at one's ideas'. Like a fever dream it goes on and on until you desperately hope that it can be achieved at one blow. You lay the breakfast the night before, you have even been known to light gas under the kettle for tomorrow's tea, wishing that by breakfast time everything could be over with by 8 a.m., the children washed, teeth cleaned and ready for bed: tucked up, *the end*. (Quoted by Rowbotham 1974, pp. 71–2)

Even the one redeeming feature of housework—that you have a

relatively high degree of control over your timetable—can be undermined with the arrival of children:

CAROL: Before I had Leon, I used to please myself when I did housework. But now you've got to do your work. I think you work harder at home than what you do when you go out to work. My friend Mai says that. She wouldn't swap with me. She says, 'Washing again?' I says, 'You've got to do, because of him. You've got to keep on going.' She says, 'Oo, I go once a fortnight and that's it.' (E2, p. 27)

Each day is very similar, for many jobs have to be performed daily. There is no clearly delineated weekend, separated by a change of scene and activity. Sheila Rowbotham describes the treadmill excellently:

Get up, breakfast, wash up, make the beds, dress the children, take them to school, come back, cleaning, polishing, wiping, shopping, make lunch, collect children, wash up, take children back, sort things out, washing, prepare tea, husband comes home, eat, wash up, watch television, put the children to bed, make some coffee, watch television, talk to husband, go to bed, make love. The day is carefully delineated, the operations are repeated again and again but the context changes every day. The whole series of tasks present themselves within a new total situation. So every day is the same and yet not the same and sucks you into itself as a person rather than a 'worker'. (1974, p. 71)

The monotony swallows life. Days become indistinguishable. They fly by. The best characterisation of this process comes from literature. Thomas Mann in *The Magic Mountain* describes the deadly habituation to sanatorium routine which overtakes Hans Castorp. Mann warns that 'Great spaces of time passed in unbroken uniformity tend to shrink together in a way to make the heart stop beating for fear . . . complete uniformity would make the longest life seem short, and as though it had stolen away from us unawares' (1975, p. 104).

Ann Tate has worked outside the home for fourteen years, and at the time I talked to her she had only been home one full year, so the novelty had not worn off. Even so, the monotonous ethos of home life had already descended. Ann's days were sufficiently indistinguishable to make the memory of yesterday tantalisingly elusive:

ANN: What day was yesterday? Er—Wednesday, yes—(pause)— Do you know it's incredible but I've forgotten—er—, (long pause). I lit the fire, and had a cup of coffee, and then another cup of coffee. Then it was time to get her done. She doesn't get up the same time as me. She gets up when the fire has burned up at it's bit warmer for her. Then I washed out her things. Washed my dishes. Went up the shops. Then—em, (pause)—I came back and had my dinner, er, then I went up to me mum and watched television. I go every day. Then I came back and got tea. (A2, p. 42)

The specific nature of 'yesterday' eluded Ann. What she managed to describe was her daily routine; she did not describe 'yesterday'.

Some women commented directly on the monotony of their work, and their attempt to overcome it. Jean for example:

JEAN: If he wants to do anything or suggest anything he'll say so, but my husband rarely does, he's, em, he's wrapped up in his work. He notices when he comes in from work, if I've done anything. So if I've moved round in here he'll say, 'Moved round again'. But when you're on your own you're looking at everything. You're in seven days a week looking at four walls. You've got to make a change somewhere: so I just move round a little bit, and just make it different, I think that's something every woman does. It's through being in the house all the while. (C2, p. 65)

And outside employment is valued partly because it represents a temporary escape from the house:

CAROL: When you go out to work you see different—well when you're working you see the same people more or less, but sometimes you see different people, who you haven't seen for a bit. I like being at home, you know, but sometimes you think—you do the same thing day in and day out when you're at home. And it's all the same, it's one long—what's it! (Words fail her.) Whereas when you go work you've got a change to when you come in. (E2, p. 30)

This all important change of scene is denied to full-time domestic workers. The prospect of release that outside employment can offer is clearly illustrated in the case of Jean Spencer, who some months previously worked each evening as a barmaid:

JEAN: At night when you're meeting different people it seems as if it gives you a break *from* the home, because during the day as far as I go is to the shop or down to the school to fetch Robert, and that's as far as I go. I can't say I'll get ready and take the kiddies for an hour, unless it's a nice day and I've got nothing to do. But it seemed like a nice break for me at night. (C2, p. 57)

The fact that housework is performed in isolation adds to the sense of being trapped. Janet Austin sees her mother two or three times a week, and being Silverdale born and bred she is surrounded by acquaintances. She claims that she cannot walk down to the village without meeting at least fifteen people she has known for years. Despite this Ann is able to say:

ANN: I hate being on my own. I like company. When they were babies I hated being on my own with them, I felt so trapped, you know.
Because of the responsibility?
ANN: Oh no. I was never worried about that. But you know I loved being at work, and I loved the freedom that went with work. But being pregnant straight away, all my married life I've only known it with children. So I've never known what married life would be like if I did go out to work. I think I'd like to try. (G2, pp. 9–10)

As well as desiring greater financial independence, Ann would like to work outside the home so as to become part of a collective enterprise. The latter motivation is itself testament to the loneliness of housework. Occasionally leisure compensates for occupational isolation, as in the case of Mary Chamberlain's bell-ringing housewife:

What I really like about it all (bellringing) is the feeling that you're one of a team and that if you don't turn up you're letting the team down, so that they can't practise properly with one missing. You feel that you belong somehow. (1975, p. 150)

If the experience of being constantly at the family's service, with all the resulting isolation and tedium, continues for several years, the domestic worker loses touch with the drama of her own lifetime. Before marriage she was a self-acting individual. The scenes of courtship and marriage may be relived many times, but the following years tend to fade into the ceaseless reality of housework and childcare. As was noted in the previous chapter, this emotional divide between the glamour of courtship and the following reality of marriage was distinctly evident in Carol Parker's interview.

If the years after marriage are felt to lack sparkle, the women do recognise that raising children is an important job which has its rewarding aspects. Their husbands have the freedom of non-involvement, they on the other hand reap the advantages of being involved:

JOYCE: I don't think my husband has had the contact with the children that I have had. So I think I've had the best end of the stick. And that appeals to me much more than being involved with customers. (I2, p. 58)

Janet Austin feels the same:

Do you think the job you do is as important as the job Andrew does?
JANET: Well, washing and cleaning, jobs like that, to me they're not important. But then again with me being at home I'm seeing far more of my children than somebody who's at work, therefore they're going to get influence off me a lot more. They do get their influence off me I think. (G2, p. 54)

It should be noted that the ability to influence children's behaviour and the power to decide family practices are different capacities which are not always, or even usually, exercised by the same person:

Do you think you have as much say in the house and about the upbringing of the children as Janet?
ANDREW AUSTIN: Probably more than Janet I would say. (H2, p. 20)

Furthermore, the breadwinner's power to take decisions carries its own influence.
Despite the fact that running a home and raising children does

offer some scope for interest and initiative, the factors that have been touched on here—dependency, servility, tedium and isolation—combine to sap the confidence of the houseworker. As time goes by, houseworkers begin to feel they are so immersed in domesticity they have little individuality left. Maureen Clark, for example, says:

MAUREEN: I think I'm most boring actually, because I don't have an awful lot to say to my husband. I don't go out very much. If I go out I go to my mother's, or his mother's, or one of his relations; I go and spend an hour after shopping. And sometimes I can go and not see anyone at all that I know. So I can't talk to him. It's not like going out to work and spending the day out or the morning out and talking, admittedly to the same people, but talking about their families, their son or daughter, or somebody they've seen, you know, and you've got something to say.

My husband's always tired. He goes to sleep most evenings. He gets up at five, but I suppose I'm not very exciting. (J2, p. 33)

Although Maureen thinks she has little to offer conversationally with her husband, she recognises that her domestic experiences have given her more conversational scope with women:

What do you think are the best things about being a housewife?
MAUREEN: Sharing I think.
What do you mean?
MAUREEN: Well, not sharing things with your husband particularly, but experiences with other people, you know.
What kind of experiences?
MAUREEN: Women used to talk about what it was like when I had so and so, or when so and so was little, and I used to wonder, well I wonder what it is *like*. Now I like having something to say. (J2, p. 53)

Maureen's admittance into the maternal world does not, it seems, altogether compensate for her non-involvement in industry. The maternal world seems to be narrower and less exciting. This feeling of being 'backstage' is very common. When I started my conversation with Joyce Atkin, she began by saying:

JOYCE: You don't want to talk to me. My life's not interesting. I've never been able to say I go out and earn a wage. (I2, p. 1)

As we proceeded, Joyce found she did have things to say, and three hours later commented, 'I've never talked so much!' Houseworkers have a lot to tell us, but they take some convincing that their experiences are of any interest to any one except other women who have been or are in the same boat.

We have seen in this section that many influences combine to make houseworkers feel inferior. Their role as family servant saps their independence, both as agents of action and as financial beings. The overriding importance of the breadwinner in the household is registered by the extent to which the houseworker accommodates the industrial worker. She attempts to minimise any factors the industrial worker may find discomforting, particularly those associated with children. When the industrial worker is at home, the houseworker continues to assume the main responsibility for childcare and housework, leaving the wage worker free to enjoy the comforts of the home.

This service is the result of ideological conceptions which are reproduced in daily practice. Once installed in her own home on a full-time basis, gender role expectations on the part of neighbours and kin, particularly his kin, reinforce the gender-socialisation which predated the marriage.

The separation of wage work from domestic work has the effect of releasing the wage worker almost completely from the responsibilities of the home. This is not merely because the houseworker is more often on hand to take over these tasks. The ideological impact of the wage system has a decisive impact. The contribution of domestic work in the creation of labour power as a saleable commodity is hidden. The wage seems to be earned by the industrial worker alone. This has the effect not only of enhancing the industrial worker's control of family expenditure, but also of providing legitimation for the wage earner's avoidance of domestic toil. According to this ideology not only has the wage earner put in a full day's work elsewhere, but that work is more like real work than housework could ever be. The latter appears to be merely a personal service of benefit to family members only, whereas the former commands a wage and is socially necessary.

Although the houseworker is better placed to recognise that the home comforts that the wage earner often takes for granted have to be produced, the houseworker is also bound by the wage system ideology. This reinforces an acceptance of traditional gender roles. It also creates a situation in which the houseworker is dependent, both financially and socially, on the industrial worker. Thus even if the individual houseworker was able to throw off the ideological ties which bind her to the home, she would remain bound to the home in harsh reality.

THE STATE AND FAMILY LIFE

Unemployed men frequently find enforced domesticity irksome. A newspaper article headed 'When the Cash and Confidence Runs Out' describes the predicament of Michael Evans aged twenty-nine, father of two small daughters, who has been unemployed for a year, and now faces a situation in which his dole-money will cease:

> He neither earns nor receives any money of his own and Susan (his wife) earns £39.00 as a machine operator with Lyons, to keep the family. As the husband of a working wife he is no longer entitled to any claims for himself or his children. Nobody starves, but life is bleak. Work brings in only £4 more than basic supplementary benefit.
>
> Michael stays home to look after the flat and the two children. He cannot accept or understand his new role. 'I know I've got more aggressive', he says. 'Some mornings I feel as though I could burst, I slam the doors and kick the walls. I have taken it out on the children but I felt awful afterwards.'
>
> Susan also resents their enforced role-change and its destructive effect on Michael and the children. 'Since he has been unemployed', she says, 'the least thing drives him to screaming and shouting—like a proper woman'. (*The Sunday Times*, 21 November 1976)

The economic and political structure of the labour market does not facilitate role-swaps of this type. As will be shown in the next chapter, women in the economy constitute a secondary labour force, which is paid less, has less security and less occupational opportunity than the male labour force. Susan's job is typical of secondary labour force work. Her poor wage has to keep a family of four. This sort of situation is not so unusual. It has been estimated that one in every six households, excluding pensioner households, are dependent wholly or mainly on the woman's earning or benefits.

Most of these households include children, sick or elderly relatives (*The Demand For Independence*, 1976).

A woman like Susan not only confronts a disadvantageous labour market, she is also at a legal disadvantage compared to her male counterpart. She cannot, for example, claim Family Income Supplement. This supplement is paid to families with children where the breadwinner is low paid:

> Where the family includes both a man and a woman, both must claim, and either can receive the payment. But it must be the man who is in full-time work. The Act blatantly discriminates against families where it is the woman who has chosen to be the sole breadwinner. A woman will only be recognised as a breadwinner if there is no man around. (*The Demand for Independence*, 1976)

Similarly if Susan falls sick or becomes unemployed she will not be able to claim dependents' allowance for her family. Such benefits are reserved for single women or families with a male breadwinner.

The maintenance of the family unit, within which women are by and large seen as dependents, is built into the operation of the Welfare State. The Beveridge Report (1942) clearly identifies the all important function of the family unit and woman's work within that unit:

> In any measure of social policy in which regard is had to facts, the great majority of married women must be regarded as occupied on work which is vital though unpaid, without which their husbands could not do their paid work and without which the nation could not continue. In accord with facts the Plan for Social Security treats married women as a special insurance class of occupied persons and treats man and wife as a team . . . The attitude of the housewife to gainful employment outside the home is not and should not be the same as that of the single woman. She has other duties . . . Taken as a whole the Plan for Social Security puts a premium on marriage in place of penalising it . . . In the next thirty years housewives as Mothers have vital work to do in ensuring the adequate continuance of the British Race and of British ideals in the world. (quoted by Wilson, 1974, p. 14)

All nicely put in an imperialist context as Elizabeth Wilson has observed.

Under the Social Security Pensions Act a woman will not be denied a pension because she has not paid contributions whilst looking after children or adult relatives. This removes one penalty suffered by women, despite the fact that Beveridge sought to put a premium on marriage. This change, however, still treats the family rather than the individual as the unit of accountancy. Furthermore, the family is defined in terms of relations of dependency. Thus, if a woman (or a man) in receipt of social security benefit cohabits with a partner it is assumed that the partner will provide financial support, in precisely the same way as a husband is assumed to support his wife, and social security benefit will be discontinued. In the case of a woman cohabiting with an unemployed man, it is the man who must claim, and the man who receives the benefit.

The dependence of women on men is not, of course, a legal device. The majority of women are, at least in part, dependent on men. This situation is likely to remain so long as women have more responsibility than men in the domestic sphere. In present circumstances any radical socialisation of housework and childcare would cost the establishment dear. It is only when the need for female labour is at a premium, as in war time, that the State takes over more of the cost of producing labour (CSE pamphlet).

In the present period women are assigned their labour producing tasks within the home, and at the same time they form a secondary work force in the labour market. From the perspective of the women involved this double occupation is beset with contradictions, which will be explored in the following chapter. In terms of savings to the state, female involvement in the labour market reduces the proportion of families who would otherwise qualify for State benefits: 'A Department of Health and Social Security Survey in 1971 showed that the number of two parent families with the father in full-time work whose income would have been below supplementary benefit level (the official poverty line) would have trebled if the mother had not had paid employment also' (*The Demand for Independence*).

The operation of State agencies reinforces the homeliness of women's concerns. The allocation of assistance is linked to pressure for family conformity to State determined domestic norms. I have a childhood memory of witnessing the inspection of my grandmother's home in Stockport, conducted by a National

Assistance Official. The inspection included scrutiny of the kitchen sink. This was to make sure the sink was clean, my grandmother informed me later. David Vincent has a similar grandmother recollection, from the 'other side', since his grandmother worked as an agent of state control. She was a health visitor for the poor, and in the course of a seminar on 'Childhood in the Potteries' at Keele University, David Vincent explained that if the houses his grandmother inspected did not maintain a sufficiently good standard of hygiene, benefit would be withheld. There was, he recalls, quite definitely a rigorous inspection of houses for standards of hygiene, and subsequent loss of money if the standards were not kept.

Eleanor Rathbone in the 1930s drew attention to State supervision of motherhood:

> She pointed out that at any time health visitors, school inspectors or rent collectors could drop in unannounced, putting pressure on the mothers to improve the quality of the labour power she produced and holding legal sanctions against her if she failed to meet the prevailing norms. (Quoted by The Conference of Socialist Economists.)

The authors add: 'Since the war the ideological pressure on women in the home has increased enormously and a veritable army of social workers has been trained in family case work'.

The ultimate threat entailed in such inspection is the removal of children, either because of inadequate childcare or because the parents are unable to prevent their child falling foul of the law. And as Elizabeth Wilson has noted: 'The intensity of close family ties in the small family makes this a very powerful form of social control of the parents as well as the kids' (Wilson, 1974, p. 21).

This control bears most heavily on women, particularly on mothers without paid employment, who suffer stigmatisation for any failure adequately to fulfil their State superintended responsibilities.

If another personal incident will be allowed, a young woman of my acquaintance reported cleaning through her house very shortly after the birth of her child, despite the fact that she was ill and had been medically advised to keep to her bed. She disobeyed the doctor because the health visitor was due, and she did not want to be thought of as 'dirty' and thereby risk losing her child.

The point is not whether her fears were justified or not, but that women experience surveillance of their domestic capacities. This control is likely to be felt most sharply in the most deprived families who have neither the housing standards, nor suitable facilities with which to set a health visitor's mind at rest.

The inactivity of the State, however, can be as significant as active reinforcement of women's domestic duties. Care of pre-school age children conflicts with the parents', usually the mother's, ability to go out to work unless relatives, minders or social agencies will take the children off her hands. It is unusual for relatives to take over the full-time care of young children. Non-family care is therefore the main source of care available to would-be working mums. Public authority provision for pre-school age children is, however, totally inadequate. In 1974 only 3.2 per cent of pre-school age children were provided for in Day Nurseries on a full-time basis. At that time only eighty-one employer-provided nurseries existed; and a survey of twenty-one of these nurseries showed that they were limited to female staff and were usually for one child only (Labour Research, Number 4 Vol. 65, April 1976).

Research on the education and care of the under-fives is currently being undertaken by Helen Foy, Corinne Hutt and Stephen Tyler at Keele University. The findings to date indicate that total provision in North Staffordshire covers 85 per cent of all children under five years of age. This is much better than the national average where 55 per cent of pre-school age children are provided for in some form. Figures can be deceptive, however. If we deduct those children who are attending primary school, who will be approaching five years of age, and if we deduct children catered for in play groups, which typically meet for three hour sessions with the mothers frequently in attendance, we are left with nursery schools and classes and day nurseries as being the kind of provision which would enable mothers with small children to go out to work.

Nursery schools and classes provide for 35 per cent of the under five population in North Staffordshire, although not all of these children attend on a full-time basis. If a would-be working mother obtains a full-time place for her child in a nursery class or school the hours of opening, from 9.30 a.m. to 4.30 p.m., may prevent her from obtaining full-time work. Only day nursery provision has sufficiently long opening hours to enable all would-be working mothers to look for full-time work outside the home. Day nursery provision is, however, as inadequate in North Staffordshire as it is elsewhere; providing for approximately 3 per cent of the under five population. Places in day nurseries tend to be reserved for children with special needs, children from single parent families, children with a mental or social handicap, etc. For the majority of would-be working mothers in North Staffordshire as elsewhere, child minding is the most readily available form of child care.

Child minding is the largest childcare service. In 1974, 30,200 registered minders catered for 56,700 children. The number of unregistered minders is uncertain, although a child minding project in Birmingham seems to offer some evidence that the number of unregistered minders has been grossly overestimated in the past (Joanna Mack, *New Society*, 9 December 1976).

Like other forms of homework, child minding is very badly paid. Many earn as little as 10p an hour for a ten hour day. Brian Redhead, for example, in the BBC series 'Other People's Children', interviewed a minder who took three children at £7 a week each, and was left with: 'only £5 at the end of the week after deducting the cost of food, milk, outings, equipment and allowing for wear' (Joy Tagney, *Guardian*, 14 January 1977).

The only way for the minder to increase her income is to take on more children, but then, as Joanna Mack points out, it becomes extremely difficult to get out of the house at all: 'Mary Duggan, a child minder, in the Birchfield district of Birmingham says, "I have to maintain my full quota of five children or it wouldn't pay me to stay in, with the cost of heating. But with five children from the age of four months to six years, I'm not even able to get them to the park in this dreary weather!"' (*New Society*, 9 December 1976). In this case the minder is more trapped in the home than most mothers.

Many minders start out as the mothers of young children themselves who face, in the absence of public provision of childcare services, the same lack of manoeuvrability suffered by other homeworkers. Although the homeworker, discovered by the low pay unit, who knitted gloves for 1.3p an hour, must be exceptional (*Guardian*, 7 December 1976), poor pay characterises home-work, and those who accept such work must be motivated by dire need rather than choice.

Women who are not in a position to be choosy not only get poor pay, they may have to accept a drop in skill and status, as Joyce found after working in the pottery industry:

JOYCE: I started out on vine work. It's rather a tedious job, you learn it in six months. I did get into cameo work in the factory. I was on that for about five years before I left. It was quite a come down to go back on what we call the thirteen vines. I began and ended with it! It's rotten work. It's like, have you seen the grape vine?—it isn't that, but it's a similar thing that goes round the edge, a terrible job. They're rotten minutes on that job. So people who work at home get the thirteen, the thirteen vines.

And the money would be a lot less?

JOYCE: Yes a lot less, because you've got the mess to start with, can you imagine? I had like a little outhouse, and I fixed it up in there. It was like a little glass place. And I would go down there at seven, and do an hour from seven to eight. Then I'd get the kids off to school. The two youngest would help. You have to keep the clay moist. I used to have the kids round me. Stephen, he's ever so good with his hands. Even when he started school, he's always done rather good things with clay. I say it's all the training he got when he was little. Then at night when the kids were in bed I'd go and do a bit more. I don't know how I managed really. But you were lucky to get the work. (I2, pp. 13–14)

In this chapter seven women have been compared. One woman, Gill Carter, has chosen to be the family breadwinner. Two others, Jean Spencer and Janet Austin, took on part-time jobs after I had talked to them. Jean is still employed, washing glasses in the local workingman's club, and Janet found employment at Keele University as a cleaner, during the summer holiday period. The status of full-time domestic worker is therefore far from fixed. Women move in and out of employment during the period when their children are young.

Joyce Atkin does not plan to return to work in the foreseeable future. Her four children all attend school but, given her involvement in her husband's grocery business, and given his non-involvement in the home, Joyce feels with some justice that she could not cope with outside employment.

The three other women, Carol Parker, Maureen Clark and Ann Tate, expect to remain at home without a break until their children go to school. Ann alone is satisfied with this prospect. As we have seen, Maureen Clark thinks that she has become dull since being a full-time houseworker, and she hopes that this will alter when she returns to work. Carol Parker plans to stay home until Leon is school age, but she regrets the style of life the absence of childcare facilities imposes on her. Nurseries are needed not only to enable mums to go out to work, but simply to go out:

CAROL PARKER: I think if I'd only got someone to have him occasionally, you know, so that you can just go out, even just to have a walk round, even if you don't buy anything. (E2, p. 69)

Silverdale as a whole is far from being the matriarchal suburb beloved of town planners:

> Most city architectural designers and planners are men. Curiously they design and plan to exclude men as part of normal daytime life wherever people live. In planning residential life, they aim at filling the presumed daily needs of impossibly vacuous housewives and pre-school tots. They plan in short strictly for matriarchal societies. (Jacobs, 1965, p. 94)

Silverdale has three distinct sectors. The first is Parksite, a postwar council estate. Parksite is situated close to the colliery and houses, in the main, miners' families. Since miners work on a shift system there are always some men around in the day time. The estate has a well attended workingman's club and a sprinkling of shops. All those who live in Parksite and took part in this study report that it is a friendly place, warmly termed the United Nations because of the Geordies, Welsh, Scots, Poles, Czechs, and Germans who have made it their home.

About a mile downhill from Parksite is the second sector, the old village, which dates from the middle of the nineteenth century. The village population tends to be local in origin. Although there is more occupational diversity in the village compared with Parksite, the overwhelming majority of people are employed in manual jobs, including mining. A new shopping centre has been built in the village—'The Parade'. In the day time The Parade is the social centre, not only for the village, but for the newly built private estate to the south of the village, which is the third sector.

The private estate appears to have a higher proportion of white collar workers compared to the other two sectors. It also resembles Jane Jacobs's 'matriarchal society' to a greater extent than either Parksite or the old village. Even so The Parade is only a short walk away, and the village as a whole is sufficiently small to prevent total anonymity. People from the private estate report that when they go to The Parade it is more than likely that they will meet people they can chat with, so that shopping trips are often anticipated as a morale lift.

Even so, if like Jean Spencer you haven't got many spare pennies, this form of relaxation has to be strictly limited, for the more you shop the more you spend. Furthermore the village is not a town, and The Parade is not a vast shopping centre. The products available are routine; the consumption best sellers of modern capitalism:

The massed forces of the pre-packed sliced loaf—ideal for sandwiches at work—of the baked beans, the instant wonder cleaners and the handy mops assembled in the supermarket with history on their side. (Rowbotham, 1974, p. 109)

But this routine can drag—the same groceries week in and week out, the same walk to the shops, the same daily round. The one available avenue of escape seems to be a trip to the nearby town of Newcastle, or if you really intend to spread your wings, Hanley. But with small children this escape route has its drawbacks, especially if, like Carol Parker, you don't have the use of a car.

CAROL: If it's a one-man 'bus, which it is sometimes now, I take him on, but if there's someone in the queue they'll take him on while I take the pushchair. It's alright going, but if you've done any shopping it's coming back that's difficult. It's difficult even with a conductor, 'cos last time I took him on first and went back for the pushchair, and when I got to the 'Bush' here he said, 'You're a damned nuisance with that chair!' I said to the driver, 'Will you stop the 'bus while I take him off and then get the pushchair?' The driver said, 'No, the conductor will take that off', but the conductor was calling me a nuisance. If it wasn't too far I'd walk it. (E2, p. 54)

It was reported recently that Radio Solent has started devoting air time to women who have formed network groups which attempt to overcome the isolation and frustration experienced by mothers like Carol Parker. 'Everybody after months or years of silence, coping with problems they think unique to themselves suddenly find that everyone else has them too.' One common problem was voiced by a mother: 'There's just nowhere you can go with children or do with children. Society just hates children, and their mothers too.

You lived and coped with your problems entirely alone' (*Guardian*, 7 December 1976).

Neither 'buses nor town centres are places easily negotiated with small children. Those concerned with town planning are sometimes aware of the difficulties. The Bolton town centre report, for example, recognises that parking provision for prams is needed in the town centre, and that 'buses should have ample space for pushchairs as well as luggage. It is also noted that centrally situated playgrounds staffed with attendants would enable mothers to shop unencumbered, and refreshment and rest places are needed which would enable shoppers to sit and rest while the children play safely nearby (1965, pp. 75–6).

Few towns in practice, however, have these kinds of facilities, and the anticipated hassle of a visit to town in the company of young children is not the only drawback to be faced. In inflationary times the 'bus fare will be prohibitive for some:

JEAN: I like to go Newcastle, I like to go Hanley, when I've the chance, but I don't often go. The biggest part of the food I fetch in from here at weekends.

Is it a lot to carry?

JEAN: Well not really 'cos I don't go far, and this is why I don't go Newcastle, because if I go Newcastle I've got to take two or three of them with me to carry things, which is two or three times more 'bus fare. So I'd rather go across here. (C2, p. 78)

Life is hedged in with restrictions. In the case of Jean and Paul Spencer their poverty is the major restriction. Eight years before, the family had given up its caravan at Rhyl. This meant the eleven year old child could hardly remember having had a holiday, and Paul, who liked to fish, commented: 'Since then I've felt I've lost a part of my life. I used to go there every weekend nearly—but that was before I got this job in maintenance' (D2, p. 24).

Jean had been putting her evening earnings aside to finance a week's holiday, but the next electricity bill which was higher than expected at £77, threatened to break into the holiday fund. To avoid this Jean and Paul decided to cash the children's insurance policies, which yielded a grand total of £73.

Other families in this study are not impoverished to this extent, and it is not perhaps surprising that the Spencers' view of politics is stamped with egalitarianism; and that they define classes on the basis of life chances:

Have you any views about political parties?
JEAN: When I was first married, if anyone worked they were automatically Labour. This was my impression. I've thought about it since. They say we've freedom of choice, but it doesn't matter who you vote for, they all seem to do the same thing when they get in. There's tax on petrol, tax on borrowing money, tax on bread—it's the working man who always has to pay it back . . . If you've got a car for work reasons, what do they do? Your tax goes up, your insurance goes up, petrol goes up. They're having it back off you. To me, if the news is on and it's politics I just don't listen, 'cos I know what they're promising they are not going to fulfil.

Same as school, in the old days, if you were brainy and passed the exam, you had to pay so much money; you had to buy school uniform. So if there was someone who had a little business, the mother had got a little shop or something, it seemed as though they stood a better chance. Whereas if you were a family with just enough to live on coming in each week you didn't stand a chance. Well today everybody's meant to have a chance, but it's still—if you don't pass the eleven plus you can't go. I think if you've got a school and there's a backward child there, give him a little bit of help. Give a child that's bright the opportunity of helping him.

So you feel none of the political parties represents you?
JEAN: It's just a position for them, they've got a bit further. They're not *doing* anything for the country. You take it from the war, I wasn't very old but I can remember the ration books and standing in a queue with my mother. We would be better off today with a ration book so that everyone was getting a fair share of everything. I can't remember having smoked salmon and fresh salmon; I haven't tasted any for *years* because it's so dear. A joint of meat at the weekend, I'm paying £1.80. Potatoes are so dear. I've cut down from cod because it's scarce and bought herring, but now that's scarce. You keep cutting down to the cheapest food and you're getting nowhere. You're getting cheaper and cheaper until you're buying muck. Take a man with a business, he's got someone running his business, he can go and buy fresh salmon. Take the politicians, can you see Mr Wilson's wife thinking, 'Well I'll make dumplings this week, 'cos we've no potatoes'. No. They're running this country; they're making a profit out of us . . . It's dog eat dog.

So politics, really I only talk about it if somebody asks me, but myself, I've said all along we want a bit of communism in this country—equal rights for every bugger! (C2, pp. 50–3)

When Paul talks politics it's usually with his fellow maintenance workers. Paul like Jean has a desire for change:

PAUL: At work we were talking about Labour, Conservatives and Liberals. A few of the fellows said we've had all of these governments in, the Liberals before the 1914 war, and Labour and Conservative since, and all three of them have done nothing. One chap says, 'Germany was flattened during the war and look how they've built it up'. Look at this place here, Silverdale. The only place they've built is the middle of the village. There's no go in the place at all. If you go to the cities you see derelict houses. Look round the Newcastle area . . . I could say a lot, but I don't. One chap says, 'The three parties have done nothing', another says, 'What are you hinting at?' he says. 'Well we've had them all in, why not try communism?' 'Oh that won't do!' So I said, 'What's to be feared about communism?' 'Well, Albert says, 'what about Russia and Czechoslovakia?' I said, 'Well I've heard no more about Czechoslovakia, not after the riots they've had'. He says, 'What about Hungary?' I said, 'Well they've settled down now, they're happy now'. 'Well anyway don't let's talk about communism here,' the foreman said, so that was that. (D2, p. 20)

When Paul talks about union struggles he emphasises the weakness of the workers' movement compared to the strength of the bosses. The last strike he experienced was in his view called at a time that was beneficial to management and during the second week of the strike the Government announced its pay-threshold policy which took the wind out of their sails. Paul is steeped in pessimism; which is not surprising in the light of his domestic and industrial experiences. His conception of communism seems very abstract, a vague electoral possibility.

Other couples share the Spencer's distrust of politics and politicians without sharing their radicalism. Andrew Austin and Mark Carter have a very instrumental approach to politics and trade unionism. Andrew thinks that it is a good thing that 'there are blokes like Scargill in Derbyshire, and the blokes down Kent, prepared to do something. They are the blokes who voted for a strike, and if we hadn't had a strike where would our wages have been then?' Andrew supported the strike as a suitable course of action for others to engage in, but not for himself: 'I didn't want to strike. I'd a wife and child and this house, my mortgage is £22 . . . I wanted the money, but I'm at a pit where if you wanted to work overtime you could.' (H2, p. 23)

Andrew is not interested in party politics. Two issues which impassion him is his belief that there is a vast amount of social security scrounging and uncontrolled immigration. He would like to emigrate to South Africa, but Janet is opposed to living in a racially segregated country.

Andrew would also like to be self-employed because 'You set your own time and you know that what you do is *yours*. I think if any man had a chance to work for himself he wouldn't mind working twelve hours a day, seven days a week.' (H2, p. 20)

Andrew possibly symbolises alienated labour; he resents the time he has to spend at work for the benefit of others, but he is compelled by anxiety concerning his future to take all the work he can get:

ANDREW: The time you spend at work throughout your life is terrible. You know, out of a week I'm spending half the week at work. To have enough money I'm spending half the week at work . . . But then again, you've only got a certain amount of good earning life in you. You've got to get what you can. (H2, p. 24)

As Theo Nichols and Peter Armstrong have argued, in response to Goldthorpe *et al* (1968, 1969), such instrumental attitudes, which are rooted in insecurity, express or result from a partial form of class consciousness (1976, p. 157).

Mark Carter has more freedom. Since he is supported by Gill he is free to take on as many foreigners (in undeclared jobs) as he can get. He thinks they are doing well; politics and trade unionism have nothing to offer him.

Michael Tate, a pottery worker, has a very constitutional approach to trade unionism. In his view all strikes are unnecessary, conflicts must be resolved through negotiation, because too many people suffer otherwise.

But if management will not negotiate, what kind of pressure can be used to create willingness to negotiate?

MICHAEL: It's very difficult to put pressure on without a strike I must admit. To put *real* pressure on striking is the only way. But there are many jobs throughout the country—you've got to think of people as a whole, not just individual jobs—and there are lots of jobs throughout the country where, either because of the job or because of their own personal circumstances, the people couldn't or wouldn't go on strike . . . And when the miners are on strike it involves everybody, not just those who use coal. It affects the pricing of goods, the electricity, transport. The dockers have almost the same leverage, even the motor industry to a lesser extent . . .

What do I think about political parties? I don't think any party represents the people at large. We had a vote on the common market and we were voted in, rightly or wrongly. I think *that* would be a way of voting, because members of parliament don't always represent the views of the people. The obvious issue is hanging, because all the parties are saying the same thing on this. (B2, pp. 22–3)

Alan Parker, a building worker, is the embodiment of the deferential worker. Alan votes Labour, although he can see little difference between a Labour and Conservative government. Alan disapproves of trade unions:

ALAN: They're Bolshie in my opinion . . . These executives, they're earning big money, they go round in big cars. But there's some skill to that, why shouldn't they have more than us? . . . If a man has got brains to get his own company, his own firm going, so he can keep men working, why shouldn't he get more than what his employees get? I think he should get more. The thing with these unions, they think the men should get as much as the boss—or more! Why should they? It's only through brains that he's got that firm going in the first place. (F2, pp. 9–10)

If it is thought that houseworkers, because of their confinement to a narrow home-based world, are more politically backward than their menfolk, it must also be recognised that the latter's outlook is often inconsistent and illogical. The views reproduced here seem to display a variety of ideological tendencies; reformism, deference, economism, and in one case, racism.

Two women, Janet Austin and Carol Parker, are more left wing in outlook than their husbands. Both vote Labour, support the right to strike, and see trade unions as a useful means to improve working conditions. However, both these women, along with the others, except Jean, became hesitant and reluctant to speak as soon as the word 'politics' was mentioned. Their menfolk, on the other hand, seemed to welcome the opportunity to expound their 'theories'. Possibly the men get more practice in the art of political discussion at work and in the clubs and pubs.

Whatever the reason, the contrast with women's response is striking. Joyce Atkin answered the question, 'Do you think any political party represents the views of people like you?' by saying: 'I'm not intelligent enough for this interview. I don't know a lot about it. I don't feel satisfied with any of them.' (I2, p. 27)

When Gill Carter was asked, 'Do you think strikes are ever justified?' she responded, 'It's just something that doesn't interest me, I don't know'. And again a moment later when asked, 'Do you have any views about political parties?'—'No. That sort of thing just doesn't interest me.' (K2, p. 26)

Maureen Clark, when asked, 'Does a union cover your husband's work?' replied, 'He doesn't belong to a union. I think the union there is the General Workers. I don't really know about unions at all, I've had no contact with them myself. It would be best if you asked my husband about unions.' (J2, p. 26) When asked about politics, Maureen responded by saying: 'No I don't take much interest in politics at all'. She would like the Liberal Party to 'have a go, because they can't do any worse than the rest of them'. (J2, p. 27)

Joyce Atkin and Ann Tate both react against what they see as unnecessary party bickering:

ANN: I think really they all ought to join together, for the time being, to get the country back on its feet again, instead of one party being in, and the other party fighting against it. I think they ought to pull together. (A2, p. 23)

The sense of being outside decision making processes runs through the remarks made by all the women. This tallies with the results of the *Woman's Own* survey of five thousand readers. (The five thousand readers who replied to the *Woman's Own* survey may well be unrepresentative of the readers who did not reply; in my view, however, the latter are unlikely to be more in touch politically than those who did reply.):

We asked readers: 'Who do you think makes sure your views are represented nationally?'

Two thirds couldn't think of anyone who represented them. The other third named all sorts of people but no particular group got much support. Roughly one in ten mentioned MPs and councillors, and the same number mentioned the Press. Five per cent said their trade union, while two per cent each suggested the Consumers' Association, their professional association, and the Women's Liberation Movement. Action groups and Mrs Thatcher logged up one per cent each. (*Woman's Own* Survey, 1976)

This is not simply the reflection in thought of the real under representation of women in unions and governmental processes (see table).

TABLE I

October 1974 General Election percentage female candidates:

		%			%
			Female MPs		
Labour	50 : 626	8	Labour	18 : 319	6
Conservative	30 : 623	5	Conservative	7 : 277	3
Liberal	49 : 619	8	Liberal	0 : 13	–
SNP	8 : 71	11	SNP	2 : 11	18

Success of candidates

Female		%	*Male*		%
Labour	18 : 50	36	Labour	301 : 576	52
Conservative	7 : 30	23	Conservative	270 : 593	46
Liberal	0 : 49	–	Liberal	13 : 570	2
SNP	2 : 8	25	SNP	9 : 63	14

1974 Local Government Elections

Percentage female candidates for the Labour Party		*Successful women as a percentage Labour elected*
Scotland	(regions)	11	6
Scotland	(districts)	12	9
London	(boroughs)	22	19

SOURCE: 'Obstacles', *Women in Politics* (London: The Labour Party, 1975) p. 6.

The root of the problem lies in the separation of family life, as *private* life, from public, social life, and the immersion of women in the private, personal domain (Zaretsky, 1976).

In her cloistered world the houseworker is hard put to see how elections, parliamentary debates, union conferences and strikes have any but a negative bearing on her concerns. On the whole she prefers to stay 'obstinately within the one realm that is familiar to her, where she can control things and in the midst of which she enjoys a precarious sovereignty' (Simone de Beauvoir, 1972, p. 616).

In the main, public policies impinge on her interests via her husband and older children. Those active in the work-a-day world have ongoing work projects and related experiences which sometimes bring them face to face with issues—'Should I join the union?'—'Should we stick to the pay-norms?'—'Will my job be secure if the government continues with its deflationary policy?'—etc. Since these issues bear on the interests of family members, houseworkers are not indifferent to them, but they may be sufficiently ill at ease in areas where they lack first hand experience to wish to avoid any direct discussion. It may seem wise to leave such matters to the 'man of the house'.

This withdrawal reaction is likely to reinforce the tendency for women to be under-represented in decision making processes. In the home their reaction is likely to strengthen the authority of the husband as the arbiter of the family's relation to society.

The women we have looked at here are oppressed in their personal relations to a much greater extent than is the case with their economically active counterparts. The houseworker's life is centered round the husband's activity. Her leisure and work are tailored to suit his. She cuts her coat according to the cloth he provides. Whereas for the man homelife is but one, admittedly important, aspect of life, for the houseworker the home is the bedrock of her experience.

Jean Spencer has had more industrial experience than any other woman in this group, and Jean is, as we have seen, the only woman in the group who is not slow to express a viewpoint about political and industrial matters. I think for most women the work experience prior to starting a family is defined by them as being transitory. In terms of time involved the years spent in full-time maternity is dwarfed by the long span of work in industry prior to the arrival of children and after the period that full-time maternity has been completed. But the significance of the intervening period of maternity cannot be comprehended in terms of the time it takes. The transition from childlessness to parenthood is seen as a qulitative change of the utmost importance by most women. This is not simply because the lack of social provision for children does indeed give their presence a decisive influence on the life style of the parent. It is also because the effect of the ideology of 'woman the homemaker', discussed in the previous chapter, inclines most women to define the transition from childlessness to parenthood as being of key importance. In an ideological sense their life leads up to this turning point.

I think the period at work between school and parenthood has for most women a temporary quality. It is expected to give way to a maternal break which, however short that break may be, offers, as a result of gender socialisation, an emotional fulfilment which work cannot match. Most men do not, I think, experience the work period prior to parenthood in this way, that is, as an occupation performed in the anticipation that in the foreseeable future it will give way to a more fulfilling activity. I think that this difference between young male and female workers will show itself in the more pronounced non-involvement of the latter in the work-a-day world, particularly in the case of those employed in unskilled and semi-skilled occupations. In such occupations young women may only 'put their backs' into the work then marriage is round the corner and the money is needed to set up a home.

A pottery shop steward made precisely this point to me. The women most responsive to trade union questions were married women returning to work after a full-time period at home, whereas young girls, until they get engaged, 'have no sense at all; it's no good talking to them. They may give their mothers £3 and the other £15 is for themselves, to spend on anything that takes their fancy. Then they get a steady boyfriend and you see them change overnight. They work like hell they really do.' (Pauline Hunt, 1974)

It is likely, therefore, that the work experience of most full-time houseworkers has not been so absorbing as to provide them with either an interest in, or knowledge of, the affairs of organised labour of sufficient depth to make them feel involved in industrial matters during their temporary absence from the labour market. In most cases the houseworkers' foothold in the world of labour was tenuous to begin with, and during the period of full-time domestic work most houseworkers feel very cut off from industrial and political concerns.

When, therefore, the typical houseworker returns to the labour market she does so against a background of domestic rather than previous industrial experience, and in comparison with her male partner she continues to bear the main burden of domestic responsibility. One would expect that her background and her domestic situation would influence the way she related to industrial relations at the place of work. It would seem probable that married women workers differ from married men workers in a variety of ways. It is now time to turn our atention to this probability.

3 Workers Side by Side

The typical female worker today is a married woman; the mother of school age, teenage or grown up children. In March 1973, 8,919,000 women went out to work. About 62 per cent of them were married (Department of Employment, 1974). The typical female worker has a second job in the home. This job is often longer, harder and more demanding than her paid job.

Sarah Wells, one of the women to be considered in this chapter, got a job in a book shop after being at home full-time for fifteen years. It is more usual for women to be absent from the labour market for four or five years (Yudkin and Holme, 1969). Nineteen per cent of women with children under five years of age already work outside the home and, according to a survey carried out in 1971, 41 per cent of the rest said they would like to go out to work if childcare facilities were available (Pat Knight, *Morning Star*, 6 October 1976).

The neighbourly presence of mothers and sisters make an early return to work possible. Working mothers with young children depend on their extended families. Children are taken to their grandmothers for breakfast, and they are taken to and collected from school by grandparents or sisters. Occasionally a close friend will provide this kind of service. It is very rare for kin or friends to replace the mother on a full-time basis. If a pre-school age child is cared for on a full-time basis the circumstances are usually exceptional. The mother may be a single parent, or the family may be very hard-pressed financially, as in the case of Sandra Mill:

SANDRA: I've never really not earned. The only time I haven't worked is when you've finished, you know, when you're six months pregnant and you have to finish work until you have them. The eldest boy was just six weeks old when I started back, 'cos I had to go back to keep even myself. I never had another break then until I got married and I came to have Clive. Then I started back work again when he was about two or three months old. So I've always worked.

Who looked after the children?

SANDRA: My mother, they live just up the road. (G3, p. 8)

Sarah Wells, like most women who return to the labour market after a few years absence, felt very unsure about her ability to cope in the new environment. This is not because 'women's work' is particularly demanding. The range of jobs open to women like Sarah is very narrow because the labour market is organised in terms of sexual apartheid.

> In the Sample Census of Population in 1966 it was demonstrated that 60 per cent of all female employees were in occupations where more than three quarters of all employees were female, and that 2.8 million women were in occupations where women were more than 90 per cent of the work force (Judith Hunt, 1975, p. 6).

Furthermore:

> 'Over half of all women employees work in three service sectors: Miscellaneous services which includes hotels and catering, laundries and hair-dressing, distributive trades, mainly shop assistants, and professional and scientific services, teachers, nurses, social workers . . . no single industry accounts for more than 10 per cent of all male workers' (*Women Under Attack*, 1976, p. 2).

Not only do women confront a severely restricted range of employment but *within* occupations women occupy low status jobs with poor prospects. Thus:

> women account for:
> 96.8 per cent of all canteen assistants, counterhands, etc.
> 91.7 per cent of all charwomen, office cleaners, etc.
> 91.6 per cent of all nurses. (Judith Hunt, 1975, p. 6)

The fact that women in the main find employment in mundane occupations does little to boost the self-confidence of women returning to the labour market after several years absence. Such women often doubt their ability to perform *any* job adequately. This is due to their immersion in housework, which is an extremely privatised form of work.

Domestic work is to the world of employment as the back stage work crew is to the play; without them no performance, yet how easy it is for the audience to forget they are there at all. Even the actors may decline to rank them as equals in a creative enterprise. The public effect on stage is rewarded or rejected, judged as the case may be. Backstage life is cloistered, the actors might say drab. For those who live back stage, excluded from direct judgement, it can be experienced as a sheltered place—in comparison with the open stage.

After fifteen years toil behind the scenes it feels almost insolent to walk out on to the stage.

Sarah started work in a book shop after fifteen years full-time work in the home. This change of work environment was challenging enough, but for those women who enter or return to factory work the change of environment is very distinct.

Margaret Dean's mother had worked part-time as a cleaner while Margaret was growing up. After Margaret got married she took a job in Kipling's Cake and Bread factory. On the top floor of the factory various sticky substances were mixed, and passed through pipes to the ground floor, where the mixtures became cakes and flan fillings. Only women worked on the ground floor cake section. They added trimmings to the cakes and packed them. Downstairs bread was made in huge automatic machines resembling mechanised macaroni.

Margaret's mother had once asked why no women worked in the bread section. Because, she was told, the trays of bread were very heavy to carry and the men worked in an unpleasantly hot temperature. She did not think to enquire why only women worked in the cake section.

The segregation of women workers to a narrow range of occupations, and to particular jobs within these occupations, severely limits the number of equal pay claims that can be made under the 1975 Act. This Act allows people to claim to receive equal conditions of employment and remuneration with others of the opposite sex who are employed in the same place of work, and who do the same job as themselves, or a job which is broadly similar. Margaret's mother cannot claim that her job is the same, or broadly the same, as that of the breadmakers; she cannot therefore claim that she should be paid at the same rate of pay as the breadmakers.

The Act also makes it possible for comparisons to be made between jobs which have been classified as equal under a job evaluation scheme. Since the weighting of various job factors is decided according to the whim of the evaluator, the result of the evaluation scheme is frequently a pseudo-scientific justification for the maintenance of pay differentials, as occurred in the first claim under the Act involving job evaluation (*Women Under Attack*, pp. 5–6)

As was noted in the first chapter, not all women think that they should be paid on a par with men. Gladys Kohout, who works in Rist's Wires and Cables Ltd, is hostile to the idea of equal pay for women:

GLADYS: Rist's now, they're employing men for women's work; paying 'em women's rates! If them men can prove they can do it Rist's are getting cheap labour, aren't they? It shouldn't be that a woman can have the same money as a man. Take me, I'm doing this job, it's pin money for me. Now the man over there is doing the same job, and he's got four children, and his wife isn't working. He should get more shouldn't he?

Her friend Muriel did not agree.

MURIEL: No. I think people should be paid for the work they do, for their ability. (F3, p. 79)

In reality at the present time in Britain wages are primarily determined by the impersonal requirements of the market and the strength or weakness of the workers' collective bargaining position, and secondly by the stringency of the government's wage restraint policy. We are a full revolution away from the realisation of Muriel's principle of payment according to work done. We are two revolutions away from Gladys's desire for payment according to need.

Some women decline to support the demand for equal pay because they fear this will result in a worsening of their working conditions; a point which Audrey Wise has drawn to my attention (Wise, Spokesman Pamphlet). Margaret's mother certainly would refuse to be paid on a par with the breadmakers if this meant she would have to lift heavy trays of bread and work in stifling conditions.

To trade conditions for cash would run counter to the homely approach she brought to work. She had chosen to work in the bakery because she enjoyed baking at home, but as she said to Margaret, it was not like the same job at all.

'You had to keep going all the time. You can't just go to the toilet when you want, you've got to call somebody to take your place. All the time you have to stand by your machine watching the cakes whizz past. If somebody isn't pulling their weight all the cakes pile up.' (D3, p. 4)

HOME AND WORK

Sarah found the demands of two jobs so distressing she felt that fairly soon she would give up her paid job. If social facilities existed to provide most of the services currently provided by houseworkers, the problem of coping with two jobs would largely disappear. The availability of childcare provision for every parent who desired a nursery place for her or his child would in itself transform life for working parents. Childrearing is not, however, seen in Britain as socially productive work—the production of the next generation of workers—it is, on the contrary, defined as the private affair of the parents concerned, and more particularly of the mother concerned. In my view this ideological climate serves to justify the totally inadequate provision of nursery places, and of other facilities like laundry and sewing services, and catering services, which would lift much of the burden of servicing families from the shoulders of individual women.

In the absence of such social facilities, women have only two ways of reducing the domestic burden; they can redistribute tasks among family members, or they can do tasks less frequently and less thoroughly.

The first alternative is not within the woman's *individual* control. The attitudes of her husband and children influence the redistribution of jobs. Sarah found the extra help her family gave did little to reduce the burden of two jobs:

My family life has altered completely. Len picks me up from work each evening. When we walk into the house in the evening we have to start organising what we are going to eat. We don't talk at all. And then we sit down and eat, and by the time I've cleared up and we've really got time to sit down it's time to go to bed. And I haven't read to Ellen as much as I did. And at weekends I haven't got time to do things with the children. If it's only to go for a walk I haven't got time. It's not just household things, it's things like getting to the doctor. You can do it when you're around in the day, but when you're not you have to make an appointment for half past five, and you have to come straight in, pick the child up and rush down there. It's very difficult. It's the same with the dentist, and with money affairs as well, just having time to sit down and work out the account. It's difficult when you want to 'phone people, they're not always around in the evening, it's much more leisurely in the daytime. And not being able to go to Speech Day last week. I feel this a lot on Sports Days and at Christmas Concerts. It's very difficult not being able to do these things. It makes me resentful. I get in such a state sometimes. I just feel I want to get back to normal living. (C3, p. 38)

Len Wells, who works as a technician in a laboratory, helped in the house as much if not slightly more than most husbands. He prepared the children's breakfast, and helped to cook the evening meal. He would help Sarah change the linen on the beds and he 'hoovered round' during the week. Shopping they did jointly in a drive-in supermarket. Most of the jobs Len now did, apart from shopping, he took on when Sarah got paid employment. When Sarah gave up her job she resumed these tasks again, apart from changing the bed linen which Len continued to help with.

However, at all times Len only *helped* Sarah; that is to say she carried the main burden of domestic work. During the period in which she worked in the shop Sarah gave the house a 'going over' each weekend, and she did all the cooking at weekends. This pattern is very general. When the woman isn't around, either because she returns home after her husband or simultaneously with him, the husband will take on tasks like cooking, but when she is present, notably at weekends, she reverts to her full-time houseworker role. Sarah also dealt with the family's washing and ironing, and she kept the house and kitchen shipshape during the week. She cleaned the cooker, a task much disliked by Silverdale women. Cleaning a cooker involves dismantling the parts, removing the grease and grime and reassembling the parts. Of all tasks performed in the home, this task resembles an industrial job, and it is therefore quite significant that husbands fairly often take it on because their wives find it so unpleasant.

Sarah also planned the daily menu, and she was responsible for general household management. This duty is quite a time consuming aspect of domestic work which nearly always falls to the woman to perform, as a Rist's worker observed:

JOAN WITZ: Not only do women do the shopping, they've also *got* to think what shopping to get in. It's the planning of the meals, and thinking what you've got to buy, and the things that are needed in the home, all this has got to be taken into account. Even when it comes to holidays it's the woman who thinks about the clothes and does the preparing. At Christmas, all my husband does towards Christmas is go out and get a few bottles. All the planning and everything else I do, and I think most other women do all the shopping and planning for Christmas as well. (E3, p. 49)

From my vantage point behind the drinks counter of the Silverdale Co-op, I can confirm the above statement. It was indeed primarily the men who took upon themselves the job of purchasing the Christmas booze, while their wives did the rest of the shopping, for which task they had prepared a full twelve months in the form of Christmas Club savings.

There were certain household jobs which Len regarded as the responsibility of the man of the house. Len did electrical repair jobs and the decorating. He saw to the car's maintenance and he kept the garden under control: 'It's not a woman's garden, it involves a lot of digging'. (C3, p. 29)

In their division of labour Len and Sarah are fairly typical. Gardening, decorating, household repairs and care of the car— even when the car is purchased by the wife and they both drive— these jobs are mainly done by men. Occasionally a woman will take on one of these jobs if her husband shows great reluctance to do it himself:

ROSE HARRIS: He saddled me with the decorating donkey's ages ago. I'd still got a few inhibitions about swearing in front of the children. And I asked him to decorate. Well he started. He put up these three strips of wallpaper, it was an all morning job, you know. Well he was fed up to the back teeth, 'cos he can't bear decorating, and I walked in and opened my big mouth straight away. 'Oh', I says, 'you've put that middle strip on upside down.'—She drew in her breath—I ushered the children right round me, 'cos the air went blue, you know. He just downed tools and left, and I finished the job, well I had to do. (A3, pp. 51–2)

Carrying in the coal to maintain the fire also emerges as a man's job, although tending the fire, lighting it and cleaning the grate is woman's work. Since Silverdale is a mining village most houses naturally have coal fires.

As noted previously, washing windows outside is also the man's job, whereas washing windows indoors is another female duty.

Typical masculine jobs: household repairs, gardening, decorating, cleaning the cooker, washing windows outside, are performed sporadically, whereas typical feminine jobs: planning meals, shopping, cooking, washing dishes, getting clothes ready, putting things away, making sandwiches, are *daily* jobs. Even the most helpful husband is often less tied to the daily round of household tasks than his wife.

The weekend is a very different experience for the husband as compared to his working wife. During the week, if the need arises, he will be prepared to care for the children, help with the cooking, washing up and shopping, but the weekend is his time to relax. He may like to go fishing or to a football match, to the club or pub, or just stay put with his feet up in front of the telly watching the weekend sport. For their wives the weekend presents itself as an opportunity to catch up with household chores and do the weekly wash. And, as already mentioned, they take on the same responsibility for childcare and the cooking as they did in their houseworker days. During the week these women loosen their ties with the house, at weekends these ties reassert themselves. For their husbands the process works in reverse. During the week they are more involved in the house than they used to be, at weekends the previous normality asserts itself. It is difficult for the women to demand more help at weekends because their husbands can say they did their share during the week, and in some cases they can argue:

MICHAEL DEAN: I didn't ask you to work. If you can't cope in the house chuck the job in. (D3, p. 15)

The inequality of workload between husband and wife is the general rule in Silverdale. It looks somewhat improved if we compare present day relationships with the past. Most couples grew up in households in which the male head did next to nothing in the home. This was often correctly interpreted as the assertion of masculine authority:

DON HARRIS: My dad was an old fashioned man, very Victorian. He thought everything to be done in the house was woman's work. The only thing I can say he did was keep his clothes tidy. He wore solid tweed clothes. When he went out he always wore breeches and tight lace-up gaiters, and black boots. It was always our job, not the lads, but the girls' job to keep them clean. And he would sit there and put his trousers on and have the girls put his boots on and then lace his gaiters up. He always had the girls do that. But he never did anything in the house, he never did a hand's turn. (A3, p. 18)

It is hard for these people to imagine their fathers behaving other than they did:

JOAN WITZ: My father was a big man of sixteen stone, and the thought of him with a duster seems a bit hilarious really. (E3, p. 9)

Against this background current practice represents an improvement. But the past in which the husband 'never did a hand's turn' is the present of some families. Michael Dean, one such husband, explains his domestic arrangement by saying, 'She's the boss'. What this means in practice is that he has opted out of domestic duties and she is left to get on with it.

Peter Lewis also left his wife, Dilys, to cope with their home while, for years, he was involved in the union and miners' club. When the children were still young they went on holiday in Blackpool with a group of friends. Peter took part in a pram pushing race with the other fathers, and that, as far as Dilys could remember, was the only time he had pushed a pram. Peter would occasionally cook something. His speciality was chocolate cake. Each day he came home and took his dinner out of the oven—a step forward from the miners who expected their dinner on the table (Dennis *et al*, 1969). Even young women will sometimes try to conform with this expectation, until their involvement in paid employment prohibits their ability to have their husband's meal ready on the table.

Peter rationalised his non-involvement in the home by arguing that most jobs men did were heavier, and harder than housework, so that housewives were merely evening up the score when they took on a second job outside the home.

PETER: I think women are just starting to work on a par with men. By going out to work they're starting to work on a par. Before they went out to work they didn't have enough to do. (B3, p. 60)

Peter and Dilys, like most Silverdale families, did not take measures to control their family size until they already had a family. They had four children. Peter did not want to have children at all, and Dilys would have prefered a family half the size. She has reached this view after the experience of bringing up four children single handed. Peter is not, however, convinced that this was a full job of work, not as compared to the miners' work at any rate. Only now, in his opinion, is Dilys beginning to work on a par. At the same time, Peter points out that mechanisation in the mining industry has transformed his job: 'all I do now at work is push a button'. He does not, however, seem to feel that this conflicts with his view that women are just beginning to work on a par with men.

This is because the difficulty or ease of domestic work in comparison with industrial work has little to do with the real reason why Peter devalues housework. As I have argued previously, domestic work is socially productive; it contributes to the reproduction and maintenance of labour. The productiveness of domestic work is, however, obscured by the fact that it is performed in privatised family units. The result of this privatisation is that the domestic worker appears to be performing a personal service for the family, whereas industrial work is seen to be socially productive. In terms of this comparison domestic work does not seem to be a real job at all.

Dilys receives more help from her daughter Carol and son Paul than she does from Peter. Carol keeps her room tidy, helps to cook the evening meal and takes it in turns with Dilys and Paul to wash up. Few parents in Silverdale impose household tasks on their children. Those below the age of thirteen do very little indeed. Help from teenage daughters was often more noticeable than help from either sons or husbands. However, such help remained 'help'; the person helped in each case was the mother, who shouldered the prime responsibility for caring, cooking, cleaning, washing and ironing.

The general picture which emerges from this study of households in Silverdale corresponds to the findings of a National Opinion Poll of 422 working wives, 393 non-working wives and 412 married men described in *The Sunday Times*, 27 February 1977. It was found that:

an overwhelming majority of men take it for granted that wives, even working wives, take the main brunt of housework and childcare . . . More surprisingly their wives mostly agree . . .

they do not, apparently, expect more than token help with the washing up, cleaning and shopping.

The reasons for this are, I think, fairly complex. The privatised nature of domestic work and socialisation into gender roles are involved. These have been discussed in previous chapters. Additional reasons have to do with the life cycle of the family.

Husbands in group three households, where both parents are employed, do more in the home than husbands in group two households, where the wife is usually employed full-time in the home. This is not, I think, surprising since in the latter households the woman has become involved in the house on a full-time basis. What is less predictable is that husbands in group three households do less in the home than husbands in group one households, where the couple is childless.

I would suggest that during the period in which women work full-time in the home, husbands get accustomed to their wives doing jobs which were previously performed jointly. The more marked sexual division of labour which develops in group two households is not easily uprooted when women return to the labour market. If the wife's employment is deemed by the husband, or by the husband and wife, to be unnecessary or at least of secondary importance, the husband can use the marginality of the wife's employment as an argument in favour of maintaining the domestic status quo. The marginality of the wife's job will be discussed when we consider family finance. For the moment it is enough to recognise that women may lack both the conviction that household tasks should be redistributed in the home, and the bargaining power which a non-marginal job would give them in an attempt to secure such a redistribution of tasks.

Rather than attempting to redistribute domestic jobs, most women try to cut them down to size. This has a direct impact on the family's pattern of consumption. As Jean Gardiner (1975) has pointed out, the real consumption of the family is influenced by the organisation of the family budget. This organisational task is usually a female duty. To save money the housewife will prepare food herself rather than buy pre-prepared convenience food. The married woman worker, however, will turn to convenience food products far more frequently. Sarah was reluctant to adopt this practice. She felt tinned and frozen food had less nutriment than fresh food. The pressure of time, however, forced Sarah to use more prepared products, although for her and others there is a financial ceiling to her willingness to purchase such products. Inflation is bringing us close to that ceiling.

'In 1971, for the first time in ten years, the quantity of convenience food purchased in Britain went down. Thus it seems likely that women were substituting their own efforts for commodities which the family income was insufficient to buy.' (*Women Under Attack*, 1976, p. 25)

The family budget is also made to stretch further by shopping around for bargains. Of all the household jobs which have to be cut down when the woman goes out to work, shopping takes the biggest cut:

NORMA WADE: We go shopping on a Friday night. We go to the supermarket, and then to the greengrocers and bakers. We get it all done in one go for the week. It was different when I was at home full-time. When I think of the time I wasted! I used to come straight from playschool, and go to the parade. I'd draw my family allowance, and think, 'Do I need anything else? Oh yes, go in the fish shop. Do I need some cotton? What colour?' So it would go on. I'd stay up there until they closed for lunch. Really what a waste of time. (H3, pp. 64–5)

To experience this time spent in the past as a 'waste of time' implies a recognition that there are competing alternatives for the use of time; in this case recognition that time is money. It is the experience of selling labour power that makes this recognition possible. If you are a houseworker for several years the idea that time is money gets blunted. If you have never sold your labour services you don't think in time saving terms at all.

This situation is aptly described by the experience Zygmunt Baumann recounted in conversation with me, concerning the introduction of laundries in Poland. Baumann and his associates were asked to find out why Polish housewives were reluctant to use the laundries which had been built for their convenience. The housewives had totted up the cost of using the laundry, in contrast with the cost of doing the washing without the use of mechanical aids in their own home. They concluded it was cheaper to do the washing at home. The one cost factor they had left out of account was the cost of their own labour time. Since at that stage there were no paid productive outlets for their labour there was no means by which their labour time could acquire exchange value in their own eyes. As employment opportunities became available to them the laundries also became more widely used.

Rose liked to shop around, but her husband Don, highly conscious of the exchange value of labour, argued it wasn't worthwhile:

DON: If she runs down the bottom of Newcastle, and then goes up to the top she may find out things are a bit cheaper at the bottom. Then if she goes back to the bottom again it's to save maybe ten pence. But that's taken her an hour. It's not common sense to do that when she's going out to work. (A3, p. 64)

Other household jobs are axed, not only because time has taken on new value, but because the double job really is too much work:

JOAN WITZ: In the beginning I tried to keep up with the housework, doing the same more or less. But I found it too much because you had no free time. I found I was spending every night cleaning. You see, for instance, when I didn't work I would wash the paintwork down every week. I would go through the house each day and hoover every room, and each room would be thoroughly turned out once a week. I only go through the house at weekends now, and I only wash paintwork occasionally. I used to wash dishes and glasses that were not in use, and put them back in the cupboard, I used to do that a lot more often. The pantry was emptied and cleaned more often than it is now. You just can't keep up with working full-time *and* keep your house like you used to keep it.

There are things that you've *got* to do. You've *got* to cook to eat, and you've *got* to wash and iron. Even then, when you're at work you don't iron all the things you used to iron. I think when you're working you will only iron the bare necessities, whereas when you're not working you go to extremes and iron everything in sight, you know, you fold this and you fold that, whereas now I concentrate on nipping through it. I think you're bound to do less housework because you're not there to do it. When you're at home you've got all day to do the housework. (E3, p. 28)

This was said by Joan, the mother of a teenage daughter. For those with more children it is harder to keep housework under control. 'You dread every speck of dirt when you're working,' said a harassed mother of four (G3, p. 34).

What is regarded as necessary and unnecessary work in the home is relative. Some houses are very tidy and polished, others, like mine, are untidy and a bit dusty. However, jobs like cleaning out cupboards, polishing furniture and glasses and washing paintwork tend to be reduced drastically in all households. Other jobs like ironing towels are cut out completely.

Ironically as the hard pressed working mother is forced to lower her domestic standards her family may well become more rather than less appreciative:

GLADYS KOHOUT: One job I used to do regularly and don't now is that black polished floor. I used to wipe it everyday, and polish it everyday 'till it shone like mirrors. But I was miserable with myself at the time, and I was miserable with the kids. Oh that floor! I'd worked hard on it and nobody seemed to appreciate it. But now, I only do it when it needs doing, and when it's done they say, 'Oo, that looks nice!' It makes you feel appreciated. (F3, pp. 50–1)

FAMILY FINANCE AND WORK IDEOLOGY

Sarah had decided to return to work. Most men in the village didn't decide, they never thought of doing anything else. Most of these men had grown up in a home geared to their father's work routine. When their time came they had slipped into the rhythm of work as a matter of course. For some work had always been one long hard dominating fact of life.

Don Harris, for example, came from a family of twelve.

DON: When I was a child I always had a lot to do. At the bottom of our street there was a small milkman who used to keep half a dozen cows, and he used to deliver the milk in half quart cans. And as I ran up and down delivering the papers in the morning, I used to pick up four or five of these cans and drop them off, and pick up some more on the way back. And, well, at this time of the year we were dependent a lot on the food that we grew, and we used to have three or four allotments on the go the whole time, so there was always work to do . . .

On leaving school at fourteen, I went in the saw mills for a short period. Then I had two farm jobs. I remember digging potatoes, doing it by hand, you know. I used to be paid about 2/6d. for a good crop. I might sow as much as 200 potatoes for about half a crown. After that I went into a forestry job, and I got fed up with that and came up here, and went into mining. When I first came up here I did two years on haulage before I did any contract work. They're fairly repetitive jobs, and some are difficult to pick up, but once you've picked them up they're dead easy. I was doing some rough work, you know hard work, but I was being paid accordingly and I didn't mind that. I mean, before no matter how much you used to do, on farm work or forestry work, you were on a flat rate. (A3, pp. 39–40)

From such a background as this it is not surprising that hard work is second nature to Don.

Where poverty is an ever present threat a woman will also not hesitate to earn what she can when she can.

The DHSS in 1970 found that the number of *poor* two parent families with fathers working full-time would have nearly trebled if the father's earnings had not been supplemented by the mother's. (Land, 1975)

In the majority of households it is felt that you can do without the wife's wage but not without the husband's. The NOP survey discussed in *The Sunday Times* on 27 February 1977, found that, 'Even at a time when living standards are falling, three quarters of working wives say their families could manage if they did not work'. This is not the case in families with dependent children where the husband earns a below average wage. Fairly obviously the more hard-up the family the more likely it is that the woman's contribution is seen to be as indispensable as the man's.

Sonia Dale comes from such a household. After the birth of their third child the council moved them to a new modern house:

SONIA: Which was better in every way but one. With the change the rent went up from £1 to £9.35 a week. It leaped from £1 to £9.35 a week! (I3, p. 16)

Sonia went to work at Rist's so that they could afford to live in the new house. Shortly afterwards Sonia's husband also started work in the factory. Each week they brought home almost identical amounts of money. There was no question of one wage packet being less important than the other.

In this respect the Dales are somewhat exceptional. In most households the woman's wage is seen to be the family's means of maximising its earning capacity:

> If the man is on a fairly normal wage . . . then any pay increases he may win will be taxed at the standard rate of 35p in the £. The woman, on the other hand, can go out and earn up to £675 before she pays any tax . . . What this means is that if the family needs to increase its disposable income substantially, it is far easier to do so through the wife taking paid employment than through the man winning the same amount through higher wages . . . to increase the family's disposable income by the average full-time woman's take home pay of £1500 (April 1975), he would have to earn an extra £2300 gross—(whereas she only earns £1950). That would have required, at the time a 73 per cent increase in the average full-time man's wages. These figures . . . do not take account of NI contributions and other deductions, which do, however, presently tend to favour the woman's wage on this basis. (*Women Under Attack*, 1976)

Extra cash can buy security. Being a mining village Silverdale had felt the impact of the 1972 and 1974 national miners' strikes. The first was the big one; after three months overtime ban the miners went on strike for seven weeks. People became very short of money. The majority, with nothing at all to fall back on, were living from day to day. After that experience people began to put a bit by. These savings mostly came from the wife's earnings.

Norma Wade for example now saves some of her pay from her job in a tax office:

NORMA: It was difficult paying the mortgage during the miners' strike. It wasn't a lot, about £17 a month, but it got in arrears. Mind you, we straightened it out with the Building Society. Of course it was nationally known, so we didn't get any eviction orders, but it took *ages* to catch up. I remember friends bringing me eggs. At first it was just half a dozen. And they didn't say, ''cos you must be hard up', sort of thing. She said, 'We get them from the farm, so you may as well have them'. And Frank's brother came on Friday night with a smashing car load full of food. I don't get on particularly well with his brother, but to me that was smashing, and all the good stuff, you know. But it took us about eighteen months to pay back this mortgage.

Now I'm working I've been able to save. For the first nine months I just treated it as pin money, and I renewed things in the house like lamp shades, that were dead tatty, and I had a new hoover, things like that. Then about nine months ago I went to the Trustee Savings Bank. I said to Frank, 'I've taken this book out'. He said, 'Please yourself'. But one month I paid in £20 and the next nothing. So I arranged to have my wages paid in the bank. And I've found I've got this little bit, I said, 'little bit', but it must be £247 something that I've *saved*. I can't believe it! (H3, p. 27)

Most women say that their wages enable the family to have a higher standard of living. The first item Sarah brought was an automatic washing machine because the one they had was broken and Sarah was determined to buy something 'to help *me*'. She also paid for Mike to have a holiday in France with his school. They calculated that if Sarah stopped working they would be able to live as they had always lived, merely forgoing such extras.

What is defined as 'extra' depends upon previous circumstances. For one family it means the difference between staying at home and having a holiday, for another it is the difference between having a holiday in England or a holiday abroad. The extra cash pays for domestic aids and consumer durables, for a car, for the children's piano and ballet lessons, for their clothes as well as for her clothes. Norma spent one week's wages on jeans for her three youngsters, which she said they would otherwise have had to do without.

NORMA: I don't begrudge it, and John at fifteen, he's like a man. Up until a year ago he'd say, 'The other boys are having such and such, ma, but I realise I've got a brother and sister, so it's difficult'. But *now* it's different and I realise at that age your friends and others in your age group really matter, it's so important to him to keep up with them. (H3, p. 29)

In most households the husband's earnings are reserved to pay for the necessities that had to be met *before* the wife returned to the labour market; that is rent or mortgage payments, food, basic clothing, heating and lighting bills. The woman's earnings tend to be used to purchase additional items which make life easier, more secure and more enjoyable.

It would be quite possible for all families in which both the husband and wife work outside the home to use the wife's earnings to lighten the burden of unavoidable bills and expenditures, thereby releasing more of the husband's money for 'luxury' spending. In practice it works the other way. One income—the husband's—is kept to pay for basic items, the other income—the wife's—is used to buy 'nice' things to wear, eat, have and do.

There are a number of interconnected reasons as to why families make such gender related financial divisions. Once again the ideology of 'man the breadwinner' and 'woman the home maker' exerts its influence. The NOP survey referred to earlier shows that married men want different things from work as compared to married women. Three aspects of work were chosen by men to a far greater extent than by women, namely a secure job with a steady income (60 per cent men, 33 per cent women), high wages (42 per cent men, 25 per cent women), good promotion prospects (37 per cent men, 10 per cent women). These choices indicate that men survey the labour market with a breadwinner's eye, and the women folk back them up; three quarters of the working wives who participated in the NOP said that if unemployment were to get worse, men should take priority over women.

Four aspects of work were chosen by working wives to a much greater extent than by working husbands, namely, work within easy travelling distance (47 per cent women, 26 per cent men), pleasant working companions (39 per cent women, 25 per cent men), management that understands the difficulties of working mothers (25 per cent women, 5 per cent men), opportunities for part-time work (25 per cent women, 2 per cent men).

At least three of these choices indicate that women select jobs which fit in with their domestic responsibilities, despite the fact that the NOP survey highlights an interesting change in self definition. In 1971 two out of three working wives considered themselves mainly as 'housewives with a job'. In the current survey almost half regard themselves as 'working women who also run a home' (*The Sunday Times*, 27 February 1977).

There are, however, many traditionalists around:

DILYS LEWIS: My family comes before my job. I mean, I would give my job up tomorrow if anything happened to the family. If a woman's still got a young family, then the family comes first. Unless of course they're in dire need as far as money is concerned. Possibly the husband isn't earning enough for the family. Then of course it's different altogether. These women *need* the money, and the job is very important to them. (B3, p. 21)

In Silverdale this seems to be the generally accepted truth:

LEN WELLS: A man's got to work, whereas a woman hasn't. (C3, p. 48)

MURIEL: He's everybody's meal ticket a man is. I mean, he's the wage earner, he's the mainstay of the family, a husband is—when he's working. (F3, p. 58)

GLADYS KOHOUT: If I had an accident tomorrow and I had to pack in work, all I'd be looking for is a holiday. But if Joe had an accident and he had to pack in, I'd be losing my light, my fire, my food—the whole parcel. I mean he's the backbone in the family. (F3, p. 58)

It is felt by many that man is and should be the breadwinner. When a woman works it is of secondary importance, both to the woman—she has accepted that her domestic role comes first—and to her family—her money merely buys the icing on the cake, not the cake itself. On this basis unemployment is a far bigger tragedy for men than for women.

> Reporting this month's unemployment figures, the Press Association (whose agency material is widely used by newspapers, especially outside London) said that the government felt that an 'encouraging factor is that in the last three months most of the increase in unemployment was amongst women'. (Rob Caird, *Morning Star*, 28 August 1976).

This brings us to another factor: the woman's job is likely to be more temporary than the man's. Labour turnover rates in 1972/3 show a much higher average rate for females (40.1 per cent) than males (26.0 per cent) over all manufacturing industries. The New Earnings Survey for April 1971 showed that among full-time adult workers 12.2 per cent of men and 19.5 per cent of women were 'recent entrants' who had less than twelve months service with their present employer (*Women and Work*, Department of Employment 1974, p. 36).

Women working part-time are particularly vulnerable. Sandra Mill, for example, used to work on the evening shift at Wedgwood's Pottery factory. The evening shift was all female. These women were released from their maternal duties in the evening when their husbands came home from work. When Wedgwood's became short of work the evening shift was closed down. It has since been re-started, but Sandra now works for Wedgwood's full-time on the day shift. Such full-time work is difficult for Sandra who is the mother of three lively boys. She chose to go full-time because of the vulnerability of the evening shift:

SANDRA: It could finish tomorrow, or it could last three months. (G3, p. 8)

Sandra is quite right. Where work is for less than sixteen hours a week an employee has no statutory right under the Contract of Employment Act 1972 to a minimum of notice, no statutory right to a remedy under the Industrial Relations Act 1971 for unfair dismissal, and no right to redundancy payment under the Redundancy Payment Act 1965.

Over three million out of the total female labour force work part-time—'rather more than one in three were part-time workers, compared with about one in twenty of the men' (*Women Under Attack*, 1976, p. 18).

It is advantageous from the employer's viewpoint to take on part-time workers even while they are dispensing with the services of full-time workers, if they anticipate a short-term boom to be followed by a slump. This calculation seems to have occurred in the second and third quarters of 1974 (ibid. pp. 17–18), and again in the economic slowdown between September 1974 and September 1975 in the distributive and service sectors. Although women concentrated in these sectors suffered a net loss of jobs, all the loss was among full-timers, 'since part-timers were able to increase their numbers in both services and distributive trades. To some extent, then, it appears that there may have been some substitution of part-time for full-time women workers.' (Werneke, 1978)

Such part-time workers can be shed without the contractual liabilities full-timers are likely to represent. Thus, as Werneke notes, over the same period in production industries 'a far higher percentage of women lost their jobs than men. These women were part-time workers whose jobs were probably the most expendable in the prevailing economic conditions.' (Werneke, 1978)

The insecurity of the female labour market is an important reason why families try to prevent themselves becoming over-reliant on the woman's wage. Another factor that has to be taken into account is that women earn less than men. In the case of manual workers a little under a third of the difference in earnings between male and female workers is due to men earning more overtime pay and shift allowances (see table).

Average earnings and hours of full-time adults in April 1977

	Cross Weekly earnings (£)	Overtime pay (£)	Make-up of earnings PBR pay (£)	Shifted pay (£)	Average weekly hours (£)
	a	b	c	d	e
Men (21 and over)					
Manual	71.50	9.80	5.70	2.00	45.7
Non-manual	88.90	2.60	2.10	0.50	38.7
All	78.60	6.80	4.20	1.40	43.0
Women (18 and over)					
Manual	43.70	1.30	4.10	0.70	39.4
Non-manual	53.80	0.50	0.30	0.30	36.7
All	51.00	0.70	1.40	0.40	37.5

SOURCE *Labour Research* (Feb. 1978) p. 39.

For most families the woman's earnings alone would not be enough to buy the basic necessities required by the family. If one source of income is insufficient and uncertain it helps if it is regarded and used as a useful windfall, not as a basic source of supply.

Thus the way productive relations are organised in a capitalist society, and the gender divisions which characterise the labour market, create a situation in which families are wise to reserve the woman's earning for what the family defines as non-essential purchases. In its financial policy the family is cushioning itself against the, quite probable, need to revert to being a one income family.

The effect of this practice is to reinforce the ideology that woman's place is in the home. Because the man's labour market role *is* primary in terms of hard cash and job stability, his wage tends to be used as the primary income. This usage reinforces the ideology that man is the breadwinner, and one practical result of this is that most women bear the main burden of domestic work, even when they also work outside the home on a full-time basis.

The man emerges in thought and practice as the breadwinner. He has pride of place in the labour market. She works to make life more comfortable for her family but she doesn't *have* to work.

UNFREE AGENTS

Although both parents may be ideologically wedded to a situation in which the man is seen to be the breadwinner, the situation is fraught with difficulties which find expression in tension between the spouses. Sarah, for example, felt that although Len helped more in the home than he had before she went out to work, she really had two full-time jobs to his one. She tackled him about his attitude towards his family:

SARAH WELLS: I think the job I do here is more important than the one I get paid for. I mean, thinking about the children and what they're going to put into life. I think I contribute quite a lot to their failures and their successes. But it's not the same for you is it? You don't think your job here is more important than the one you get paid for.

LEN WELLS: No, purely on a financial basis it couldn't be. I suppose my main function in life is to provide food and shelter for the people who are dependent on me. So obviously I've got to go and earn in order to do that, and any other function I may perform in the home is secondary to that. I don't think there's any other way I can look at it. (C3, pp. 48–9)

Sarah did not have a ready answer, but she recounted an incident which had occurred on the previous day, which demonstrated, she felt, Len's casual attitude towards domestic duties. Len always cooked breakfast for their three children while Sarah did other jobs. On this particular day the children did not put in an appearance and Len simply left their breakfast on the table and went to shave. Sarah asked him to send the children down. Len replied that he had told them once, and that it was now up to her to get them down. At this Sarah complained that she was always the one who had to pester the children. Len simply replied, 'Alright if they don't come throw it in the dustbin'. (C3, p. 58)

Neither he nor she fully realised that this would go against the grain of a lifetime's socialisation into a good mother, good houseworker frame of mind. She could not throw good food away, and she could not let her children go to school on empty stomachs. The fact that Len could suggest this indicated that he was not tied by a lifetime of mothering in the way that she was tied. She resented his freedom.

However resentful she may feel Sarah can do little about her situation because she is dependent on Len, and she is well aware of the fact:

SARAH: Len thinks I've got my duty to the family, to their welfare— looking after them and seeing to things like doctors and dentists, and seeing that they are clothed. He thinks all he has to do is provide the financial side. I don't really agree with this, although you see, I couldn't go and earn anything like the money he can. So I suppose we're stuck in this situation. (C3, p. 49)

One reason why women face such a lack of occupational choice is that they take on occupations which fit in with their domestic duties. They take part-time jobs which finish at the same time as little Johnny comes out of school:

NORMA WADE: I used to drop him off at school and be at the factory by nine o'clock. And at about twenty past three I used to look out the window to see him coming out of school. And he came into the factory to me, which was great. I caught a 'bus at half past three. It went on like that until I had Colin. (H3, p. 33)

Shop work is another favourite occupation because it can often be arranged so as to fit in with school hours. Carol Adams and Rae Laurikietis (1976) make this point when they contrast the comments of three employees working in Woolworths. One of the three, Rose, aged fifty-one, states:

It's my fourth year here. I've always done jobs that *fit in with my family*. I've got three children, one boy of eleven is still at school. I work 9.30 to 1.30 five days, that way I can get him off to school before I go to work . . . I get £11 for a twenty hour week . . . I'm quite satisfied with the money, but it's not good if you are young—they can go for better work . . . They can't get women to do full-time—most of us are part-timers—well, if you've a family you've got to cater for them. (Italics theirs)

The second Woolworths worker, Margaret, aged sixteen, demonstrates that the anticipation of a future domestic role conditions current work experiences. She says:

I thought *I might as well* do full-time . . . I don't really fancy the idea of going out to work after I'm married, so I'd look after the kids . . . I'm not *really ambitious* . . . I wouldn't call it a cushy job here, but the work is easy . . . Sometimes *I get bored* if there's no stock.

The third worker, Tony, aged twenty-three, has a Woolworth's job which is more involving and which, in contrast to Margaret, he experiences as the opening of a career:

They offer prospects here, I'm a trainee manager . . . The training here is better than in most places, it holds good if you go to work in other stores . . . I like it here—there's always something new—*you never get bored*. (1976, Book 1)

Thus for Rose shop work represents a way of assisting her family financially. For Margaret the job is merely a stop gap situation until she starts a family. Only Tony approaches his job as part of his life project.

Domestic commitments may result in a woman worker being demoted:

ROSE HARRIS: I started in the mill on leaving school. I got about 25/- a week. I left there to have the baby. I was about eight months over Cathy when I left. That was because of the breast pockets on men's coats. My boss was the only one who could do them. She had trained me to do them, and she was off sick with ulcers. Alf said, 'Couldn't you stay on a bit longer and train someone?' It took about a month to train someone. I said, 'Well fair enough, provided you're willing to turn midwife'. I was huge at the time, you know. Well I had Cathy, and John and Paul. It was about nine years before I went back. I was only doing part-time work, but I was getting full-time wages, you know, it was a bonus system and I could turn the work out. Well, I'd only been back, what, about nine months, and I told him I'd got to have about six weeks off with the children. He said, 'Well fair enough'. Then, after about five weeks, he sent me a letter saying I'd have to start on trainee pay. So I told him to go whistle for it. (A3, pp. 28–9)

And sometimes the clash between the domestic and the paid job finds expression in people turning down promotion:

JOAN WITZ: I was offered promotion at Rists a few years ago. I did accept it, but then I had to turn it down. It meant working overtime, and Caroline was still a young girl at the time and it meant leaving her. I had to tell them I didn't think I could do it, and I might as well tell them at the beginning than take the job, start it, and then say it was no good. (E3, p. 54)

Joan had also curbed her job ambition:

JOAN: When Caroline was still little I hadn't got over this longing to be a nurse. There were some people doing midwifery courses and this appealed to me very much. But shift work was involved, which with a young child I couldn't have done anyway. (E3, p. 53)

The greater your maternal responsibilities the less manoeuvrability you have in the labour market.

'Only seven per cent of those without children were doing the worst paid jobs, like being a shop assistant or machinist, compared with 23 per cent of mothers.' (*Woman's Own*, 20 March 1976)

Sarah had to face the fact that she could not equal Len's financial contribution. He felt she made up the difference by running the home well and by caring for her family's needs. She felt this meant she had two jobs to his one.

Neither Len nor Sarah Wells is happy with the situation they are faced with. Their awareness of their difficulty may be unusual, but the social factors which give rise to tension in their marriage is, I would argue, present in most marriages. Both of them envy the illusory freedom of the other. Sarah envied Len his relative freedom from domestic duties. Len envied what he saw as Sarah's freedom from ties with the labour market. If she really wanted, she could drop her job. After a while, if she wanted, she could look round for something else to do. On the other hand he *had* to bring in a steady income. He could only change jobs, not drop out of work, and the change would have to be equally remunerative.

In the early days Len's job had seemed to be the opening of a career which would represent a genuine challenge. By mastering the work he would, it seemed, develop his creative powers and secure a social position in the community. The experience of work would provide his life with a purposeful structure.

Over the years the excitement diminished. There was some satisfaction to be gained from what they had been able to acquire:

LEN: There's a certain pride in having your own house. I suppose I've gained a certain sense of achievement after twenty years, to see I've got a few sticks of furniture. (C3, p. 65)

Len also thought that work fulfilled a basic human requirement, but increasingly this meant work unconnected with employment:

LEN: I think people have a basic need to work. In the summer I bolt my tea down and I'm out in the garden till nine and ten o'clock. And at weekends I used to decorate. I don't so much now, but you feel you've got to be doing work of some sort. If I was in such a fortunate position that I didn't have to go out to work I would probably have a very large house and be decorating all the time, and digging the garden. I wouldn't want to sit on the beach and things like that. (C3, p. 67)

Len's paid work had lost the significance it had once held. It was no longer a means by which not only his employer's interests would be served but by which he could acquire an expanded sense of self. Now the job consisted of a certain set of functions which had to be performed for a certain number of hours in order to gain the indispensable meal ticket. This shift in focus had transformed his job from a life enriching to a life reducing process. Hours spent at work were hours subtracted from real living. Work stood like an unavoidable life sentence eating up vast chunks of the time that was left:

LEN: You feel you've got to go there every day, and no matter how good your job is it's basically repetitive. You may be a cabinet maker, and be making a chair one day and a table the next, but you're using the same movements, and you know you've got to go there five days a week for fifty years of your life. This is the worst part of work. (C3, p. 66)

Len and some of his colleagues are 'Non-Careerists' (Hearn 1977) for whom the work experience has turned sour. They thought it would be ideal to get work over with in one chunk so as to have the rest of the week to themselves:

LEN: We've discussed it at work. We think the ideal thing would be to work three twelve hour days and half a day, so you would have half a week's work and half a week's leisure. (C3, p. 67)

So Len continues to perform his job but now with a minimum of enthusiasm. As Hearn has suggested, the detached stance of the 'Non-Careerist' may help him to withstand competition, stress and threat:

LEN: I think it just leads to an early grave if you think about work at home. At one time it used to worry me if I went on holiday. I would worry about what was going to happen if I went away, and what I would find waiting for me when I got back. But now it doesn't bother me. (C3, p. 55)

Most workers in working class occupations never expect a great deal of personal fulfilment from their work. They have already lost out in the race for qualifications for what could be self-developing work. However, the rewards that some people reap within employment others can experience in 'outside' involvements. This is one form of the 'uncareer' option discussed by Jeff Hearn.

Dilys's husband Peter made his voluntary work in the Labour Movement a life long 'career'. As secretary of the Silverdale NUM branch he was the chief union negotiator at the Silverdale pit. In addition, for many years Peter was secretary of the miners' Working Man's Club.

His ability to speak, to capture thought on paper, to seek out information in libraries, bookshops, journals and newspapers, his ability to keep accounts, to spell and order his thoughts, this had all been taught in the movement. The union branch and the club succeeded where school and college had failed. Peter blamed his lack of progress in school on the leniency of the teachers; if only they had stood over him cane in hand and made him knuckle under. Yet in the labour movement he accepted posts of responsibility which demanded that he equip himself intellectually. The issues at stake concerned the struggle against exploitation, the struggle to make their views heard, the struggle to stand up.

PETER LEWIS: We had a two day strike before, but that's going back, it must be fourteen years. The old tyrant himself was here then. He wouldn't pay, well he would only pay so much. We got involved in a claim for 70/- a shift, and the branch committee they came out and accepted 55/- in front of us. They wouldn't stick out for what they were entitled to, they took the 55/-, and they were quite happy that was the best of it! He was one of those managers you doff your cap to, you know.

And another thing, when you walk from the job to pit bottom you're supposed to have walking out time. When I first came to Silverdale people didn't dare come off their job until it was time to be at pit bottom. Some had three quarters of an hour to an hour's walk from their job to pit bottom, and they didn't dare leave their job until it was time to be at pit bottom. Now they get walking out time. There's been all sorts of improvements down here over the years. (B3, p. 54)

In the movement that became his college, Peter learned the realities of class conflict with a vividness and immediacy denied to those who approach this as the subject of an academic discipline.

PETER: On the first strike the coal board were certain that Silverdale would be the odd one out, that they would work during the strike. They were expecting to try and break the strike through Silverdale. I don't know, I don't like making a speech, you know, I try to take a minute or a couple of minutes to get across what I want to do. But on the first strike I knew this was a big problem as far as Silverdale was concerned, and so before I went to the meeting I told the committee I would be Chairman, 'cos I knew that would give me a strong hand to start with. I wasn't long, I spoke for about twelve or fourteen minutes, but when the vote was taken they were 100 per cent for the strike. This has never been heard for Silverdale.

This was enormous. I was staggered myself to be truthful, because I was expecting to get defeated. This wasn't only our branch either, the Power Group were there as well, and they're very un-militant. If they promised them a Saturday and Sunday shift as well, they'd work for £5 less during the week. That's the type of person they are; give them some overtime and they're quite happy. (B3, p. 55)

Peter continued:

The first day I went to Saltley, on the Monday, the police threw us about. One police chappie came running up about forty yards and kicked us. I was that annoyed. When I got back home that night I got straight on the 'phone to John Golding. I demanded that either he come himself the next day, or that he send some other MP there. The amusement was, the first MP that walked in on the Tuesday, they grabbed hold of him, the very first one. They grabbed him straight away. He got it straight away he did (said with great satisfaction).

This wasn't the Birmingham police, we got on all right with them. But a squad came in, about 150, I saw some of them in London when we went down on the parade, so some of them definitely came from London. They still swear blind there were only Birmingham police there, but that's not true. We were getting on alright with the Birmingham police, then this other lot came. They were different people altogether. They came in just to smash it up. Mind you they didn't smash it up when they came on the Thursday. (B3, pp. 30–1)

On that Thursday:

almost 40,000 workers struck from scores of Birmingham factories, and 10,000 of them marched to Saltley to join the 2000 miners and the 1000 police (at Saltley). When the police saw this massive gathering they realised the gates of the coke depot would have to close; which they were at 10.42 a.m., to a deafening roar of approval from the crowd. (Nichols and Armstrong, 1976, p. 13)

As with most working class men Peter had been brought up to see himself as a wage worker:

PETER: I've never thought of not working to be truthful. I've had a work routine ever since I started going out to work. Generally I get up at quarter to five, and I'm at the colliery by quarter to six. I should finish at quarter to two, but I usually come up half an hour before the shift ends to do union business. Usually I leave about three o'clock, sometimes a bit later. When I get home at half past three or four o'clock I have my dinner, which is in the oven ready. Then I used to go to the club at about seven o'clock. Many a time it was one o'clock before I got to bed, but I don't go so much nowadays. Between work, the union and the club I didn't have much to do with the family really. (B3, p. 49)

Not only was work experienced as a fact of life, Peter accepted a further limitation of choice:

PETER: If I could have my life over again I think I would end up in mining anyway. You see, I think to get on in anything as far as management's concerned you've got to be 'yes men', 'three-bags-full men'. I don't think I could do it. I might last six months but I know I would go after that. I mean, I could have had jobs of this type before. In the past I may have taken them but I wouldn't now. I'd answer back, and that wouldn't suit. So I'd have to go in the end. No I think I would end up in mining anyway. (B3, p. 44)

Peter, like Len, felt his life had been something of a sacrifice. Unlike Len, however, he felt he had chosen his course. The choice had been dictated by the existence of social inequality, class exploitation and conflict, but in recognising this class struggle Peter had chosen to position himself with the labour movement. That choice transformed him from an exposed onlooker caught up in ongoing events, into a party to those events.

Peter's effectiveness and his understanding of class struggle is, however, curtailed by the prevailing party-political contest, and by his commitment to the Labour Party. In my view the Labour Party has attempted to advance the well-being of working people within the limitations imposed by Capitalism. The result has been that when the contradictions characterising Capitalism have become intensified, Labour administrations have attempted to overcome the difficulties by avoiding some forms of control and introducing others, which have had the effect of undermining the living standards of working people. Peter, as well as his neighbours, has suffered as a result.

In this situation it does not seem to me to be surprising that many working people feel detached about Labour Party politics. Sarah voted Labour, and that was an end of it. Most of the voters of Silverdale seem to be equally unenthusiastic. They don't expect much change to result from a different party holding office. Their passiveness is tinged with suspicion:

SONIA DALE: I don't think it matters much who gets in. They seem to be only out for themselves. When I vote I vote Labour, but I was in two minds whether to vote or not last time, but then they came for me in the car so I went. (I3, p. 17)

It is not surprising that some of this suspicion rubs off onto anyone who takes on a job of work in the Labour Movement. Peter has been on the receiving end of such mistrust:

PETER: Back in the old days after finishing at 2 o'clock I would stay at the pit 'till 5 and 6 o'clock in the week. This happened regular. You see, everything was done in your own time in those days. I was one of the first to complain about that. Yet now, when I come up early to do union business they say, 'You're going out the pit early'. You're going out for their own good really. That's what you're going out for. But they don't realise this. They don't see how things have changed since the days when you couldn't do any union business in the firm's time. (B3, p. 56).

Such mistrust takes its toll. Peter has invested his life in the movement, but increasingly he experiences union work as just another job.

PETER: I used to often go and see the manager at one time. But this last few weeks I haven't gone to see him a great deal. But I'm at the colliery bank on a Friday, all day on a Friday, so if anyone wants anything done I'm there. And more or less I'm available during the week. I tend to catch the three shifts. I can see most of them if I want. I don't bother too much about the overtime men on a Friday. If they want to stop overtime that's their lookout. If they want to see me they have to come up and see me as far as I'm concerned. They do sometimes contact us. I had one come up last Friday. I gave him ten minutes. He'd been on the night shift, and he thought I should stop all day talking to him, but I wasn't going to. I used to at one time, but not any more. (B3, p. 34)

If union work is a job like any other, you judge a union worker in terms of his technical negotiating skill, and his understanding of procedure. If you professionalise the negotiator's job in this way as Peter seems to, it follows that the class position of the official is of secondary importance:

PETER: The last three union presidents we've had, the first one he's now our materials officer, the next one he's at Staffordshire House (the NCB district office) in the industrial relations department, and the other one, he's a deputy down here, and in fact I wouldn't be surprised if in the next four or five years he became an overman down here. The only thing I really object to with him is he's always trying to prevent other people from doing the same—changing to the coal board. Of course, when they change they've got to be on the management's side more, but they also understand what we're fighting for. I've had a lot of help from them all. I still get a lot of help off the first president. (B3, pp. 56–7)

Once union work becomes simply another job it can become subject to the same process of disillusionment which creeps into a career turned sour. Peter's 'uncareer' stands in danger of becoming as much a 'non-career' as Len's. Their history of non-involvement in the home prevents either of them gaining much compensation in that quarter. The home for these men is a place of relaxation, not a scene of work entailing all the struggles and accomplishments of creative enterprise. Women tend to take their domestic pre-occupations to work, they plan when they can take their child to the dentist, they think, 'Now what am I going to give them for tea tonight?' and in fine weather they think wistfully, 'If I was at home I could be doing my washing'. Since most men are not this involved in the detailed management of domestic affairs, the family does not intrude into their place of employment in this way.

In mining circles the family features in conversation primarily as the scene of sexual exploits, as an opportunity to tease or as a means of projecting masculine status. As Don explained:

DON: Nothing is sacred, not wives or children, mothers or mothers-in-law. Anything goes like. There's one young bloke, Paul, he lives at Knutton. They're buying their own house. He's been married about six months. Well, he used to come to work, and we'd have our round of snap-in—we have a round of bread like before starting work—and as soon as he sat down Paul would fall asleep, just for a couple of minutes like. Well we teased him that much over it. He was always making excuses, he'd been out late the night before or something—anything but what we knew was the cause like. In the end he came up with the excuse that his wife used to get up to go to the toilet two or three times each night, and each time she would wake him and say, 'I'm going to the toilet Paul', and when she got back, 'It's O.K. ducks, I'm just getting in bed again'. That was the excuse he came up with! So now, whenever he comes to work tired they say, 'He took his wife drinking again last night, and she's been in and out of bed all night'. (A3, pp. 57–8)

Times haven't changed much since the 1950s when the authors of *Coal Is Our Life* noted:

> The use of the sexual swear words in the pit is only part of a general attitude of toughness and near callousness in conversation . . . Men in exclusively male company talk very lewdly about sex in general and about particular women without any consideration or feeling for the personality of such women. Men will say, pretending to joke, 'A woman's only good for two things—looking after the house and lying on the bed'. One collier—although his workmates showed some disgust amid their laughter—said, 'When a woman's in her teens and her twenties she's worth having—she's just what a man wants. After that she's finished!
> 'After she's thirty, what is she?'
> 'She's just an old cow!'
> These are but two examples of the typically loose and unrestrained conversations about sex which take place in the pit. (Dennis, Henriques, and Slaughter, 1969, p. 215)

Although women feature in miners' pit talk as the subject matter of banter, other aspects of family life and household management are absent from both thought and speech in the enclosed world below ground. Just as home is shut out of work, work is shut out of home. Most working people do not talk about their jobs when they are at home, or even think about them if at all possible. Peter attempted to extend such separation to all of his activities.

PETER: When I'm at work I'm thinking about work, and when I'm at home I'm thinking about home. When I'm at the club I'm thinking about the club, and when I'm on union business I'm thinking about the union. I more or less shut off one part while I take on another. (B3, p. 57)

In reality things are not so sharply demarcated. Peter's club and union work lend to his experience of employment a significance it would otherwise lack. His involvement in the Labour Movement has shaped his intellectual development and it accounts in part for his low level of participation in domestic affairs.

Furthermore, the home situation which Peter seeks to disassociate from other areas of life, is not thought of as being a second place of work. When Peter and most other Silverdale men think of their domestic hearth they do so as a retreat from the never ending round of work. The men feel that the advantages of family life reside in 'home comforts' and the security of companionship which can be seen as a shield against the cold winds of instrumental capitalist relations.

Most Silverdale women feel unable to separate home and work as distinct worlds. For Sarah Wells the home itself is a workplace concerned with domestic production and the job of caring for the wants of others. And as Margaret Stacey wrote in her earlier study of Banbury, the houseworker cannot easily leave her form of employment:

Most Banbury women are housewives only, and of them it is true that a wife cannot resign from her work without breaking from her husband and children, nor can she leave her husband without losing her job. Her occupation is rightly returned as 'Married Woman'. This is a unique status in a society otherwise based on individual contract, specialisation, and separation of function. (1960, p. 136)

The mother's family work is so personalised it can subsume her whole personality. A telling account of a middle-aged woman's fight to regain a sense of selfhood is to be found in Doris Lessing's *The Summer Before Dark.*

Not only is the domestic job often experienced by working women as the basis for their self-identification, despite the fact noted earlier that nearly half of them regard themselves as 'working women who also run a home', the media image of women tends to treat a woman's family role as her total status.

Thus women in full-time employment are often described as housewives in newspaper reports. The *Guardian*, for example, printed the following news item recently:

> Housewife Mrs Jean Ullyett has won a £444,420 football pools jackpot at only her fourth attempt at filling in the coupon. She will give up her £49-a-week job as a machinist but the family will continue to live in their semi-detached home in Barnsley Road, Wombwell, South Yorkshire. (*Guardian*, 30 March 1978)

If Mr Ullyett had won the jackpot he would have been described in terms of his paid occupation, or his lack of paid occupation: unemployed, retired, etc.

The identification of women with their domestic role is even more blatantly illustrated in an article printed in the *Evening Sentinel*, a local Staffordshire paper, under the heading:

> Housewife is top secretary.
> Britain's top secretary for 1975 is 27 year old Portsmouth housewife, Mrs Christine Eveleigh.
>   She has beaten 342 other candidates for the title awarded by the London Chamber of Commerce and Industry.
> Mrs Eveleigh works for Portsmouth Council as a public information assistant, having previously been a personal secretary on the council staff. (*Evening Sentinel*, 20 August 1975)

Occasionally readers retaliate, and point to the ideas being perpetuated by this type of reporting. The following letter, for example, appeared in *The Times*, under the heading 'THE HOUSEWIFE LOOK':

> Sir, I have read with great interest the news item in today's issue of your paper (April 1) of the first recorded bank robbery by a woman in Vienna. The report describes the woman as looking 'to be aged about 30 and a housewife'.
>   While I hold no brief for the extremists of Women's Lib. I

would be fascinated to learn the features which render the lady in question immediately recognizable as a housewife rather than as, say, a doctor or a poetess or a secretary or, indeed, as a bank robber. So would my wife.

Yours truly,
Geoffrey R. Marks
(*The Times*, 6 April 1976)

Even if an individual woman declines to identify herself or be identified by others as primarily a houseworker, she is still more likely to be more involved in home life than her husband. An evening's relaxation within the home is often experienced differently by the husband as compared to his wife, particularly if she works full-time in the home. She remains conscious of the arena of work surrounding her on all sides. Lee Comer describes this experience well:

> While she is talking with her husband or watching television she is minutely aware of her responsibilities—the ashtrays which must be emptied, the cups and glasses which must be washed; the husband's and children's clothes which must be sorted for the morning and she must break off a conversation to put a note out for the milkman and all the time she must remember what she has to do the next day—the child to the dentist, clothes which need mending, sugar which has run out, ad nauseam. She goes to bed and the evening which her husband enjoyed, or merely relaxed in has, for her, receded behind the weight of things she has done and things which she still has to do. The joke that the woman lies there planning the following day's menus while the husband is making love to her is no joke to the woman. Doing housework and being a housewife are indivisible. (Comer, 1974, pp. 85–6)

The magnitude of domestic work can be extremely oppressive when the woman has full-time paid employment as well. Margaret Dean, for example, thought it would be so nice to be able to say:

MARGARET: 'Right, I've done my eight hour shift, now I'm completely finished with work for the day.' I'd like to be able to just go out to work; it would be so much simpler, to have nothing to do when you come back—like a man's life. Many men go out to work and then come home and relax, whereas a woman goes out to work and comes home and starts again. (D3, p. 24)

Len experienced work as an unavoidable life sentence. Work was a necessity from which there was no escape. It was different for the woman, Len thought. She wasn't the breadwinner, work for her was not a necessity. Len was not completely right if the *Woman's Own* survey is representative, since this indicates that 14 per cent of working women are the main breadwinners in their households. Len would, I think, accept the existence of this minority but insist that the majority of working women have more freedom than their husbands.

LEN: If men aren't doing a job properly they're told to go and find another job, and this would bother them, whereas I don't think it would bother women so much. They are not so financially dependent on the job. I think this is true of a lot of women. Because they're not dependent on the job if they don't like it they're just off and away. (C3, p. 70)

This view overlooks the extent to which the family comes to rely on the *joint* income of husband and wife. If the *Woman's Own* survey is correct it would seem that a majority of women workers regard their earnings as an important part of their family's income. Although, as was pointed out earlier, the family is more likely to choose to purchase less essential items with the wife's earnings.

However Len is basing his argument on an assessment of the situation he and Sarah occupy. Sarah could give up her job whenever she wanted without their family suffering greatly, whereas such an action was unthinkable in his case. Not only would it contravene a lifetime of socialisation into acceptance of the breadwinner role, but his family actually did rely on his earnings.

Len was preoccupied with his own proletarian servitude. This preoccupation blinded him to the servitude inherent in Sarah's position, which she was quick to point out:

SARAH WELLS: You say I'm more free than you, but I've *got* a job, another job, this wretched job in the home. This year I've been doing two jobs. You should feel lucky you've only got one job. Housework is a horrible repetitive thing, that keeps going on and on. When a job's done it doesn't stay done. And I don't see there's anything I can do about it, I just keep going. You're just as free as I am really. (C3, p. 30)

It would have been more accurate if Sarah had said Len was equally unfree.

THE CLUB AND PUB

The work-a-day world is a component part of club life:

DON: They dig coal all the while at the club. This old woman was sitting with a bunch of miners in the club the other night, there were other wives there like. Well, they were all on about pit work, and this old woman says to her husband, 'Well shut up about bleedin pit work. When you're down the pit all day you're talking about women, and up here you're talking about nothing but pit work.' (A3, p. 54)

The club is a man's world. Many women do not feel at ease in the club without the company of their menfolk. Some women don't feel easy in the club at any time. Gladys Kohout, for example, who moved to Silverdale from a village near Wrexham says:

GLADYS: It was quite a different environment, quite different from what I'd been used to. I came to live here five years ago, and I've been married seventeen years in May. In Wales the women were always at home, they never went to work. I never went to work. I had my children, I had to rear them, they were mine. I mean, no one reared them for me. To go out to work just wasn't known. It still isn't really. There are more now who go out to work, but people say, 'She goes out to work!' you know, like it was a disease. And I never went in a pub before I came here. Even now in Wales very few women will go in a pub, especially not on a Sunday. Men yes, but women no, only very, very few. I would say, going back to before I left Wales, if a woman went in a pub she was tainted, she was a bad woman—even if she wasn't. (F3, pp. 8–9)

Gladys's retired friend Muriel listened and confirmed her tale. Gladys continued:

When I first came here to live I only went once in the club, with Muriel on a Sunday, didn't I?

'I took her', Muriel agreed.

GLADYS: She said, 'Come with me to the club'—this was Sunday dinner time. 'We'll have a game of bingo!' I said, 'Never, I can't!' She said, 'Come on', and Joe said, 'Go on, no harm'. But I still said, 'No, I don't think I will'. He said, 'Listen, you're in bloody England now, do as the English do'. So I came, didn't I? 'Cos I'd worked really hard in the house, we'd just moved in. But as soon as I went in I felt like a fish out of water. I felt so *guilty* about being there. I should have been *home* doing the dinner.

Then I saw this woman come in with a baby in a pram, and it was crying its head off wanting a bottle. And I said, 'Oh Muriel, I've got to go'. Fancy, *bringing a baby in a pub like that.* She should have been *home* with it, not in the club. I felt *embarrassed* for her, you know. I thought 'Oo, a young woman like that, with a young baby, has to come here to drink of a dinner time. I mean, there was something wrong. I was that embarrassed for her I had to come out. I said, 'I'm sorry Muriel, I know you've bought the bingo tickets'. But I couldn't sit there, I was ever so uncomfortable. And I've never been in that club after. We go in the pub together now. I would never go in the pub on my own. I would never go in after him and join him there. I always go in *with* him.

MURIEL: And when we're in the pub he always pays, he thinks it's the gentleman's prerogative. Whenever I've gone in with them Joe wouldn't let me pay for a drink.

GLADYS: No he won't. Now Muriel will bear me out on this, she used to never drink nothing but beer. But when she comes out with us he won't let her drink beer. With him you've got to drink whisky. To him beer isn't a woman's drink.

'To him it isn't, but I'm much happier with bitter—I'm a bitter woman', said Muriel, without a trace of irony. (F3, pp. 15–17)

Gladys may be an extreme case, but most people in Silverdale regarded the club and pub as a male domain.

Families will go together to the club, and re-form themselves on peer-group lines once inside. Women form themselves into groups of bingo players, youngsters gravitate to the pin-ball tables, the serious drinking is done by the men in groups. It is the men only who can become members of the club, and only they can serve on its management committee.

The club and pub, the union and the pit, form together a male network. This network expresses male camaraderie, and raises to high status those of its members recognised for what the community defines as manliness.

As Ann Whitehead (1976) has shown, in the male domain of the pub the social control exercised over women may serve to express both solidarity and ambivalent rivalry between men. Control may take the form of making it plain, in acts of aggression thinly veiled as teasing, that particular categories of women, notably those without male accompaniment, are unwelcome. As we have seen in the case of Gladys, women may become so highly sensitive to the atmosphere of male exclusiveness that they control themselves by avoiding situations where they may be subject to the censorious pressure of a male dominated assembly.

Control of women can also take the form of a man exercising sufficient 'manliness' in his marriage to establish his 'right' to go drinking with the lads whenever he pleases. In this situation a wife's desire to spend more time with her husband may conflict with the status pressure exerted by his drinking companions. He may prefer to endure her displeasure than risk the loss of face entailed by being labelled as a man who has to kowtow to his wife.

The male drinking scene can have a magnetic appeal for adolescent males. As Don said of his lads:

DON: They like coming out with me in the evening once in a while. And, er, I always talk to a bunch of men, there might be six of us like, and they like to feel accepted as men. And I like to see them joining in and talking away with no inhibitions. I sort of appreciate that as they get older. (A3, pp. 72–3)

The man who likes his beer will leave his wife in charge of the family for a few nights each week, or he will go out most nights after nine o'clock for a quick one. And as Gladys realised, Sunday lunchtime belongs more than any other time to the drinking man. This sometimes causes tension between husband and wife, particularly if the wife is starved of social contact because she works in the home full-time:

JANET AUSTIN: On a Sunday I do get a bit angry sometimes. I say to him, 'I'm doing dinner for one o'clock, sometimes it's two o'clock, be in'. Now it doesn't matter what time I say, if he wants to go for a drink he'll stroll in twenty past two. That really gets me! I mean, it takes more or less all morning to cook. I say to him, 'the children very rarely see you anyway'. Mark you, sometimes they go with him if he just goes to the club. Sometimes I say to him, 'Well, why can't I come?' and he says, 'Well come'. But then again it's not—I suppose I could walk down there and take the children with me, but that's more or less not the done thing. People say, 'Oh, look at her, she can't let him go for a drink on his own'. You've got no right to be there sort of thing. (G2, pp. 19–20)

And if a woman does pluck up courage to go with her family to the club, as Gladys pointed out, her responsibilities go with her:

GLADYS: If a woman's going to take her children out with her drinking it's not going to be a break for her is it? You are still *tied* with them. The men don't seem to bother, I've heard them—'Oh, it's alright, give him a drink, he's alright'. All the time you hear them, 'Go to mum'. (F3, p. 19)

FRIENDSHIPS

Woman's greater involvement in the home, as compared to man's, limits her range of social contacts. It is acceptable nowadays for women to work outside the home, and they have greater social freedom, however, as Sullerot (1971) has observed, women 'are tied to the house with a lead which gives them an impression of freedom' (p. 41). So, for example, maternal duties accompany them to the pub, and if they don't, nine times out of ten it is the woman who has fixed up a baby sitter.

An employed mother doesn't have a great deal of relaxation; the leisure pursuits she does permit herself are often in some way connected with domestic work, for example, when she knits or sews. Such domestic 'relaxation' is indulged in privately, within the home, and does not enable her to increase her circle of acquaintances.

Don and Rose recognise this:

DON: I've an enormous range of acquaintances. It started with me going out for a drink, mainly of a weekend when everyone's about. ('Everyone' in this case means by and large men.) And you know, I think men get a lot closer to men than women do to women. (A3, p. 67)

Mining is, of course, a type of employment in which the communal ties formed in work are reinforced through residential and social contact within the mining village. Furthermore, the job brings men into close physical contact not only underground, but in the Pit changing rooms and baths. After a visit below ground my observations stopped at the door of the baths, but my associate Ron Frankenberg was not similarly excluded by virtue of his sex, and he observed how uninhibited the men were, pausing in the cleansing process to discuss economic policies and political questions with neighbours as naked and unashamed as themselves.

Rose conceded at least half Don's case:

ROSE: Well, apart from anything else, as with me, I'm interested in sewing and things like that. It doesn't take me out. Mabel, who lives on the end, she knits. Well that doesn't take her out either, does it? Sometimes when the sun's out we'll congregate on the front and have a natter. But even then it's just the three of us. Mary may trot across. Mary knows more on this estate because she goes to bingo. And Mrs Williams goes bingo as well. They make a lot of friends that way. (A3, p. 68)

There are no formal institutions on the Parksite estate which might involve the local women. There is no Women's Institute or guild. Those who wish to attend a chapel or church service do so down in the village or, in the case of Catholics, in the nearest town, which is three miles away. The only public building on the estate is the workingman's club.

It is, however, easy to underestimate the impact of informal contact. Jean Spencer, who was discussed in the previous chapter, and Sarah, are supported emotionally in their interaction with their children. Both were able to confide in their children and to receive confidences in turn. Rose also felt herself to be very close to her children, and all three had formed lasting friendships at work. 'Oh I like my workmates,' said Rose. When she first went to work in a factory she formed a particularly close friendship:

ROSE: With a little woman who used to sit opposite me. She was old enough to be my mother. Don used to write me letters and she read them all. It was almost twelve months to the day after meeting him that we married. Of course there was gossip. She said, 'If you won't tell them I'll tell them you're not pregnant, I will!' She used to stretch herself to five foot nothing in her cotton socks. She was lovely. (A3, p. 40)

Molly, who worked alongside me in the Silverdale Co-op, believed that: 'A woman's best friend is her mother; a mother's more to a woman than her husband even!' The women around spoke out their agreement. They were all over forty, at a stage when matrimony is likely to spell compatibility rather than romance. Silverdale is, however, another Bethnal Green, at least as far as the mother-daughter tie is concerned (Young and Willmott, 1957). Mum's presence is met with everywhere. She helps with the shopping and cooking, sometimes she does the washing and ironing, she minds the child and if the need arises she minds her daughter's husband. It is not as uncommon as one might suppose for her to foster her daughter's illegitimate offspring.

Neighbours sometimes loom larger on the horizon than either mums or sisters. Muriel and Gladys have formed one such neighbourly partnership. On Gladys's first shopping expedition in the area Muriel acted as a guide. Now they do the week's wash together on a Saturday morning, and they spend many evenings together. Gladys's daughter Clare goes to Muriel's house after school until Gladys gets home. When Clare had 'flu, Muriel tended her. They say of their relationship:

GLADYS: Muriel's a friend I know I can depend on. I could put my life on her, you know. She's the type of friend I can call on and say, 'lend me £50', and she'd give it me, no questions asked about why I needed it, or when would she have it back, you know. (F3, p. 13)

MURIEL: I go up Gladys's and say, 'Glad, can you give me this?' And she gives it me. There's no such thing as borrowing. We don't borrow *we give*. Glad. will come and say, 'Oh, I've got visitors coming', and I'll say, 'alright, what do you want?' And then if I'm having visitors she'll say, 'Don't worry we'll fix it between us'. To me that's a friend. (F3, pp. 13-14)

The difference between men and women is not that women fail to make friends with other women, but that their circle of friendship is more confined. Only one, two or three people may be included in the circle of close friendship, and these friends are likely to be drawn from female relations, neighbours or workmates. For men the catchment area is wider, it embraces the mine or factory, the club and pub, the neighbourhood, the union and sometimes the political party.

In one activity, however, women fraternise with other women for evenings on end, spending money on themselves just as though they were men. Bingo is the cause of this metamorphosis. This game may be dull, competitive and acquisitive; it has, however, opened doors. Gladys describes its impact:

GLADYS: The younger ones won't take it now. Women I work with will say, 'I'm going to a dance tonight', another will say, 'I'm going to bingo'. I'm going here, I'm going there on all sides. I think bingo has opened a new scope for women. It's *that* that's made them go out. (F3, p. 9)

A miner's friendship is influenced by the circumstances of his work which, for all that safety has improved, remains a dangerous job. Silverdale women may assess their contacts on the basis of neighbourliness, a Silverdale miner is more likely to do so on the basis of a man's trustworthiness at pit bottom. And if, as in the case of Don, the miner is an active unionist, the assessment is tinged with class content.

DON HARRIS: I haven't a great deal of time for many officials. There are exceptions; about 20 per cent of the officials I work with have been good workmen. But a large proportion of them get to think like bosses. And while I'm working I get to think about this—say there are seven men in our area, and while the machine's coming up I've got nothing to do, it's a practice of mine to ask myself, 'If anything goes wrong who do I turn to?' I know all the men. And in my mind I strike so many off the list, and I put others at the top, you know. After a few years of working with them in the same team you get to know who you can depend on like. And when I make this reckoning it's not often I put an official in the top, in the top ten say. You couldn't count on many of them if it came to the final crunch like. (A3, pp. 43–4)

The loyalties that people form in this situation run very deep. In Silverdale as a whole friendships span a good chunk of life, for both men and women. The fellow feeling that miners form for miners, and women for other working women, can run as deep and be as emotionally and intellectually rewarding as the friendship between husband and wife. And since the latter relationship may sometimes be less than friendly, these secondary relationships can assume primary importance. In Silverdale the closest affinities are not bounded by the walls of the nuclear family.

AUTHORITY IN THE FAMILY

Frederic Engels has put his finger on the connection between earning cash and exercising authority within the home. In the absence of changed social conditions Engels deplored the cases of role reversal between husband and wife which he came across in Manchester in 1844. His tone is at times a little at odds with the modern era:

> In many cases the family is not wholly dissolved by the employment of the wife, but turned upside down. The wife supports the family, the husband sits at home, tends the children, sweeps the room and cooks. This case happens frequently; in Manchester alone, many hundred such men could be cited, condemned to domestic occupations. It is easy to imagine the wrath aroused among the working men by this reversal of all relations within the family, while the other social conditions remain unchanged. (Engels, 1969, p. 173)

Engels goes on to present the contents of a letter written by a working man to Oastler in which a friend of the writer looked up an old acquaintance and found:

> Why he sat and mended his wife's stockings with the bodkin, and as soon as he saw his old friend at the doorpost, he tried to hide them. But Joe, that is my friend's name, had seen it, and said, 'Jack what the devil art thou doing? Where is the missus? Why, is that thy work?' and poor Jack was ashamed and said, 'No I know this is not my work, but my poor missus is i' th' factory; she has to leave by half past five and works 'till eight at night, and then she is

so knocked up that she cannot do aught when she gets home, so I have to do everything for her what I can, for I have no work, nor had any for more nor three years . . . she has been the man in the house and I the woman, it's bad work, Joe.'

Engels comments:

'Can anyone imagine a more insane state of things than that described in this letter? . . . which unsexes the man and takes from the woman all womanliness without being able to bestow on the man true womanliness; or the woman true manliness'. (Engels, 1969, pp. 173-4)

If some of the assumptions contained in this passage are questionable, Engels correctly sees that matters of hard cash underlie authority relations within the family, and that this unsavoury reality is not redeemed if the woman rather than the man flaunts the breadwinner role:

If the reign of the wife over the husband, as inevitably brought about by the factory system, is inhuman, the pristine rule of the husband over the wife must have been inhuman too. If the wife can now base her supremacy upon the fact that she supplies the greater part, nay, the whole of the common possession, the necessary inference is that this community of possession is no true and rational one, since one member of the family boasts offensively of contributing the greater share . . . The same relation exists on the part of those children who support unemployed parents . . . In this case the children are the masters of the house, as the wife was in the former case, and Lord Ashley gives an example of this in his speech: A man berated his two daughters for going to the public house, and they answered that they were tired of being ordered about, saying, 'Damn you, we have to keep you!' Determined to keep the proceeds of their work for themselves, they left the family dwelling, and abandoned their parents to their fate. (Engels, 1969, pp. 174-5)

Some men today are equally ashamed to be seen doing 'women's work', as ever 'poor Jack' was in Engels's day. Joe Kohout is a helpful husband by Silverdale standards. Joe would do any task *asked* of him; it was of course Gladys Kohout's job to do the asking.

When Joe was on early shift he made up the coal fire. He regularly cleaned the cooker, and Gladys and Joe shared the cooking. Joe did most of the washing up, and he was quite willing to clean the house from top to bottom. This last job Joe had taken on when their children were young. He did not, however, like his domesticity to become public knowledge, and this shyness extended to childcare. Inside the house Joe was more than ready to change baby's nappy, but being *seen* with baby outside was a different matter:

GLADYS: He would never wheel a pram out. He would say, 'Take these children out, and everything will be done when you get back'. And the house would be like a new pin. He'd do everything. He'd do the house all through, and I mean literally all through. He'd pick up all the lino and wipe underneath it, he wouldn't just wipe the floor surface. *But,* he'd stop when he got as far as the back door step; that was that, because he wouldn't want nobody to see him with a scrubbing brush and mop, or a bucket or whatever in his hand. (F3, p. 73)

This behaviour represents an implicit acceptance of masculine status and authority. A minority of couples openly support masculine authority. The statement that the man should be the head of the family often occurs in discussions about money—a fact which would not have surprised Engels. Rose and Don are a case in point. Rose explains how they make decisions about purchases:

ROSE: If I was going to decide on anything I wouldn't decide on it on my own back, I'd ask Harris here what he thought, more or less. Mind you, if I was going to lash out I'd generally ask him when he's deep in a book. I'm dead crafty! He'd say anything then to shut me up, he'll say, 'Yes duck, of course', and I've got his go-ahead then. But no, I think he's the boss in the house. I don't like it very much, but I think he is the boss. It's easier now we're both earning money, and you feel it's yours 'cos you've earned it, you know. That gives you a bit of independence, though Don's never kept me short of money. (A3, p. 75)

Don thought in other families it was different:

DON: There are some houses where women are the boss. There are some very aggressive women, and I think men will give more in an argument than a woman will. There's a couple round the corner where the woman is aggressive. They've got a daughter around sixteen, and the daughter's got to the stage where she talks to her father just like the mother, in public, in the garden.

Rose agreed this was a bad thing:

> I clipped her only the other day, tongue wise, she spoke to her father and I didn't like it, and I told her. (A3, p. 77)

Although Don and Rose could agree about the respect daughters should show their fathers, they disagreed on the question of financial independence.

DON: Money upsets me more than anything. I query something she's spending money on, she'll say, 'It's *my* money'. Now I never say 'It's *my* money'. I always say, 'It's *our* money'. She says, 'Well, that's my money, that is'. I say, 'It's not your money, it's our money'. You see, I don't say I've got this and I've got that, I always say 'we'. Even when I was the sole wage earner I never said it was *my* money like. We used to save money, and I used to say we can afford this or we can afford that. (A3, pp. 77–8)

It is difficult for Don to see that his ownership of the money is expressed by a relationship in which ultimately *he* says what they can or cannot afford. Lee Comer, writing about houseworkers, argues, I think correctly, that the '*our* money' concept which is emphasised by the ideal of joint discussion, is something of a myth:

> It sounds nice in theory but what it amounts to in practice is the means whereby the woman talks her husband round, gets his *permission* to buy a washing machine, vacuum cleaner and so on . . . do they honestly sit down together and discuss how he shall weigh up the relative merits of £2 on a horse or a pubcrawl? . . . what husband however wealthy would fail to ask how much those (new) boots cost?

And if a wife should challenge her husband's expenditure he could argue logically that:

> He works his balls off all week so that she can have the things she

wants and if he isn't entitled to some enjoyment, just what is he entitled to? . . .' All her lines of attack are circumscribed by her dependent position. She too works all week, but it doesn't merit the label work because it isn't paid. And, without a moment's hesitation he can sweep away the nonsense of shared money, merely by stating the truth. He earns it and he *gives* it to her. (Comer, 1974, pp. 124–6)

Houseworkers are financially dependent on their husbands. When a woman goes out to earn money this dependence is modified but in most cases not eradicated. If this were not the case, the possessiveness of women like Rose would be puzzling. Rose feels guilty about her attitude because she is reacting not to Don's open possessiveness but to the possessiveness implicit in their situation, and because, as we have seen, the husband's rather than the wife's money is reserved to pay for unavoidable expenses so that his money appears to be more tied up than his wife's. Sarah once again lives out individually a general predicament:

SARAH: I've got a different attitude towards the money I earn compared to the money Len earns. Actually Len pointed this out to me some months ago, and he's right about it. I felt the money I earned was mine. I don't admire myself for it, but I can't bear any of that money to be spent without me saying what it's going to be spent on. It's very selfish. As Len says, the money he earns he really can't decide how it's spent, because he knows how it's got to be spent. This money I've earned, I haven't put it away to spend on myself, but I've decided how it's going to be spent, every penny of it. (C3, pp. 32–3)

Other women feel less guilty:

MARGARET DEAN: My money isn't all that, but it's my own. It comes in for holidays and things for the home, and I buy more clothes now. I decide what to spend my money on—else I wouldn't go out to work. I feel more independent now. If I want something in the home I just go out and buy it. I don't have to ask for it, you know. Whereas before I had to get round Michael, you know, how you are. Now you've got your own money in your pocket you're alright, you just go out and buy what you want. I usually go and buy something and then tell him after. (D3, p. 17)

The determination of most women wage earners to control the money they have earned expresses their endorsement of the ideology that industrial wages are payment for individual work. From this ideological standpoint the contribution of domestic labour, in the form of reproducing and servicing wage-workers, is overlooked. If this socially productive aspect of domestic work goes unrecognised the houseworker's job seems to be merely a personal service for the benefit of family members. Therefore when women wage earners insist on controlling 'their own' earnings they, like their husbands, help to recreate the ideology which devalues domestic work.

Although as houseworkers women suffer most from the ideological devaluation of housework, when they return to the labour market they, to some extent, turn the ideology to their own advantage by insisting on their ownership right to 'their' wages. Not infrequently, however, women wage earners feel ambivalent about such possessiveness. As we have already seen, this arises from the way the second income is used. Until the houseworker returned to the labour market, the family relied on the husband's earnings for basic requirements. After the wife's return to the labour market the family continues to pay its way with the husband's earnings. This is partly because the wife's earnings are insufficient to support the family and uncertain, and partly because of the ideology that the man is the breadwinner. As a result the bulk of the husband's earnings are spent on meeting unavoidable expenses, leaving the bulk of the wife's earnings for more varied and non-routine purchases which permit her, to a greater extent than her husband, to exercise choice as a consumer.

Some wage earning women worry about the fairness of this arrangement. I would argue, however, that despite such ambivalence most working women are determined to control their earnings because they are reacting to their experience as full-time houseworkers, when their husbands exercised, however implicitly, unilateral control of the money supply. This is why financial independence is a heart-felt theme:

SANDRA MILL: Them few weeks I was out of work I was miserable, 'cos I'd always been used to having my own bit of money. Can you understand what I mean? I'd always had my own bit, so I didn't have to keep going to Jack and saying can you give me a pound. I've never had to ask him for money you see. I've kept my independence.

We both work and pool our money together, but you see I've always had a little bit on one side, for myself. If it's only £5 it's my own isn't it, to please myself. But he was pretty good, when I wasn't working he would give me a bit of pocket money for myself like. But you couldn't save it. (G3, p. 19)

In a minority of cases couples did seem genuinely to share their money. This was the case with Frank and Norma Wade. Their arrangement represented a break with the past as far as Frank's family of origin was concerned. Norma describes how this fact came to light:

NORMA WADE: We lived up Parksite, and Frank's mum lived up there, although she didn't often come round, we had to go and beg her to come or go and fetch her. Anyway this Friday she just followed Frank in. He just came in, threw his wage packet on the table and went through the back to hang his coat up. And she said in a shocked whisper, 'Frank, is this your wage packet, you dropped it', you know, it's accidentally slipped out of your hand in front of Norma sort of thing. You see, she had never seen how much her husband had got. She wasn't horrified, but she was a bit shocked to learn Frank wasn't like his father. Mind you, it was a bit tactless really. (H3, p. 28)

Silverdale women twenty or more years ago were far more likely to be in the dark about their husband's earnings than they are today. They were also likely to be very short of cash. It was the woman's job to make the little she had go round:

MARGARET DEAN: My mother paid all the bills. My father hadn't used to give her very much, only housekeeping. That's why she had so many different jobs. But he'd save it, he'd save money, you know. But he never gave her a great deal. He used to go out a lot, he used to go out most nights.

Your father would buy the big items for the house?

MARGARET: Yes, he'd buy furniture or anything big like that, but we'd have to be desperate.

Did your mother go out much?

MARGARET: No. She used to listen to the wireless. We'd got one of those big old fashioned wirelesses. She used to sit and unwind these old woollies, you know, and wash the wool out and knit them up again. She used to sit hours doing them. Woollies that were too small, she'd undo them and knit something else with them. And sit darning socks, for hours. (D3, pp. 16–17)

The change in authority relations within the family is part of a wider process of change, which also finds expression in women's readiness to go out, be it only to play bingo, and in the inequality of pay between men and women being seen by more working people as an issue, as well as being expressed as an issue in government legislation. The general improvement in prosperity and full employment—currently under threat—has also eased the domestic struggle for money. This change in prosperity over a twenty year period has made itself felt in financial arrangements between parents and children. From a period in which children either had no pocket money at all, or had to work for the small amount they got, we have moved into a situation where children expect a weekly sum of money with no strings attached. In the past when children went out to work they used to 'turn it all up', and be given pocket money. Now their position resembles that of the breadwinner, they pay board and keep the rest.

Mums who go out to work are less subject to their husbands' subtle and not so subtle exercise of authority than their houseworker counterparts. The difficulty of coping with two jobs quite frequently prompts women to challenge previous arrangements in the home:

MARGARET DEAN: I used to do all the decorating. I had more time when I was at home, and I used to think it was my job sort of thing. I leave it to Michael now. I just think, well I do housework, you do decorating. I stick up for myself a bit more now. (D3, p. 25)

But such changes are not simply due to the pressure of holding down two jobs. As suggested at the beginning of this chapter the world of work is on-stage, where things are seen to happen. By comparison the back stage world is an isolated world where the level of skill and effort expended is often overlooked or devalued. The occupational disease backstage is demoralisation. For those employed persons who inhabit the stage, off-stage life is confined to a wait in the wings and dressing room. It is the place where you prepare for the next performance, and where tension is released after the show. It is almost impossible for such employed persons to comprehend the backstage world from the viewpoint of its permanent inhabitants. As Engels noted, the aura of the breadwinner's authority is carried backstage partly through the medium of the pay packet. After the initial shock of finding herself on stage the houseworker may recognise that the important thing about working is 'finding you have the ability to earn your own income'. (C3, p. 31)

The question of money is tied up with the question of self-esteem. The boost to the ex-full-time houseworker's confidence from the discovery that she can make good on stage can and does spill over into the domestic sphere. Sarah and Len Wells recognise the change:

SARAH: I feel I've changed a lot. I don't think I'll ever be like I was before. I was the little housewife before, and now I tend to throw my weight around a bit. And I feel more independent now. I know I can work and stand on my own feet. If I finish at the shop I will get another job, but it will be on my own terms next time. I've changed so much you see. Before I would put up with things. I really was the little housewife. Now I do things I want to do much more often.

Len agreed, and added, 'I think we will probably go our separate ways more than we did before'.

Sarah accepted that. 'Yes we will. Before I went along with your opinions a lot, but now I'm able to disagree. And I think my relations with the children have improved. I don't nag at them the way I did, and I think I like them better than I did before, although I think I've neglected Ellen in terms of giving her attention at an important time in her life, 'cos she's going to bed at eight o'clock when we've only been sitting down for half an hour or so, and I've attended hardly any of her school things. (C3, pp. 39–40)

At home, as at work, a basic safeguard is the right to walk out. Married women in paid employment tend to be the mothers of school-aged children. The fact that they do earn money, and that their children are older makes the decision to separate from their husbands conceivable, at least in comparison to the more tied position of the full-time houseworker. On the whole, though, the freedom to set up a home for themselves and their children is not real. These women don't earn that kind of money. They would in most cases require the help of another wage earner, most probably another man. So their reduced dependence on their husband—or man—is marginal. This is one reason why their increased tendency to stick up for themselves at home is likewise marginal. It is not the only reason, as the case of Gill and Mark Carter discussed in the previous chapter, illustrated. Gill has the economic means to get up and go—and she may do precisely that one day—but their relationship continues to be partially shaped by their socialisation into gender roles and the pervasive ideology that 'women serve men'.

WOMEN AND THE TRADE-UNION MOVEMENT

It is to women rather than to men that the task of reproducing and maintaining labour mainly falls in our society. Since in this respect the social situation of women differs from that of most men, we may ask if this difference affects the way women respond as workers at their place of paid employment.

Juliet Mitchell has a reply at the ready:

> work as a housewife isn't work—it's 'being at home' (the place of leisure), work in the office or factory isn't work—it's 'getting out of the house for a bit'. Working at home she is isolated, working outside the home she is enjoying some social life. There is no possibility here of comradeship or unity in struggle—the relationship of women workers is simply the counterpart of the loneliness of the home, it is friendliness or its opposite . . . Their exploitation is invisible behind an ideology that masks the fact that they work at all—their work appears inessential . . . Cut off from other women at home, going to work 'for the company' she yet brings—at times of crisis—the isolation of the family to bear on the collective possibilities of the work situation, she does not have even a divided loyalty, for where dependence is intrinsic to the situation, loyalty is redundant. (1971, p. 139)

As full-time houseworkers women are cut off from the direct experience of class struggle on the shop floor. When such women re-enter the direct labour market they find themselves in the non-career, low paid job sector. It is easy to see how such female labour could represent a threat to the hard won gains achieved by organised labour. However, to present the problem in these static terms, as Juliet Mitchell does, is to obscure the actual process involved.

Women like Sarah, the mothers of school age children who have been at home for several years, return to the labour market doubting their ability to hold down *any* job for long. From the employers' point of view such women represent willing and reliable labour power. Sarah, for example, went out of her way to prevent her domestic responsibilities interfering with her job:

SARAH: When the children are ill I find it difficult. Mike had this 'flu that's going round, and I went to work although he was quite poorly. In fact he shouldn't have been left. I suppose I could have stopped home, but you're very torn. You've got your responsibilities at work and your responsibilities at home. I feel I'm pulled two ways. (C3, p. 38)

Unmarried more youthful workers will, now and then, take an odd day off because they feel like it. From the employers' point of view such youthful workers may be far less reliable than women like Sarah.

The initial desire to serve willingly extends to matters of pay. Norma Wade describes her attitude like this:

NORMA: We get equal pay with the men. When I first started here I thought £24 a week, I thought, 'that's great'. Now it's £40, and I still think it's alright.

This seemingly confirms Mitchell's opinion that such workers have a dampening effect on the 'collective possibilities' of the work place. However, as Norma herself recognises, the situation changes:

'Now I hear of people earning—after seventeen years of earning only pin money I was dead satisfied. But now, I believe I'm worth £40 at least. If they offered me more I certainly wouldn't feel that I didn't deserve it. But it's taken me two years to think like that, I'm afraid.' (H3, p. 45)

Once again those who are younger and unmarried may be more ready to accept low pay than married women returning to work, for, as a pottery worker recollects:

SANDRA MILL: The young girls don't seem to be bothered about working to get money. I've been like it myself so I know. I don't think you realise the value of money till you get married and come to have a family. When you're single, and you're living at home, you're working for yourself, to buy yourself clothes and make up. You're not really working for anything that's important to you. When I was younger I could not have cared less. I went to work, laughed and talked. When I look at these young girls I see myself. Some of the older ones forget, and they think, 'silly devils!' but I don't 'cos I'm sitting there thinking, 'I used to be just the same myself!' (G3, pp. 26–7)

Expectations concerning pay tend to expand with experience. This is also true of solidarity. Gladys describes the ties that have grown up between women workers in the section of the wire factory where she works:

GLADYS: The shop I work in is a closed shop. They don't call it that now, but it's 100 per cent union. Now, a woman came to work there who wasn't in the union. When she came in she was asked, 'are you in the union?' I didn't ask her, it makes no difference to me. But, see, this was a new shop I'd gone into. The shop I worked in for a couple of years before wasn't a completely union shop. Well, she said she wasn't in the union and everybody downed tools. 'We'll not have a non-union member in this shop,' they said. She said she would not join the union. She said it was a waste of money and a waste of time. Well where I'm working there are women who have been there twenty-five years—the biggest majority of them. Apart from me the shortest time someone's done is fifteen years. They've all stuck together through thick and thin. I mean, they've seen more or less what we've fought for. You know, better conditions and more money. Why should one spoil it? You know, break the bond that they've got there. So I thought to myself, 'Gladys, you've either got to join them or be called a blackleg'. Well I went with them. I've got the intelligence to see that they had fought for it. So she was moved to another shop. (F3, pp. 41–2)

It would seem that the docility of the ex-full-time-houseworker is temporary. The money they earn represents an important contribution to their families' standard of living, and within a few years they are as determined as their male counterparts to stand up for their rights as paid workers.

Nevertheless women employees are not as involved in the trade-union movement as male employees. The overall employment rate for females in 1971 was nearly 43 per cent. This proportion is not, however, reflected in their union membership. Women comprise approximately 25 per cent of the membership of trade unions. Furthermore those women who do join unions tend to be less involved in the running of the union than their male counterparts. There are few female full-time union officials; for every thirty-two men there is one female full-time official (Judith Hunt, 1975, p. 20). Women are drastically under-represented on union national executive and district committees. This remains the case even when the majority of the union's membership is female. The same under-representation occurs in union conferences and congresses. For example, at the 1975 TUC out of a total of 1030 delegates there were only eighty-four women. Out of the fifteen affiliated unions with more women than men in membership, five sent delegations to congress which did not include a woman. (Judith Hunt, 1975, p. 10)

What factors underlie this lack of involvement? First, some unions are very male oriented in their style of work. This shows itself in a number of ways. Sometimes male trade unionists think that women should support the union on the men's terms, that is, without making any alteration in the way the union operates. The relationship between Peter and Dilys illustrates this dilemma. Although Peter's extensive involvement in the union had left Dilys to raise their family single handed, this had not undermined her commitment to the trade union movement.

DILYS: I've never been hostile as far as unions are concerned; not to the NUM itself. I was concerned about the time it was taking up. I mean Peter's time. But unions are absolutely necessary as far as the working class is concerned. I was resentful at times, about the time Peter used to spend with the union. But I wasn't resentful as far as the union itself is concerned. (B3, p. 64)

Dilys thought women sometimes opposed strikes because, while it was plain for them to see the effect the strike would have on their family, the reason for taking strike action escaped them. This, she felt, was largely due to a lack of discussion between husband and wife.

DILYS: Women don't like strikes because they know it's going to affect the family as far as money is concerned; they're going to have to tighten their belts. But if they discussed the strike—some women just aren't interested in their husbands' jobs, they take the pay packet and that's it. But if they discussed it with their husbands, and found out more about the conditions they have to work in, it would be different. (B3, p. 22)

One obstacle to this kind of dialogue was pointed out in 1955 by Alvin Gouldner. In terms of the dominant ideology in industry, a lot of grievances seem to the workers themselves to be of dubious legitimacy. Frequently such background grievances are collapsed into strike demands for 'more appropriate' remedies like more money. When this occurs it is 'hard for the strikers to verbalize their reasons to outsiders, for they have not clearly articulated the principles involved even to themselves' (1955, p. 36).

Dilys identified another difficulty standing in the way of female participation in union affairs:

DILYS: There again, I think the family has a lot to do with it. Women don't have time enough to get involved with things like that. But I think women should take a bigger part in trade unions. I don't think that men would agree though. I think women could improve the unions because women have got a different outlook to men, haven't they? I think they have a different outlook. I mean, men are mainly wage structure, hours of work, things like that. Whereas a woman would probably be more involved with social activities, such as nurseries and things like that. (B3, pp. 22–3)

Dilys didn't expect Peter to agree. 'He thinks this is a load of bullshit!' She was right.

PETER: Men are involved in that sort of thing. We've had all sorts of things as far as social do's are concerned. We've even run a Gymkhana up the cricket field, and done children's sports and everything. And to be truthful 90 per cent of the time on these occasions the women have let us down. I mean, they are involved just as much as we are in getting the children into races. Last year we put the forms out in plenty of time. The women knew these forms were out, but they couldn't have cared less about telling the men to go and get one.

'There again,' answered Dilys, 'there aren't the women there who could go forward and get these other women involved. The union's such a male thing.' (B3, pp. 23–4)

Audrey Wise (n.d.) has pointed out ways in which the unions recreate situations which reinforce male dominance. It may be that women are relegated to roles which fit in with their domestic image. The larger policy issues are often seen, frequently by women themselves, as matters that don't concern women.

The language used in union meetings and literature may reinforce the male atmosphere. Audrey Wise gives two examples: the use of the expression 'dear brothers', when women are among those being addressed, and the phrase 'trade unionists, their wives and families', which ignores the fact that a quarter of trade unionists are female.

Women, to a greater extent than men, care for dependents, often adult dependents in the case of single women. If the unions want to involve these women adjustments in union arrangements are required. Too often union meetings are held in the evening when it is difficult for women to get out. A report illustrating this difficulty appeared in the *Morning Star*. It concerned a group of women members of the NUM, who served in a pit canteen. They supported the strike 100 per cent:

> There's not many hands rest on our canteen counter that haven't got a finger missing, or the tips sliced off. It's a dangerous job mining . . . The miners are out only for what they need, and we're out with them. We support them all the way.

Yet, for all this loyalty, when questioned as to whether they felt involved in the decisions taken by the NUM locally they replied,

> 'not really. Getting to the branch meeting means a 'bus ride in the evening, there and back . . . and after getting home from work and fixing a meal you're too tired. If we could have branch meetings in canteen, that would be different. We're always at any meetings held in canteen. We discussed taking strike action at a canteen meeting.' (*Morning Star*, Friday, 1 March 1974).

If evening meetings are held in traditionally masculine environments like pubs and working-men's clubs, social inhibitions are added to the practical difficulties which deter women from attending meetings.

Child care facilities provided at all union congresses and

conferences would make it easier for those with young children to attend.

Such issues as these weigh more heavily on women than on men, because women are more involved in domestic production. I think that these differences would find expression in different policies if women were more involved in the unions. For example, work place creches and improved maternity allowances would enable more women both to go out to work and to play a part in union government. Pat Knight, secretary of South Norwood ASTMS reported that in answer to a survey on discrimination at work, ASTMS groups in Number 8 Division, creches and maternity provision were frequently mentioned as issues on which the union should take action. Creches, in fact, were mentioned more than any other issue, although they have been regarded until recently as outside the normal sphere of trade union activity (Pat Knight, *Morning Star*, 6 October 1976).

Since unions up till now have mainly been run by men, it is men who have defined what is 'the normal sphere of trade union activity'. Given this situation, Richard Brown's question is very relevant: 'Do the different priorities at work held by women as compared with men (e.g. hours and conditions) mean that their main concerns are given second place to men's (e.g. overtime) in male dominated work place union organisations, which thus continue to fail to attract their interest and support?' (Brown, 1976, p. 37). I think the narrow range of traditional trade union concerns has deterred women from becoming more actively involved in trade unionism.

Occasionally situations arise within which men seem to gain objectively from siding with management against women workers. Nichols and Armstrong (1976) provide a striking example of this in their chapter on six women. They also make the point that the only group who benefited from this division in the workforce was management.

Where the interests of male and female workers are apparently in contradiction, unions have been known to demonstrate their male dominance by taking the men's part. The Union of Post Office Workers is a case in point. For years this union has fostered policies which harmed its female members. Until forced by the Sex Discrimination Act and the Equal Pay Act to mend its ways, the UPW accepted the classification of post women as 'temporary unestablished'. This classification entitled post women to only three months paid sick leave, compared to the men's six months paid leave. More important, 'temporary unestablished' post women had no seniority or promotion rights.

The ideology which justified the post office union's discriminatory policies was the familiar ideology that man is the family breadwinner. Thus, when the Birmingham District was faced with the prospect of thirty-six postmen being made redundant, the local UPW branch passed a resolution that no man should be compulsorily retired or made redundant while part-time labour was being employed. So instead of thirty-six jobs being lost seventy-two part-time women workers were told they had to go. The remaining part-time women workers were informed that their hours would be reduced from twenty-five to eighteen. The union encouraged these women to accept voluntary redundancy, but as the post woman telling the story observed, 'There was nothing voluntary about it because eighteen hours didn't pay enough' (*Women Under Attack*).

Given the existence of such prejudice, women's lack of involvement in collective struggle and the trade union cannot be explained exclusively in terms of the women's immersion in domesticity.

TRADE UNION CONSCIOUSNESS

Involvement in the trade union movement is not necessarily or even usually associated with a marked degree of class consciousness. This is due to a number of reasons, one of the most important of which is the disassociation between private family interests and collective class interests referred to in the first chapter. Where this disassociation of interests occurs the collective struggle is weakened, as Don discovered:

DON: It was during the strike that I got pretty deeply involved with the union like. One of the reasons why I did was, despite what the popular press says, the NUM, especially in this area, is very weak. Very weak. And when we came to the final crunch and went on strike I was surprised at the lack of active support we got from the rank and file. I was a member of the rank and file myself at the time, but I felt sort of beholden to go and do something like. You see it was a common practice to go to the doctors and get on the club. That was while we were on strike. They took part-time jobs, full-time jobs some of them. It rattled me more than a little bit that did.

Well, I went on the picket for at least twelve hours a day like. That was for seven weeks. And there was another practice which caused a bit of bitterness among the workers themselves. I brought it up at a meeting when they asked for pickets. It was the first time I had ever spoken at a public meeting. There was always a fair attendance at these meetings. They wanted to know what was going on in their own branch, to see if there was a chance of starting work. So they used to attend. But when it came to go on picketing they were very few on the ground. Now at the pit there were stacks of coal on the banks that the men were making sure wasn't moved. And a lot of pickets used to come just as it got dark. They'd roll up in vans and cars. All they'd come for was the coal you see. These pickets, two would come in a car like, one would go and fill three bags of coal while the other stood on the picket line. And as soon as those three bags were full they'd go. They would go. It was shocking! Well, as I say that was the first time I ever spoke at a public meeting. Peter was the secretary at the time, and he was asking for pickets, and I brought this point up. 'We don't want this type of picket on the line,' I said, 'because they just come and show their faces while they get half a dozen bags of coal, and then they're away again'. And it wasn't just the odd one or two, there were quite a few of them. (A3, pp. 45-6)

Rose had her experiences during this time.

ROSE: Everyone was saying to me, 'you can get cheap dinners for the boys at school'. So I went down to social security. I sat there. I felt a bit of a fool, you know, 'cos I'd never gone with my hand holding the begging bowl in my life before. But he says, 'Well Mrs Harris, how much money have you got in the bank'. I looked at him. I said, 'What on earth has that got to do with it?' He says, 'Oh, if you've got over a certain amount in the bank you can't draw a penny'. I said, 'Well, I'm not telling you how much money we've got in the bank. You can go an whistle.' It was the same with my friend Peg, her Derick hadn't got much at all. He asked her what wages she got, and she couldn't draw a penny either. Bloomin marvellous. (A3, pp. 46-7)

Many working people find asking for welfare a humiliating experience. The application of pressure through the strength of their union organisation to take what they need is quite a different experience. It is mainly the women of Silverdale who are driven to state welfare agencies, particularly during strikes.

Don continued to lament the lack of militancy shown by the Staffordshire miners:

DON: A lot of things happened. When we were at Saltley the engineering unions came out and supported us. Without their support we wouldn't have closed Saltley down. But we did. Well the Saturday after it was closed down the engineering unions had some march in Birmingham. I forget what it was for, but they asked for support from the miners of this area. Well, eight 'buses went round the collieries and villages in this area picking up support for this march. Well, it was announced on the radio that only eight people had turned up. We ended up in Wolstanton Miners' Club at Smallthorne. And the 'buses came up with these eight people. Some 'buses were totally empty. They got into the one 'bus and went to Birmingham. That was the total amount of support from this area, right after the support they had given us at Saltley. It was—oh it was terrible. But funnily enough, this area is recognised for that sort of thing.

'I must like the men,' Don continued, 'or I wouldn't enjoy working with them. But I can't understand them. I think it's partly this affluent society, you know, there's too many people take too much on their backs in the way of repayments. The first thing they think of when there's mention of a strike is their mortgage and their car, and all the rest, you see. They've got more commitments than they ever had in the past. In the old days if they had a meal and clothes on their back, that was as much as they ever had. But nowadays they've tasted the good things, and a strike is going to interfere with that. This pit's a bit of an exception 'cos there's a lot of overtime worked down here, so nobody's got to do without at all you know. So if a time ever comes again, and it will do some time or other 'cos the NCB control the purse strings, when they say, "right, cut down on overtime severely", then we'll get a flood of complaints. We'll get a flood of complaints, I know that like. But at the present time we've got very little work to do as regards management and men at pit level. There will be trouble between the *union* and management about this "Health and Safety at Work Act" over the next year or two. The managers have got their backs up about that. These managers don't like being dictated to. But as regards *men* and management, we seldom have any disputes to settle.' (A3 pp. 48–50)

Don rightly sees that what can incline workers to be non-militant at one stage, in this case the affluence made possible by the availability of overtime, can at another intensify the class struggle, when that relative affluence is threatened.

Each place of work has its own peculiar features which intensify and/or detract from militancy. So, for example, the Ford stewards are personally involved in struggle at workplace level, in a way that Silverdale miners are not—at the moment (see Beynon, 1973). However, miners are members of a union and an industry which confronts issues at a national level, and this can, potentially at least, enable Silverdale miners to situate their struggles in a wider framework. In all circumstances, however, class consciousness tends to remain very limited. This is mainly because the political agency which could enable lessons of struggle in diverse situations to be pieced together into a comprehensive picture of class realities is as yet embryonic. The result is that workers often hold a number of inconsistent and conflicting viewpoints; some viewpoints based mainly on personal experience, others influenced by the mass media. For example, Karl's knowledge of industrial relations in the motor industry is based on what he sees on television and reads in the press. Like many people, his attitude towards car workers is tinged with hostility:

KARL: Sometimes you have to strike. Striking isn't a good thing for anyone is it? Not for the government or anyone. But sometimes it's necessary. I don't agree with striking over every little row, like the car workers, I've never known anything like it! But the miners wouldn't do that because it's a different kind of production, you know. But striking is necessary because you fight for your living you see. I could say, 'I want to work, I'm not striking', but then I couldn't go against the others could I? I mean, there's a lot of others. Although everybody's got their own opinion, you've got to stick together don't you? (E3, p. 17)

Karl recognises that to make a living you have to put up a collective fight, and that collective action is in pursuit of a specific objective. This view is more experienced than the elementary collectivism of the Pilkington workers described by Lane and

Roberts (1971), many of whom followed the walk out without any idea of what the strike was about (1971, p. 88).

Even so Karl accepts uncritically the media image of car workers, but not the media image of miners which can be verified against personal experience:

KARL: . . . people like newspaper men are educated people, they must be, and most of them have never had hard times in their life you see. They just find things out and they start to write. Some of them don't know anything about mines, only what they hear like, 'a miner gets £60 a week'. It isn't true of every miner, only face workers, and there's only a few face workers. You get other workers on the surface earning far below that, but all you hear is £60 a week. (E3, p. 18)

Thus Karl accepts that car workers are ready to strike over trivialities, although he recognises that strikes entail considerable hardship for the strikers. The difficulty of explaining why hard-headed workers are willing to make sacrifices over trivial matters is not confronted by Karl; he avoids the issue by arguing that car workers are different beings; 'miners would do that because it's a different kind of production'.

Theo Nichols and Peter Armstrong (1976) have pointed to many such inconsistencies in the thinking of chemical workers who conform to the pattern of 'instrumental privatization' described by Goldthorpe and Lockwood. These workers separate their industrial from their social experiences so that the ideological position taken in one realm of experience, is contradicted by the ideological stance simultaneously held with reference to the other realm of experience. Although this means that workers are susceptible to divisive ideologies, the situation is potentially volatile, for as Nichols and Armstrong note, 'Systems of thought which contain some inner incoherence . . . may be expected to contain *within themselves* the possibility of change' (1976, p. 152).

It is not only the social scientist who needs theory in order to be able to elaborate concepts which make one situation comparable with another. Until the employed population are able to see what is of general significance in their particular experience there can be little development of political awareness.

The Marxist tradition has throughout emphasised the need for theory, which is a political weapon insofar as it enables the working people to break away from bourgeois theories of political economy.

Marx said of struggles confined to the attempt to secure wage increases and better conditions: 'the working class ought not to exaggerate to themselves the ultimate working of these everyday struggles. They ought not to forget that they are fighting with the effects, but not with the causes of those effects . . . they are applying palliatives, not curing the malady.' (Marx, 1970, pp. 225–6)

To get to the roots of the question a different kind of organisation was required. Thus as Lozovsky points out:

> Marx always adhered to one major thought—to set up a part of the proletariat on the basis of a revolutionary programme, to clear the minds of at least the vanguard from all ideological confusion . . . which hindered the development of the labour movement. (1935, p. 117)

Led by such a revolutionary party trade unions would become 'schools of communism', organisations which would serve to link the party with the masses (Lozovsky, 1935, p. 175).

It is well known that Lenin posed even more sharply the case for a revolutionary party which could '*convert* trade union politics into Social Democratic (Communist) political struggle . . . *utilise* the sparks of political consciousness which the economic struggle generates among the workers, for the purpose of *raising* the workers to the level of *Social Democratic* political consciousness' (Lenin, 1970, p. 177) (his italics). Thus, 'Class political consciousness can be brought to the workers *only from without*, that is only . . . from outside the sphere of relations between workers and employers' (Lenin, 1970, p. 182).

Gramsci also thought that trade unions were inherently conservative since they seek to further the interests of their members within the framework of existing class relationships, and by so doing recreate those relationships. Trade unions were for Gramsci essentially defensive institutions. He believed, however, that some forms of working class organisations could provide workers with the positive experience of initiating policies and practices. This would, in Gramsci's view, provide workers with the confident image of themselves as a potential ruling class. Guided by a revolutionary party Gramsci thought such experiences would enable workers to move on to the offensive in political struggle.

Corrigan (1977) has applied this perspective to an analysis of struggles around the question of social welfare: 'If the working class is to gain hegemony in this country, then it must learn to administer and formulate specific policies rather than allow the state apparatus to work out those specifics . . . In short the class has to build up within itself a form of alternative civil services that can formulate policy in great detail.'

This is fully in accordance with Marx's stress on the importance of working people schooling themselves in struggle, and developing their own class organisation by means of which the working class would emancipate itself.

We need to ask, along with Gramsci, if workplace experiences ever lend themselves to the development of a more positive, offensive form of class consciousness than that usually engendered in trade-union struggles. We also need to know how women's domestic experiences influence the development of class consciousness. To do this it is necessary to explore the process David Morgan has called 'alienation in reverse'.

ALIENATION IN REVERSE

The alienation experienced by houseworkers is closely tied to the privatised nature of that employment. Domestic work is cut off from public recognition, a point made by Littlejohn in his study of a rural community:

> A farmer can become known as a good stockman, a shepherd can become known to his fellows throughout Britain as an excellent craftsman, but no woman can become so widely famous as a good wife, mother and housekeeper . . . Woman's work is not publicly judged and priced every year as the man's is at the lamb and tup sales. (Littlejohn, 1963, p. 129)

On occasion women are able to demonstrate some aspect of their domestic skill in public, as in the case of the women discussed by Frankenberg (1976) as being united by gender—when they rather than their menfolk were asked to prepare the church for a harvest festival—and divided by class, when working class women cleaned the church while middle class women decorated the altar.

Yet the price for such limited recognition can be high in terms of hard labour. Norma Wade's mother was good at washing, but this only became known in Silverdale when she took on the washing for her son's football team. Sometimes, however, performing domestic skills publicly can be genuinely gratifying. Dilys enjoyed keeping the picket line supplied with food during the miners' strike:

DILYS: Two of us women did all the cooking. There's a kitchen down the Parksite club, and we used that you see. We made these big pans of soup, and filled flasks, and cut up sandwiches, things like that. I enjoyed it actually. And another thing I was involved with was cheap shopping. We went to all the supermarkets and got goods at trade prices, and then we sold them in the club to members at wholesale prices. (B3, p. 31)

But these moments are either exceptional or very marginal in terms of a redefinition of domestic work itself. After a period spent as a full-time houseworker the chief desire is often to escape into paid employment, which apart from having the advantage of social recognition offers semi-independence financially, company versus isolation, and involvement versus boredom.

David Morgan (1969) is alert to the restrictive nature of the domestic environment, and he attempts to situate the response of women workers to paid employment against this domestic background. He discusses their response in terms of the concept 'alienation in reverse':

The work experiences and expectations of women are different to those of men. This difference springs, in the case of women, from the expectation that the primary focus of her interest is in the domestic sphere. Thus even for the working wife or mother there is a decision whether or not to go out to work. For the majority of working men, no such point of decision arises.

The situation of home and work, corresponding roughly to the situation of female and male, are two sides of the same coin. If it is possible to see men as being alienated in the context of their work experiences (although alienation is not always seen just in terms of work experience) it is also possible to see women as being alienated in terms of their domestic experiences. Aspects of this domestic alienation include the relative degree of circumscription of the domestic and female roles, the separation of these roles from the work and male roles and the tendency for the 'real world' to pivot around the latter rather than the former.

As there is partial alleviation for the male, alienated in his work experiences, in his domestic and leisure life, so there is a partial alleviation for the female in the context of her work experiences. The work place becomes a context where there is potential at least for the development of relatively uncircumscribed expressive relationships and where domestic experiences can be carried over and transformed in the framework of these relationships.

This, in brief, is an outline of the ideas behind the theme of 'alienation in reverse'. (Morgan, 1969, pp. 6–7)

In terms of time-span a woman's main job in life is as employee rather than as mother and full-time house-worker. Approximately half of all women complete their families by the time they are twenty-six or seven. Sullerot (1971) summarises what this means:

When the youngest child starts school the mother has 40 years of her life before her . . . This is a truly revolutionary change; in the past woman has always been defined by reference to her maternal role, yet at present the years devoted to maternity hardly add up to a seventh of her total life span. From now on the longest phase in her life will be that which follows the completion of her family. (1971, p. 75)

In the light of this it might be thought that women see their role at work as their primary role, but this fails to take into account the effect the woman's domestic duties have on her position in the labour market, and the influence of the all pervasive 'woman in the home' ideology. I think at present most women put their domestic duties first. Even if this were not the case, if the focus of the woman's concerns were not primarily in the home, David Morgan's conception would not be invalid. If the woman's concerns were *more* focused on the home than the man's, it would be likely that this difference would influence her attitude towards social relations at the place of work.

David Morgan is mainly preoccupied with the rewards women have reaped at work in the form of sociability. My main interest concerns how the woman's place in the domestic sphere influences class consciousness in the industrial sphere.

PRODUCTION CLASS CONSCIOUSNESS

Women's desire to find satisfaction in the work experience finds expression in their concern with working conditions. A woman shop steward working for GEC in Stafford told me the following story which illustrates the point:

> In the paint shop last week they changed the paint. They couldn't get the usual one. The women came in and smelt it. They went through the whole day, it takes time, talking among themselves, 'How strong it is getting', and, 'How is it affecting you?' They built up a case among themselves. The next day when they came in they found it just as bad. By the time they got to the point of reporting it to me they knew how many felt sick, and for how long, how many had passed out, how many couldn't eat their dinner. They had a complete picture, which is very useful to have when you're going in to see management.
>
> They had reached such a pitch that management said, 'Yes we recognise the problem, it's terrible. Just stick it as long as you can, go out for fresh air any time you want. Have breaks at regular intervals (this was breaking the normal factory rules where you just have a ten minute break in the morning). Anyone particularly sick can go and lie down in the rest room.'
>
> But the women simply said, 'No. We're not working in it.' The men working nearby said, 'You can't be so unreasonable'. But the women still insisted that the smell had to be put right or they would go home. The management argued that their job was essential to the continuity of production. They still replied, 'We're not working in it'. The men walked away saying, 'They're irrational. They won't listen to reason.'
>
> After a bit management said, 'Alright, go home and we will pay you for the lost production. We will change the paint, and seeing as we are giving you this concession will you give it a try again tomorrow?' The women said that was fair enough, went home and got on with the jobs around the house. While they were at home they had had management running round like wild things. You wouldn't get that happen in a man's shop. I must say I'm proud of them for it! (Pauline Hunt, BSA, 1974)

It is useful to contrast this with the outlook of the chemical workers described by Nichols and Armstrong.

One of the men recalls that when he came to the factory a manager said, 'You've got to expect to put up with some shit you know. This isn't a sweet factory.' And the fact is that though they resent their conditions most men accept the logic of this . . . 'Nearly thirty-six quid a week. Flat money. So for me, coming from twelve quid a week to three times that amount I'm bloody glad of the job. You know, no matter bloody what' . . . A minority brag about the conditions they put up with at work. Many more experience a feeling of pride in having withstood what the world has done to them . . . But above all the Chemco workforce, at least for most of the time, is characterised by the fatalism of men who do not control nor see any way of controlling, the world in which they live. (1976, p. 49)

These men, and most workers, understand that their labour service is a commodity like any other, for which they can but do the same as any other seller—get the highest price. The employers' calculation, like any other buyer, is to pay the least possible. Marx and Engels first identified the impact on social relations wrought by capitalism which, 'put an end to all feudal, patriarchal idyllic relations ⋮ . . and has left remaining no other nexus between man and man than naked self interest and callous "cash payment"' (Marx and Engels, 1965, p. 43).

As productive workers in the home, women have been less subject to the full force of the calculative relations characteristic of capitalism. In terms of the development of class consciousness this is a drawback. It is, however, also an advantage in that it means that to some extent women have been less adequately socialised into seeing themselves as wage earners above all else. Audrey Wise has come near to expressing this distinction by arguing that when women work in industry they put up a struggle to stay human.

I would say that as a result of their caring for people, job in the home women may well return to work with a greater sensitiveness concerning capitalism's capacity to transform workers into the means to profitable ends. But this sensitivity is reinforced by another factor, noted in *The Sunday Times*: 'More women may be openly admitting what was true all along—that they work for their own satisfaction as well as for money' (*The Sunday Times*, 27 February 1977). Women workers tend to make more positive demands of their work situation than their male counterparts, and if one is concerned with working people having a greater say in running their own lives this tendency is advantageous. Women who are out to find self-satisfaction in their place of work can be more politically assertive than men who see their home as their haven, and who have dismissed industry as a place of self-fulfilment. It is precisely because women are alienated from the home environment that they are more likely to place greater, more positive, demands on the industrial environment.

The men who deplored the 'irrational' behaviour of the women in the paint shop were out of sympathy, not only with the women's concern with working conditions, but also with their obstinacy.

This obstinacy is partly due to inexperience. As more women come to hold office in the trade union movement, women in general may increasingly learn to play the game according to established rules. On questions of pay, political principles are less obviously involved, and on pay questions women are frequently more keen to reach a compromise solution than men. Sometimes, however, the question of a pay rise is seen to involve matters of principle. Rose gives an example:

ROSE: They were going to give us a rise on our bonus. If you were earning over a certain amount the rise would go on that. If you didn't get to bonus level you didn't get no rise. And we kicked against it. The comical thing was, those who didn't come out weren't on bonus. Most of the girls that came out were high bonus workers, who were wanting to get a share for the girls who weren't getting nothing . . . It's queer the things they will strike over. They'll come out in mass *if* there's anything wrong. You know, if the toilets are dirty you can back on it they're out. But otherwise it takes a hell of a lot to get them to move. (A3, pp. 30–1)

Questions concerning toilets become political if workers balance their treatment and the facilities provided against the profits being made from their labour. This frequently occurred during the Upper Clyde Ship Builders' work-in. To give but one example, a UCS steward commented:

They were always taking money out. If you go down where they work you'll see there isn't even a cloakroom for the workers' coats, or somewhere they can wash their hands . . . During the first five years of UCS they were paying out money as profits, which is ridiculous. (Pauline Hunt, Edinburgh, 1974)

Ordinary people have little control over their lives. (By 'ordinary people' I mean low-status white-collar workers and manual workers and the houseworkers in their homes. In short, the term 'ordinary people' refers to the Silverdale families here described and their social equivalents elsewhere.) They have little ability to determine their own purchasing capacity, or the type of products available for sale. The kind of instruction their children will receive in school, the skills they will be equipped with and the jobs they will enter, their control of these matters is strictly limited, as is their control over medical services, and their general environment. So long established is this lack of choice that it is not experienced as deprivation. People make few plans:

> What would you like to be doing in ten years time?
> 'Oh, I never think that far ahead.' (G3, p. 27)
> 'Working hard, just the same as I am now.' (I3, p. 24)
> 'I'm looking forward to a rest when I retire.' (C3, p. 48)
> 'Well in ten years the children will be grown up, and Joe and I will be able to go out on our own, whereas now we've always got the children with us.' (F3, p. 76)
> Do you have any ambitions about your work?
> 'Yes, to get a well paid job.' (F3, p. 53)
> 'Well, the only other job I could do is cleaning and I'd rather stay at Wedgwoods.' (G3, p. 22)
> 'I hated school, and I always wanted to work in the mill, 'cos I liked sewing, so I've been happy there.'(I3, p. 9)
> 'We were going to start our own little business, selling things like handbags and dresses, but then baby came.' (G3, p. 18)
> Do any of the political parties represent people like you?
> 'They're good liars, the lot.' (E3, p. 40)
> 'I was in two minds whether to vote. I think they're only out for themselves.' (I3, p. 17)
> 'If a black cat puts up for Labour I'd vote for it.' (A3, p. 30)
> 'I vote Liberal, but I get the impression it doesn't matter who's in power, we're not affected greatly.' (C3, p. 35)

Within their own organisations ordinary people do get a chance to expand their capacities and their horizons. In Silverdale this means, in the main, involvement in the Transport and General Workers' Union at shop floor level, and in the National Union of Mineworkers at pit level.

But as Gramsci said of trade union experience, 'In the trade union workers' solidarity was fostered by the struggle against capitalism in suffering and sacrifice' (*Soviets in Italy*). Revolutionary initiative is not generated in trade union struggle, which is essentially defensive.

In one aspect of her life Sarah did not feel inadequate:

SARAH: To think that I've produced gives me a lot of pleasure really. I've managed to produce children. This is something in itself. I don't think there are a lot of rewards in it really. There's a lot of heartache; but it is something I've done. (C3, p. 63)

Other women emphasised the weight of responsibility associated with parenthood:

NORMA: Colin was a naughty child. He clung all the time. But I thought, 'he's got to go'. And he used to peddle his bike along here when he was about two. And people would knock at the door and say, 'Do you know he's on the road?' 'Yes', I'd say, 'And if anything happens I've only got myself to blame! But I used to think, 'Am I doing right letting them play?' (H3, p. 33)

Dilys, like Sarah, saw parenthood as a creative experience.

DILYS: You worry about what your family is going to be like. But seeing the children grow up, and not having any problems, seeing each one make a life of their own, and seeing them make it work for themselves—this gives me a lot of satisfaction. (B3, p. 47)

Since women have more than their fair share of parenthood they also have more of the heartache and more of the satisfaction entailed in that experience. Women are also on the whole more involved than their husbands in the management of the home. This sometimes finds expression directly in the way they perform in the labour market. For example when Sarah started work in a bookshop:

SARAH: Soon after I'd started there this friend of mine, that I'd known over a number of years came, and we're similar types and a similar age. Well we sort of re-organised that shop. Jobs were done in an easygoing way, so we could re-organise in between, and we got certain jobs done at certain times of the day. I think I just carried on as if I was at home really. (C3, p. 57)

Women like Sarah return to work lacking self-confidence, but after they have found their footing these women have the challenging aspects of their domestic experiences to fortify them in the world of industry. They have more opportunity than most men to develop a sense of their own worth, and they often have a greater desire to find self-fulfilment in paid work.

These factors result in women being less adequately socialised into the ethos of capitalist industry. Their resulting behaviour sometimes seems audacious:

ROSE: Me dog had pups, and I had a couple of days off with her, you know. And I went to work and the boss says to me, 'What's been amiss like'. And I said, 'Well me dogs had pups'. He said, 'Christ Almighty! Don't have any cows off the field!' (Chuckles). (A3, pp. 50–1)

Which just goes to show that despite the line of argument presented earlier, Juliet Mitchell is right: sometimes, women don't have even divided loyalty.

Their involvement in domestic management gives women enough confidence to take matters into their own hands. This is evident sometimes in the behaviour of young women who have not yet started their own family, but who have undergone the lifelong pre-training for that role. Joyce Atkins, who was discussed in the previous chapter, describes an incident where self-help seemed called for:

JOYCE: When I first went to Wedgwoods conditions were much worse than they are now. In hot weather we sat with our feet in bowls of water. The girls were sweating and sitting with their feet in cold water. Fancy, putting people under a damned glass roof! I felt very very mad about it. And in the end I got on the glass roof, and I put wet clay on the glass roof to cut the sun out. Of course I got told off for that. I was really stripped off for messing the windows up. But the clay was left up there.

Such action is not in itself indicative of class consciousness. However, it does illustrate a point of view in which productive workers are felt to have rights, and sufficient self-assurance to take action in defence of those rights. If schooled in the class struggle this disposition can give the workers' movement a more assertive dynamic.

The opportunities for working people to appropriate a positive image of themselves are few indeed. The UCS work-in was one such opportunity. In this dispute the workers identified themselves as members of the socially useful class, whose interests coincided with the expansion and performance of 'their' industry. They contrasted their interests with those of private investors in the industry who seemed to be only concerned with a quick financial return, so that when 'quick returns' were not forthcoming, they were quite prepared to see the shipyards starved of capital and equipment, and to hell with the 'national interest' (Pauline Hunt, Edinburgh, 1974).

This kind of positive class experience was, Gramsci thought, necessary to the growth of revolutionary potential. He comments, 'For the individual worker the junction between the requirements of technical development and the interests of the ruling class . . . must be conceived as transitory . . . technical requirements can be conceived . . . in relation to the interests of the class which is still yet subaltern' (Gramsci, 1971, p. 202). To recognise that expertise is not the monopoly of the ruling class, Gramsci argued that the workers needed to mobilise the expertise of the whole workforce through the medium of the factory council. These councils would, Gramsci thought, enable the workers to develop new forms of government based on the workplace, which would, in embryo at least, be the foundation of a new social order.

Gramsci's ideas, it seems to me, are very relevant to the question, 'What are the preconditions for socialist revolution?' He has less to say about the actual seizure of power. As Gwyn A. Williams says, 'One sees the muscle. Where's the punch?' (1975, p. 155). The question brings us back to the necessary function performed by the revolutionary party in the co-ordination of the struggles, and the focusing of the movement on the seizure of state power.

Gramsci's writing does, however, enable us to recognise the political potential of certain features of contemporary society. One area of political potential identified here concerns the effect their work in the home has on the way women workers respond to paid employment. I have suggested that ex-full-time houseworkers seek self-satisfaction from their experience of paid employment, and that their management of domestic affairs equips them with skills that can be utilised in an attempt to expand their control of their industrial environment.

The question as to which struggles develop class confidence is wider than a consideration of industrial conflict alone. This question could enable us to situate the political importance of social movements outside industry itself. These movements are an integral part of the working class movement to the extent that they are concerned with extending control over the conditions for the reproduction of labour. For example, the various campaigns by women's groups to improve and extend social facilities, particularly in the areas involving the care of dependents and improved health facilities, are *class* campaigns outside of, but not unrelated to, the industrial sector. The women's movement to control fertility through the extension of contraception and abortion facilities represents a direct attempt to control an important aspect of the reproduction of labour power. The Claimants' Union, community food co-ops, and the organised defence of local facilities represent attempts by working people collectively to control their own lives.

These developments represent an enlargement of the possibilities facing working men and women. From taking defensive measures against the effects of capitalist social relations, working people on occasions, and perhaps increasingly, adopt offensive measures through which they can begin to shape their industrial, domestic and local environment. I have argued that married women who return to the labour market come with a pre-disposition to gain satisfaction from industrial work. As a result, although women as compared with men are less involved in the trade union movement, when it comes to offensive struggle at the place of employment women are likely to be as, if not more, assertive than their male counterparts.

The impact of working class struggle is not solely to be assessed in terms of the concrete improvements secured, but also in terms of an expansion of the workers' organising capacities, and in terms of their ability to relate their particular struggle to the struggles of producers in industry, and to the struggles of producers of labour in the home and community.

Since women employees are more immersed in the domestic arena than most male employees they are better placed than the latter to formulate demands which relate social concerns and industrial concerns. It was precisely the tendency to isolate 'society' and 'industry' as separate domains which Nichols and Armstrong (1976) identify as the major factor in the ideological inconsistency which characterised the class consciousness of the male working-class Chemco workforce. Women's involvement in the home and community as well as in industry may go some way to overcome such inconsistency. Sheila Rowbotham (1972) discusses the consciousness of women working in the national workshops in the 1848 revolution in France in these terms. Basing her account on the articles appearing in the socialist feminist paper *La Voix Femmes* she says:

> Nor did women confine themselves to the work situation. Again this indicated the interlocking nature of women's oppression. *La Voix Femmes* is full of all kinds of schemes for every aspect of life which affected women. In March 1948 women workers petitioned the Provisional Government for creches . . . The women suggested large houses, built in large gardens, for the working population in the area. These would contain a reading-room, bathroom, communal dining-room as well as a creche where the children would have 'enlightened care'. There would also be a school. The training of young girls and a medical unit are emphasized as well. (pp. 117–18)

Such historic episodes are exceptional. Nevertheless it is through the educative experience of this type of positive collective struggle that the fatalistic posture of the workers described by Nichols and Armstrong (1976) can be overcome.

4 Conclusion

One of the things I have been concerned with in this research is how individual and collective ideas influence individual and collective behaviour and, conversely, how individual and collective behaviour influences ideas. When an idea is held in common by a group of people, which has the effect of making these people unaware of the contradictions contained in their situation, the idea in question is an ideology. When people are unaware of the contradictions contained in their situation it becomes difficult for them to envisage things being other than they are; in this sense ideologies are inherently conservative. When a particular form of behaviour occurs on a wide basis it is a social practice; so, for example, the common tendency for married women to return to the labour market when their children start school is a social practice.

Two related ideological conceptions have been treated at some length in this work, namely the idea that in general the woman is the homemaker, and the idea that in general the man is the bread-winner. These ideological conceptions are, like all ideologies, based on social practice, that is to say, it is on the whole true that women in general take on the main responsibility of servicing their family and men in general provide the main financial support for their family.

Ideology is not, however, simply a summary of prevailing social practice. At an individual level ideology exerts an independent influence. For example, the personal practice of Peter and Mary Arnold conflicted with the ideology of man as family breadwinner, since Peter Arnold had retired and Mary Arnold worked part-time. Nevertheless, for both Peter and Mary men, by virtue of their role as breadwinners, dominated the world of industry, trade-unionism and politics. The Arnolds thought that this masculine dominance of the non-domestic world equipped men with the capacity and the authority to head their households.

Similarly, in the case of Pam and Bill Ross the conflict between the ideology of man as breadwinner and their own situation, in which for a time Pat earned more than her husband, left the ideology unscathed. In fact, the Ross's criticised their own practice because it did not tally with the ideology they both endorsed.

It seems to me that at least three factors need to be present for personal practice to undermine conventional ideology in the eyes of the practitioners. First, it seems necessary that the practice in question is shaped by conscious choice rather than the force of circumstances. Thus the enforced role-change of Michael and Susan Edwards (reported in the *Guardian* 21 November 1976) has, if anything, strengthened their commitment to traditional gender roles. Unable to find work, Michael stayed home to look after their flat and two children while Susan held down a low paid job in Lyons. Both bitterly resented their enforced role-change, and continued to direct their efforts towards finding work for Michael which would enable them to revert to their 'proper roles'.

By contrast Gill and Mark Carter, who chose to swap roles, feel relaxed with the minimal gender division of labour which characterises their home. Even so, in the Carters' situation external circumstances exert an influence. As well as being breadwinner Gill does as much work in the home as Mark, so that instead of being equally beneficial their overall arrangement seems to be somewhat weighted in Mark's favour. I suggested that the atypicality of Mark's willingness to stay home gave him a strong bargaining position which may go some way to explain his favourable circumstances.

Secondly, personal practice which conflicts with conventional ideology is more likely to weaken the hold of that ideology if the practice in question is widespread. Thus because it is usual for ex-full-time houseworkers to return to the labour-market, it is much easier for them to adopt many aspects of the employee role than it was for Michael Edwards to conform with the unusual role of man as full-time houseworker. In particular, ex-full-time houseworkers readily acquire an employee's attitude towards money; they are possessive about 'their' wages. The explicit nature of their possessiveness represents a reaction against their former experience of financial dependency, a dependency which previously had been more successfully concealed by the ideology of joint money. In this case a change in individual practice, which was in accordance with social practice, highlighted a contradiction previously more successfully hidden by an ideology.

At the same time the wage-possessiveness of ex-full-time house-workers reinforced the ideology that wages are payment for individual work. As was argued at some length, the socially productive nature of housework and childrearing is obscured by its privatised form of organisation. Housework seems to be beneficial as far as family members are concerned, but it is not seen as an indispensable contribution to the capacity to labour which is remunerated in the form of wages. As a result wages are seen, incorrectly, as having been earned solely through the efforts of the industrial worker. The contribution made by domestic work cannot be discovered simply through the experience of being a house-worker, because the social contribution of domestic work is concealed by the privatised form in which it is rendered. The social contribution of domestic work can be revealed only through the theoretical elaboration of the interdependence of domestic production and industrial production.

This brings us to the third factor: conventional ideology is undermined by conflicting social practice which is informed by theory. For social practice to be so informed the theory in question must be widely available and responsive to social practice. This raises the question of the theoretical and political adequacy of existing political parties and institutions, a complex question which has been touched on in this work only in passing.

A large part of this study has been concerned with investigating how behaviour reinforces, rather than how behaviour conflicts with, prevailing ideology. One example of conformity between behaviour and ideology discussed in the text was the tendency for families to reserve the woman's earnings for the purchase of items defined by the family as non-essential. This practice reinforced the ideology that the man rather than the woman provides the family with essential financial support.

In the childless homes of group one households there appeared to be more discussion, companionship and a willingness to share domestic tasks than in either group two or group three households. It may be that most households set out with a less rigid gender division of labour, but that in the course of passing through the experience of group two families, the roles of husband and wife become sharply delineated. Full-time houseworkers become almost totally responsible for childcare and housework, leaving the husband free to enjoy the home as a place for recuperation rather than toil. I suggested this was not simply because the houseworker was on hand in the day to do the work, but because housework was seen ideologically as personal service. The houseworker did not seem to have a real job, so it was difficult for the houseworker to insist that the wage-earner should work in the home when the wage-earner had already put in a 'more essential' day's work elsewhere.

To the extent that the different work-roles of the husband and wife have become entrenched during the group two period it will be difficult to break down the gender division of labour when the woman returns to the labour market. Obviously the ex-full-time houseworker stands to gain more from a fairer share-out of domestic tasks than does the breadwinner. The ex-full-time houseworker is, however, in a very weak bargaining position because in most cases it appears as though she chose to return to the labour market, and her job tends to be of secondary importance financially. The latter disadvantage partly results from the low-paid and insecure character of the female labour market. In practice the employed married woman tends to retain primary responsibility for domestic matters, and her husband retains primary responsibility for the family's financial support. The movement from a group two situation into a group three situation does little, therefore, to weaken the conventional ideology which defines gender roles.

The separation between industrial, public production and domestic, private production is the form the gender division of labour takes in capitalist society. This separation influences the outlook of workers. In the case of your workers I have suggested that the young working class woman's anticipation of her future immersion in family life serves to distance her from her initial industrial experience. She tends to pass the time at work, whereas her young male counterpart approaches work as a life project, central to his adult status and his future role as breadwinner.

More generally I have argued that both men and women see the family-unit as the site for the fulfilment of life-projects and consumption aspirations. The individual worker's involvement at the place of paid employment tends to be seen as a means through which finance can be secured which will enable the individuals to live a satisfactory life in the privacy of their families.

This conception of the personal and private nature of family life is illusory since domestic production is an integral part of social production. Nevertheless in terms of the houseworker's experience of her role the home emerges as a very privatised place. I have suggested this domestic isolation shields the full-time houseworker from the full force of instrumental capitalist relationships. When she returns to the labour market her inadequate socialisation into instrumental relationships becomes apparent. In particular, she often sees adequate and pleasant working conditions as a matter of workers' rights, that is, as a matter of principle, rather than as a matter for negotiation in the money-effort bargain.

This non-instrumental disposition is accentuated by another factor. Although women share with men the ideological conception of family life as a private, non-socially productive domain, their continuous and thankless labour in this domain encourages them to seek personal satisfaction outside the home. Whereas most working class men work in order to find satisfaction in their domestic and leisure life, and work in industry is seen as a means towards this end, their female counterparts work in industry to earn wages but also with a view to gaining satisfaction in the course of their employment. They therefore make positive demands in their industrial place of work, demands which are felt to encompass their rights as people, as ends in themselves. Furthermore, the challenging aspects of the domestic worker's role may give her more confidence in her ability to define her own objectives than is the case with her male co-workers, because they have had few opportunities to discover their decision-making capacities.

This assertiveness on the part of ex-full-time houseworkers, which in the text I call production class consciousness, could prove to be an asset in any movement aimed at increasing the workers' control of their work situation.

In part the ex-full-time houseworkers' assertiveness arises from their lack of familiarity with the procedures and attitudes of the trade-union movement. To the extent that the hitherto male-dominated trade-union movement embraces female participation, the spontaneity of production class consciousness may be somewhat curbed. Influence is, however, unlikely to be one-way only. As was noted, one effect of the increased unionisation of women over recent years has been to awaken in the unions a concern with working conditions in a broader sense. This finds expression in the interest in creche facilities shown by a few unions, and in the union movements adoption of the Working Woman's Charter.

In the future wage-earning women may find themselves increasingly drawn in to providing the basic financial support required by their family. If so they would become as tied to the role of breadwinner, and therefore to the industrial job, as their menfolk.

This is already the case in the sizeable minority of households where the woman is the main breadwinner or where her financial contribution equals the man's. In this case work outside the home is likely to be experienced less as a chosen release from domestic toil, and more as an unavoidable life sentence. Similarly men may become increasingly involved in childcare and housework on a continuous and expected basis. If so, for the man the home would then be like a second work place rather than a recuperation centre. This is, of course, already the case where the man heads a single parent household.

This prospect would seem to reduce the already meagre degree of free choice currently exercised by working class couples; albeit that the man's freedom is usually exercised at the expense of the woman's. It would also serve to dull the positive assertiveness ex-full-time houseworkers bring to the industrial work situation, which I regard as one of the most encouraging findings to have emerged in this study.

I do not think, however, that such a convergence of gender roles is likely to materialise in capitalist society in the foreseeable future. I am rather impressed with the overlapping social influences— socialisation into gender roles, the structure of the labour market, the privatisation of the houseworker's occupation, the strength of the ideologies which reinforce the cleavage between industrial and domestic production in the minds and practices of working people—which together re-create in daily life man as breadwinner and woman as homemaker. This conservative convergence of influences looks to me to be forbiddingly robust.

The situation is not, however, as I hope this study has shown, without its tensions and contradictions. I have tried to make personal experiences meaningful in terms of social processes, and conversely, social processes meaningful in terms of personal experiences. The bridging concept has been 'ideology', which enables one to situate behaviour within political and social structures.

The main findings of this research relate to the effect family privatisation has on class and gender consciousness and practice. The domestic use of money and the division of labour within the home were analysed in terms of the way these practices reinforce gender divisions. But implicitly the analyses contain pointers as to how, if the practices changed, opposite effects could result. Similarly, the finding concerning the assertive orientation to work characteristic of ex-full-time houseworkers contains pointers which could not only be developed into a more adequate theorisation of class consciousness, but could feed back into the Labour movement and the women's movement from which the original impetus to do this study came.

Appendix I

In an attempt to minimise variations based on region and occupation the people interviewed all live in Silverdale, an industrial village in North Staffordshire. The village has three distinct sectors—Parksite council estate, the old village and a modern private estate. The population of Parksite and the old village is almost exclusively employed in manual occupations. Mining is the dominant industry for men. In the main, women find employment in Rist's, Wires and Cables Ltd, a Lucas Company factory situated on the outskirts of Silverdale, in the pottery industry and as cleaners. The private estate has a much higher proportion of white collar workers.

Silverdale was chosen, not simply because it is conveniently close to Keele University, but because for several generations Silverdale men *and* women have worked for wages outside the home. In most other areas, in the course of this century, the widespread employment of married women has been a post-war phenomenon. One would expect that in an area like Silverdale, with an established history of married women's employment, the working class women would be less home centred than working class women in general. Yet in this study I argue that the Silverdale women are more ideologically and practically tied to the home than their menfolk. Although the groups of people studied here are very small, I would suggest that if these Silverdale women are primarily to be understood in terms of their domestic commitments, this is very likely to be true of working class women elsewhere. Furthermore I had some knowledge of the village as a result of my work as a WEA tutor-organiser in the area, and because as a preliminary exercise I worked for three months during the Christmas season in the Silverdale Co-op grocery shop, which is the main shop in the village. In addition, during the course of the research I lived in Silverdale for a few weeks.

In Group 1 four couples were interviewed together. It proved to be very difficult to find any young couples without children. I think couples may well start their families early, so that the childless period is very short-lived. Three childless couples in their thirties refused to participate. This may partly be due to the social stigma which childlessness attracts. J. E. Veevers, reporting on a study of fifty-five childless couples comments:

> All of the wives interviewed feel that they are to some extent stigmatized by their unpopular decision to avoid having children, and that there exists an ubiquitous negative stereotype concerning the characteristics of a voluntarily childless woman, including such unfavourable traits as being abnormal, selfish, immoral, irresponsible, immature, unhappy, unfulfilled, and non-'feminine'. (1974, p. 505)

Veever's subjects were self-selected, whereas I approached couples without children on the basis of suggestions made by people I had already interviewed in groups two and three. If couples in group one felt they would have to explain their childless state if they participated in this research it is not perhaps surprising that three couples of the seven contacted declined to take part.

I have included in group one an interview with a seventeen year old boy and a seventeen year old girl but, as will be seen in the text, when discussing teenagers I mainly rely on secondary sources.

With the exception of one couple, group two was contacted through women who came to shop in the co-op grocery during the period in which I worked there. The selection of subjects was not very systematic. In the co-op I was employed behind the wine and tobacco counter, and at Christmas time that is not a very peaceful place. Furthermore the wine and tobacco counter also serves as the village co-operative bank, and this service includes the administration of various Christmas clubs, all of which involved considerable paper work. This general workload meant that I contacted women on the infrequent occasions when I had a moment free. On such occasions I asked the nearest woman if she had dependent children and if she was at home full-time. If the answer was yes to both questions I subsequently asked her if I could visit her at home to talk about her daily life. No one refused, and when I had six I closed the list. In the course of interviewing I heard about a couple who had swapped roles; the woman goes out to work and the man stays home with their baby. I thought this atypical arrangement would be informative and included this couple in group two.

The husbands of two women in group two did not participate. Both of these men worked very long hours, one as a manager of a dairy, the other running his own grocery delivery service. With the exception of the couple who had swapped roles all the couples in group two were interviewed separately. This was because the women found it more convenient to be interviewed in the day time while their husbands were at work. By way of contrast all but one of the couples in group three were interviewed together in the evening after work.

The husbands of four women in group three failed to participate. In one case the husband was Czechoslovakian, and he felt his English was not sufficiently good. The other three husbands were reluctant to take part, possibly because the approach had been made through their wives, many of whom were contacted as they came out of the Rist's Wires and Cables factory. In the case of the three reluctant husbands I did not feel inclined to pursue the matter since I think this kind of enquiry does represent an intrusion into people's personal lives. On this point I share the view of Mrs Jones, described in W. S. Slater's poem 'The Proper Study':

> Seated before her window Mrs Jones
> Described the passers-by in ringing tones.
> 'Look', she would say, 'the girl at Number Three
> Has brought her latest boy-friend home to tea;
> And, see, the woman at the upstair flat
> Has brought herself another summer hat!
> Her daughter Daphne, filled with deep disgust,
> Expostulated 'Mother, really must
> You pry upon the neighbours? Don't you know
> Gossip is idle, empty-minded, low?'
> And Mrs Jones would murmer 'Fancy dear!
> There's Mr Thompson going for his beer!
>
> Daphne, an earnest girl of twenty-three,
> Read Sociology for her degree
> And every Saturday she would repair,
> Armed with her tutor's latest questionnaire,
> To knock on doors, demanding 'Are you wed?

Have you a child? A Car? A double bed?'
Poor Mrs Jones would remonstrate each week,
'Daphne, I wonder how you have the cheek.
And then to call me nosey!' Daphne sighed.
'Oh, will you never understand?' she cried.
'Mere curiosity is one thing, Mother:
Social Analysis is quite another.'

Although my insufficient cheek cost me some interviews it may have helped those who did take part to be more forthcoming. The reader will be able to judge the value of the verbal data collected since in the text I make fairly extensive use of interview material. This is not, however, a work of oral history. Interview material is used as illustration, and is subject to interpretation, and the quotations are selected on the basis of what seems to me to be of significance in terms of a theoretical conception of the role and consequence of the place domestic production occupies in society as a whole.

The use of verbal material here is different from the use made of such material in the work of Mary Chamberlain (1975). Apart from an opening chapter on facts and figures to do with Fen women, and a short introduction to each chapter, the work is entirely comprised of interview data, with hardly any attempt to structure the material theoretically. Furthermore no theoretical reason is given for the selection of topics—girlhood, school, marriage, work, religion, politics, recreation, outsiders, old age, each of which forms the subject of a separate chapter.

Although no work is without some theoretical perspective which influences the selection and presentation of material, Mary Chamberlain's book gives the impression of providing a record of what Fen women had to say about themselves. By contrast, in the work presented here the words of Silverdale people are used as a means whereby I can say something about them.

Where emphasis is found in the interview quotations it is always because the interviewee emphasised the point.

Altogether thirty-six people were interviewed in depth: ten in Group 1, twelve in Group 2 and fourteen in Group 3. The interviews lasted on average between two and three hours. All the interviews were tape recorded. Each taped interview was transcribed into long-hand and the pages were numerically ordered.

Chapter one in the main utilises Group 1 material, and chapters two and three utilise material collected in Groups 2 and 3 respectively.

In the following appendixes, I give details about the age, occupation, family size and residential sector within Silverdale for each interviewee. In order to enable the reader to assess the extent to which particular people have been quoted I have given each interviewee a code. The three groups are identified simply by the number 1, 2 and 3. In Groups 1 and 3 spouses were on the whole interviewed together, and the couple share an alphabetical letter. In Group 2 except in the case of Mr and Mrs Carter, the alphabetical letter refers to an individual. Thus, B1 refers to the second couple in Group 1, and B2 refers to the second person in Group 2, etc. After each code there follows a list of numbers which refer to the pages of that person's or couple's interview quoted in the text.

The object of providing this list of page references for each person or couple interviewed is to enable the reader to see at a glance the extent to which I have relied on some respondents in comparison with others. As you will see, a few individuals emerge as key informants who have been extensively quoted; notably Jean Spencer, Carol Parker and Janet Austin in group two, and Don and Rose Harris, Peter Dilys Lewis, Len and Sarah Wells, and Gladys Kohout in group three. The personal experiences of these key informants proved to be highly relevant in terms of the research questions being investigated.

The aim of the research has been to reveal complex social processes; to analyse the reproduction of a social situation that could be other than it is. Although I think the woman's focus on the home, ideologically and in practice, has the effect on consciousness identified in the text, this is not because the groups studied are to be regarded as representative in any statistical sense. The thirty-six people here studied were selected because their situation enabled me to explore the theoretical perspective outlined in the introduction and conclusion.

Furthermore, I have no doubt that in the course of talking with people I altered their perception of their own situation. To take but one example, Joyce Atkin at the end of a long interview commented that she had never talked so much. By encouraging Joyce to verbalise attitudes and experiences which otherwise would have remained unstated our talk had the effect of giving her attitudes and experiences a degree of consciousness and form they would otherwise have lacked. In my view this does not mean that her views as reported are less authentic because they have been mediated by the research experience. To me the research experience was a learning situation which to an extent helped to unveil aspects of reality which previously were hidden.

And this was as much a consciousness-raising experience for me as it was for some of the people interviewed. Although I started out with a general theoretical conception it took shape in the course of the fieldwork. The research findings are now part of my theoretical outlook, and I would now be unable to explain the one without reference to the other.

Appendix II

Code

A1   Jeff and Wendy James, born 1948 and 1949 respectively. Jeff is unemployed. Wendy works as a schoolteacher. No children. Village.

B1   Charles and Evelyn Munden, born 1936 and 1940 respectively. Charles works as a gardener. Evelyn works as a nursery nurse. No children. Parksite.

C1   Bill and Pam Ross, born 1925 and 1926 respectively. Bill has retired early from mining. Pam has retired early from factory work. No children. Parksite.

D1   Peter and Mary Arnold, born 1910 and 1916 respectively. Peter has retired from his job as a craftsman in the pottery industry. Mary works part-time as a cleaner. In previous marriages they have had eight children; they now live on their own. Village.

E1   George, born 1959. He works as an apprentice miner. George is single and childless. Village.

F1   Caroline, born 1959. Caroline is training to be a nurse. She is single and childless. Private Estate.

Interview pages quoted in Chapter 1

A1   42–3, 57–8, 1–53
B1   15–16
C1   1–19, 28–9
D1   32–3, 3–5, 36, 37, 34–5, 18–19
E1   3, 14–15
F1   15–16

Appendix III

Code

A2   Ann Tate, born 1943. Ann is at present a houseworker; she worked previously in an office.

B2   Michael Tate, born 1936. Michael works in the pottery industry. Michael and Ann have a one year old girl. Village.

C2   Jean Spencer, born 1936. Jean works as a houseworker, she has also worked as a factory and shop worker, a cleaner and barmaid.

D2   Paul Spencer, born 1919. Paul works in a maintenance job in a factory. Paul and Jean have nine children aged from one year to nineteen years of age. Village.

E2   Carol Parker, born 1940. Carol works as a houseworker, she worked previously in a factory.

F2   Alan Parker, born 1941. Alan works as a building worker. Alan and Carol have an 18 month old boy. Private Estate.

G2   Janet Austin, born 1950. Janet works as a houseworker, she worked previously as a receptionist.

H2   Andrew Austin, born 1944. Andrew works as a mining engineer. Andrew and Janet have two boys aged three years and six years. Private Estate.

I2   Joyce Atkin, born 1936. Joyce works as a houseworker, she worked previously in a factory. Joyce has two boys and two girls at school. Village.

J2   Maureen Clark, born 1940. Maureen works as a houseworker, she worked previously in childcare. Maureen has a two year old boy. Village.

K2   Gill and Mark Carter, born 1954 and 1953 respectively. Mark works as a houseworker, he worked previously as a miner. Gill and Mark have a one year old boy. Parksite.

Interview pages quoted in Chapter 2

A2	32, 35, 49–50, 37, 58, 42, 23
B2	25, 22–3
C2	55, 62, 75, 96, 91–2, 28–9, 83, 87, 65, 57, 78, 50–3
D2	15–16, 26, 24, 20
E2	49, 12, 17, 52, 62, 56–62, 44, 59, 61, 67–8, 27, 30, 69, 54
F2	17, 17, 16, 22, 9–10
G2	28–31, 17, 53–4, 56, 60, 57–8, 52–5, 57, 55, 43, 9–10, 54
H2	16, 15, 21–2, 20, 23, 20, 24
I2	46–7, 61, 59, 42–3, 52, 58, 1, 13–14, 27
J2	25–6, 15, 36, 54, 33, 53, 26, 27
K2	9–10, 5–6, 34, 26

Appendix IV

Code

A3   Don and Rose Harris, born 1931 and 1931 respectively. Don
      works as a miner. Rose works in a factory. Don and Rose
      have three teenage children. Parksite.

B3   Peter and Dilys Lewis, born 1926 and 1931 respectively.
      Peter works as a miner. Dilys works in a factory. Peter and
      Dilys have two teenage children at home. Parksite.

C3   Len and Sarah Wells, born 1932 and 1931 respectively. Len
      works in a Laboratory. Sarah works in a bookshop. Len and
      Sarah have three children aged eight to seventeen years of
      age. Village.

D3   Michael and Margaret Dean, born 1941 and 1945 re-
      spectively. Michael works as a self-employed painter and
      decorator. Margaret works in a factory. Michael and
      Margaret have one school-aged daughter. Village.

E3   Karl and Joan Witz, born 1923 and 1932 respectively. Karl
      works as a surface worker in the coal industry. Joan works in
      a white collar job in a factory. Karl and Joan have one
      teenage daughter. Village.

F3   Gladys Kohout, born 1943. Gladys works in a factory.
      Gladys has one school-aged daughter and one teenage son.
      Parksite.

G3   Sandra Mill, born 1941. Sandra works in a factory. Sandra
      has three school-age boys. Parksite.

H3   Norma Wade, born 1937. Norma works in an office. Norma
      has two boys and one girl at school. Village.

I3   Sonia Dale, born 1943. Sonia works in a factory. Sonia has
      two boys and one girl at school. Parksite.

Interview pages quoted in Chapter 3

A3   51–2, 18, 64, 39–40, 28–9, 57–8, 54, 72–3, 67, 68, 40, 43–4,
       75, 77, 77–8, 45–6, 48–50, 30–1, 30, 50–1

B3   60, 21, 54, 55, 30–1, 49, 44, 56, 34, 56–7, 57, 31, 64, 22, 22–3,
       23–4, 47

C3   38, 29, 48, 48–9, 58, 49, 65, 67, 66, 67, 55, 70, 30, 32–3, 31, 39,
       39–40, 38, 48, 35, 63, 57

D3   8, 15, 24, 17, 16–17, 25

E3   49, 9, 28, 54, 53, 17, 18, 40

F3   74, 50–1, 58, 8–9, 13, 13–14, 9, 73, 41–2, 76, 53

G3   3, 8, 34, 8, 19, 26–7, 27, 22, 18

H3   64–5, 27, 29, 33, 28, 45, 33

I3   16, 17, 24, 19, 17

Bibliography

Adams, Carol and Laurikietis, Rae, *Education and Work*, The Gender Trap, Book 1 (Virago, 1976).
——, *Sex and Marriage*, The Gender Trap, Book 2 (Virago, 1976).
Anderson, Perry, 'The Limits and Possibilities of Trade Union Action' in R. Blackburn and A. Cockburn (eds), *The Incompatibles* (Penguin Books, 1967).
Barnard, J., *The Future of Marriage* (Penguin Books, 1976).
de Beauvoir, Simone, *The Second Sex* (Penguin Books, 1972).
Bell, Colin and Newby, Howard, 'Husbands and wives; the dynamics of the differential dialectic', in Diana Leonard Barker and Sheila Allen (eds), *Dependence and Exploitation in Work and Marriage* (Longman Group, 1976).
Bennett, Arnold, *The Grim Smile of the Five Towns* (Penguin Books, 1975).
Beynon, Huw, *Working For Ford* (Penguin Books, 1973).
Bolton: Town Centre Map, Planning Consultant's Final Report (Shankland, Cox and Associates, 1965).
Braman, Olive, 'Comics' in J. King and M. Stott (eds), *Is this Your Life? Images of women in the media* (Virago, 1977).
Brown, Richard, 'Women as employees: some comments on research in industrial sociology' in Diana Leonard Barker and Sheila Allen (eds), *Dependence and Exploitation in Work and Marriage* (Longman Group, 1976).
Chamberlain, Mary, *Fen Women* (Virago, 1975).
Comer, Lee, *Wedlocked Women* (Feminist Books, 1974).
The Conference of Socialist Economics, (CSE) Pamphlet no. 2, 'On the Political Economy of Women'.
Corrigan, Paul, 'The Welfare State as An Arena of Class Struggle' in *Marxism Today* (March 1977).
——, *The Demand for Independence*, Discussion Kit, the Women's Liberation Campaign for Legal and Financial Independence (London, April 1976).
Davies, Ross, *Women and Work* (Arrow Books, 1975).

Dennis, Norman and Henriques, Fernando and Slaughter, Clifford, *Coal is our Life* (Tavistock Publications, 1969).

Durkheim, Emile, *Suicide* (London: Routledge and Kegan Paul, 1972).

Engels, Friedrich, *The Condition of the Working Class in England* (Panther Books, 1969).

Faulder, Carolyn, 'Advertising' in J. King and M. Stott (eds), *Is this Your Life? Images of women in the media* (Virago, 1977).

Firestone, S., *The Dialectic of Sex* (Cape, 1971).

Fleming, Suzie and Ronay, Esther, *Wages for Housework*, pamphlet produced by Power of Women Collective.

Frankenberg, R., 'In the Production of their Lives, Men (?) . . . Sex and Gender in British Community Studies', in Diana Leonard Barker and Sheila Allen (eds), *Sexual Divisions and Society: Process and Change* (Tavistock Publications 1976).

Freeman, Jo, 'The Social Construction of the Second Sex' in Arlene Skolnick and Jerome H. Skolnick (eds), *Intimacy Family and Society* (Boston: Little, Brown & Co., 1974).

Friedan, Betty, *The Feminine Mystique* (Penguin Books, 1963).

Gardiner, Jean, 'Women's Work in the Industrial Revolution' in Sandra Allen, Lee Sanders and Jan Wallis (eds), *Conditions of Illusion* (Feminist Books, 1974).

——, 'The Role of Domestic Labour' *New Left Review*, no. 89 (January–February 1975).

Goldthorpe, John H. and Lockwood, David, 'Affluence and the British Class Structure' *Sociological Review*, vol. II (1963).

Goldthorpe, John H., Lockwood, David, Bechhofer, Frank, and Platt, Jennifer, *The Affluent Worker; industrial attitudes and behaviour* (Cambridge University Press, 1968).

——, *The Affluent Worker; political attitudes and behaviour* (Cambridge University Press, 1968).

——, *The Affluent Worker in the Class Structure* (Cambridge University Press, 1969).

Gouldner, Alvin W., *Wildcat Strike* (Routledge and Kegan Paul, 1955).

Gramsci, Antonio, *Soviets in Italy*, Institute for Workers' Control, Pamphlet series no. 11.

Gramsci, Antonio, *Prison Notebooks*, Quintin Hoare and Geoffrey Nowell Smith (eds), (London: Lawrence and Wishart, 1971).

Hearn, Jeff. R., 'Toward a concept of non-career' in *The Sociological Review*, vol. 25, no. 2 (May 1977).

200 *Gender and Class Consciousness*

Hunt, Judith, 'Organising Women Workers', *Studies for Trade Unionists*, vol. I, no. 3 (W.E.A., 1975).

Hunt, Judith and Alan, 'Marxism and the Family' in *Marxism Today* (February 1974).

Hunt, Pauline, *The Development of Class Consciousness in Situations of Industrial Conflict* (Edinburgh University M.Phil. thesis, 1974).

——, *The Differential Response of Men and Women to Trade Unionism* (unpublished, BSA paper, 1974).

Jacobs, Jan, *The Death and Life of Great American Cities* (Penguin Books, 1965).

Kohlberg, Lawrence, 'A Cognitive Developmental Analysis of Sex-Role Concepts' in Arlene Skolnick and Jerome H. Skolnick (eds), *Intimacy Family and Society* (Boston: Little, Brown & Co., 1974).

Land, Hilary, 'The Myth of the Male Breadwinner' *New Society* (9 October 1975).

Lane, Tony and Roberts, Kenneth, *Strike at Pilkingtons* (Fontana, 1971).

Lenin, V. I., 'What is to be Done?' *Selected Works* vol. I (Moscow: Progress Publishers, 1970).

Lessing, Doris, *The Summer Before the Dark*, (Penguin Books, 1975).

Littlejohn, J., *Westrigg* (Routledge and Kegan Paul, 1963).

Lozovsky, A., *Marx and the Trade Unions* (Martin Lawrence Ltd, 1935).

Machie, Lindsay and Pattullo, Polly, *Women at Work* (Tavistock Publications, 1977).

Mann, Thomas, *The Magic Mountain* (Penguin Books, 1975).

Marx, Karl, 'Wages, Price and Profit' in *Selected Works of Marx, Engels* (London: Lawrence and Wishart, 1970).

Marx, Karl and Engels, F., *Manifesto of the Communist Party* (Moscow: Progress Publishers, 1965).

Mitchell, Juliet, *Woman's Estate* (Penguin Books, 1971).

Morgan, D. H. J., *Theoretical and Conceptual Problems in the Study of Social Relations at Work* (The Victoria University of Manchester (Ph.D. thesis) 1969).

Morgan, D. H. J., *Social Theory and the Family* (Routledge and Kegan Paul, 1975).

Myrdal, Alva and Klein, Viola, *Women's Two Roles* (Routledge and Kegan Paul, 1956).

Nichols, Theo, and Armstrong, Peter, *Workers Divided* (Fontana, 1976).

Oakley, Ann, *The Sociology of Housework* (Martin Robertson, 1974).

Oren, Laura, 'The Welfare of Women in Labouring Families: England, 1860–1950' in Mary S. Hartman and Lois Banner (eds), *Clio's Consciousness Raised* (Harper Torchbooks, 1974).

Rapoport, Rhona and Rapoport, Robert N. with Janice Bumstead, *Working Couples* (Routledge and Kegan Paul, 1978).

Rowbotham, Sheila, *Women, Resistance and Revolution* (Penguin Books, 1972).

——, *Hidden from History* (Pluto Press, 1973).

——, *Woman's Consciousness, Man's World* (Penguin Books, 1974).

Secombe, Wally, 'Housework under Capitalism' in *New Left Review*, no. 83 (January–February 1973).

Sharpe, Sue, *Just Like A Girl* (Penguin Books, 1976).

Skolnick, Arlene, *The Intimate Environment* (Boston: Little, Brown and Company, 1973).

Stacey, M., *Tradition and Change: A Study of Banbury* (Oxford University Press, 1960).

Sullerot, Evelyne, *Woman, Society and Change* (London: Weidenfeld and Nicolson, 1971).

Terkel, Studs, *Working* (Pantheon Books, 1974).

Veevers, J. E., 'Voluntary Childless Wives: An Exploratory Study', in Arlene Skolnick and Jerome H. Skolnick (eds), *Intimacy, Family and Society* (Boston: Little, Brown and Company, 1974).

Weir, Angela, 'The Family, Social Work and the Welfare State', in Sandra Allen, Lee Sanders and Jan Wallis (eds), *Conditions of Illusion* (Feminist Books, 1974).

Werneke, Diane, 'The Economic Slowdown and Women's Employment Opportunities', *International Labour Review*, vol. 117, no. 1 (1978).

Whitehead, Ann, 'Sexual antagonism in Herefordshire' in Diana Leonard Barker and Sheila Allen (eds), *Dependence and Exploitation in Work and Marriage* (Longman Group, 1976).

Williams, Gwyn A., *Proletarian Order* (Pluto Press, 1975).

Wilson, Elizabeth, 'Women and the Welfare State', *Red Rag* pamphlet, no. 2 (1974).

Wise, Audrey, *Women and the Struggle for Workers' Control*, Spokesman Pamphlet, no. 33. (n.d.).

——, *Women and Work*, a statistical survey, Department of Employment: Manpower Paper no. 9. (HMSO, 1974).

Women's Studies Group, 'Relations of Production: Relations of Reproduction' in *Cultural Studies* 9 (Spring 1976).

Women's Studies Group, *Women Under Attack*, special report by Counter Information Services, Anti-Report no. 15 (1976).

Young, Michael and Willmott, Peter, *Family and Kinship in East London* (Penguin Books, 1957).

———, *The Symmetrical Family* (Routledge and Kegan Paul, 1973).

Yudkin, Simon and Holme, Anthea, *Working Mothers and their Children* (Sphere, 1969).

Zaretsky, Eli, *Capitalism, the Family, and Personal Life* (Pluto Press, 1976).

Index

Adams and Laurikietis, 3, 25, 124, 125, 198

advertising, and women, 25

affluence, contradictory aspects of, 165

alienation, 60, 95, 127–8

alienation in reverse, 168–70

Anderson, Perry, 33, 198

authority, changes in, 153

authority, of men through money, 148

baby, 55
  battering, 54
  care for, 19, 55–6
  effect of arrival of, 37
  effect of, on leisure, 50–2

bank accounts, joint, 38–9, 44

Barnard, J., 71, 198

Baumann, Zygmunt, 113

de Beauvoir, Simone, 99, 198

Bell, C. and Newby, H., 67, 198

Bennett, Arnold, 39, 198

Bethnal Green, 144

Beveridge Report, 84

Beynon, H., 165, 198

bingo, 140, 143, 145, 153

birth control, 31, 111

Bolton Town Centre Report, 92, 198

boss
  case of wife as, 29ff.
  coming to dinner, 24, 49
  man in the home, 18
  woman as, 148

boys
  job preferences, 21, 22
  natural characteristics, 9
  necessity to toughen up, 11
  roughness of, 9–10
  segregation from females, 11

suitability of cooking as activity for, 10

tasks in home, 15–16

Braman, Olive, 14, 198

breadwinner
  and houseworker ideology discussed, 180
  as determinant of family time-table, 48–52
  implications of role summarised, 26–36, 47, 52
  implication of woman as, 45, 138
  in childless couples, 26–36
  must be man, 28ff, 120, 123
  power of, 80–1
  spending rights of, 40–1

breadwinning
  as male responsibility in London, 23
  distinguished from homemaking, 15, 47

Bronfenbrenner, 10

Brown, Richard, 2–4, 161, 198

bus problems, 91

Caird, Rob, 120

Capitalism, 1, 32–3, 122, 131, 172, 176

career
  as non-career, 128, 133
  choice between family and, 26
  marriage seen as, 24–5
  of woman, abandoned, 23
  opportunities for men and women, 125–39

car workers, 165–6

Census, 103

Chamberlain, Mary, 79, 190, 198

childbearing
  as ideological turning point, 100

childcare, 53–7
  and working women, 89
  as interference with housework, 65
  as making return to work possible,
    102
  husbands' attitude to, 68–70
  see also baby
childhood
  and gender socialisation, 7
  historical differences, 15–19
childless couples, 26–36
childlessness, 30–2
child minding, 88
child rearing
  not seen as socially productive, 106
  private nature of, 106
children
  as threat to freedom, 31
  care of pre-school, 87
  characteristics of male and female, 9
  earnings of, 17
  effect of having money, 54
  hatred by society of, 91
  postwar indulgence towards, 19
  removal into care as sanction, 86
  subordinate position of, 17
  tasks of, 15–16
  violence towards, 17, 54
  women's primary responsibility for,
    54, 68–9
class
  consciousness, 171–9
  position and gender, 9
  struggle
    and community organisation, 178
    and trade union consciousness,
      167
    inevitability of, 37, 131
    isolation of women from, 70, 153
cleaning cooker, 107–8
clothing
  expenditure on, 38–9
club
  as man's world, 139–41
club and pub, 139–42
Coal is Our Life, 63, 110, 134, 199
collective action
  family seen in contradiction to, 33
Comer, Lee, 38, 137, 149–50, 198

comics, 14
communism, 94
Conference of Socialist Economists, 85–
  6, 198
consciousness raising experience of research, 192
Conservative Party, 94, 96
consumption, inadequate basis for
  family studies, 6
Contract of Employment Act, 1972, 121
conversation
  and gender, 26–7, 134
cooking, 58–9, 75–6
Coote, Anna and Laura King, 22
Corrigan, Paul, 167–8, 198
courtship, 34–5
crèches, 161

Davies, Ross, 3, 198
day nursery, 87
decision-making processes, isolation of
  women from, 99
decorating, 108, 127, 153
deferential worker exemplified, 96
Demand for Independence, The, 84–5, 198
Dennis, Henriques and Slaughter, 63,
  110, 134, 199
Department of Employment, 102
Department of Health and Social
  Security, 85, 116
dependency, 37–47
  as explanation of gender roles, 68
dishwashing, 61–2, 63
division of labour, 47, 48, 67–72
domestic capacities, surveillance by
  state, 87
domestic science lessons, 20
domestic work
  and wage work, differences sum-
    marised, 82
  as backstage activity, 104
  as experience, 72–83, 104
  as personal service, 111
  shared, 29, 32, 107, 148
double production process, 4, 67–8, 153
drink, problem of finance for women,
  47, 140
drinking as form of male social control,
  141

dual role, 3, 67–8, 106–15, 153
Durkheim, 8, 199

earnings
    case of female's greater, 28
    of children, 17
    secrecy about, 152
    use of woman's, 118, 149–50, 151,
        156, 182
employees as unisex, 2
employment
    as escape from house, 78, 168–70
Engels, F., 146–7
equal pay, 156
    opposed by women, 30
    related to work segregation, 104
    seen as degrading, 28
Equal Pay Act, 104–5, 161–2
expenditure
    men's final say in, 26
extended family
    as facilitator of work, 102
'extras', 118

family
    and collective action seen in con-
        tradiction, 37
    and individualism, 37
    and industrial spheres distinguished,
        32, 37
    as market for consumer goods, 33
    as privatising agent, 34
    as scene of sexual exploits, 133–4
    authority in, 146–55
    business, 48
    continuity of residence, 66
    finance and work ideology, 115–23
    in relation to production, 1
    isolation from public life, 99
    job redistribution in after childbirth,
        106
    life and the state, 83–101
    limitations of, 146
    planning, 31, 111
    reproducer of social relations of pro-
        duction, 9
    seen as consumption collective, 48
Family Income Supplement, 47, 84

father
    behaviour of, 110
    childcare role of, 50, 53, 55, 58
    concern with gender training, 10
    dependence on and rebellion against,
        44
Faulder, Carolyn, 24, 199
feminist writers, impact of, 3
financial dependency, 37–48
    following motherhood, 37
financial equality
    lack of effect on gender roles, 18
Firestone, Shulamith, 2, 11, 35, 199
Fleming, Suzie and Esther Ronay, 43,
    199
food, convenience, 58–9, 67, 112–13
    preferences, 58–9
Foy, Helen, Corinne Hutt and Stephen
    Tyler, 87
Frankenberg, R., 143, 168, 199
Freeman, Jo, 10, 199
Friedan, Betty, 1–2, 199
friendship, 142–6
    class content of, 145
    differences between men and
        women, 145

Gardiner, Jean, 1, 67, 70, 112, 199
gender
    and class position, 9
    and contradiction domestic and in-
        dustrial production, 34
    as social not biological fact, 8
    deviation, tolerance of, 14
    divisions, impact on industry, 6
    divisions, impact on Trade Union
        policies, 6
    identity and sex role, 8
    sociologists ahistorical assumptions
        about, 8
    specialisation, attempts to break
        down, 10
    training, father's excessive concern
        with, 10
    training, parents' great concern for,
        11–12
gender role
    and conversation topics, 26–7
    and window cleaning, 24

gender role (*contd*)
  embedded in practices, 63
  engendered by dependency, 68
  expectations at work, 14
  ideology of, summarised, 33–4
  swapping, 83, 146–7, 181
girls
  general characteristics, 9
  helpfulness of, 19–20, 75–6
  job preference, 21–2
  marriage as objective for, 24–6
  tasks, 15–16, 110
  work in home, 19
goals, masculine, 11
Golding, John, M. P., 130
Goldthorpe et al, 6, 95, 166, 199
Gouldner, Alvin, 159, 199
Gramsci, A., 167–8, 175, 177, 199
grandparents
  and childcare, 102
Guardian, The, 25, 88, 92, 136, 181

Hearn, J., 128, 199
holidays, 51, 72–3, 92, 118, 120, 128, 150
home
  and work, 106–15
  and work, separateness of, 24
  as place of work, 49
  bedrock of women's experience, 99
  comforts, consumer and producer, 50, 52–67
  making, distinguished from bread-winning, 15
  restriction of women to, 52ff
  work, advantages of, 69, 72
hospital treatment, effect of, 59, 60
house
  ownership of, 127
  purchases for, 41
household, types of, 4
housekeeping
  money, 39–40
  standards of, 61–7, 114–15
housewife
  as encompassing role, 135ff
  diaries of, 72–3, 74–5
housework
  and childcare, 57

as basis of industrial production, 67, 71
  as personal service, 60, 70–1
  continuous nature of, 76
  monotony of, 78
  privatisation of, 103
  standards of, 63–5
houseworker
  and breadwinner, ideology discussed, 180
  defined, 5
  dependence of, modified by work, 150
  lack of individuality, 81
  position of, summarised, 82
Hunt, Judith, 103, 158, 200
Hunt, Judith and Alan, 8–9, 200
Hunt, Pauline, 100, 171, 173, 177, 200
husband
  as *helper* in domestic work, 107
  authority of, 99
  capacity to earn money dependent on women, 67
  catering for preferences of, 58
  definition of good, 20
  dependency of, 59
  earnings of, and necessities, 118
  financial characteristics of, 42
  in different kinds of household, compared, 112
  involvement in domestic work, 60
  lack of domestic standards, 63, 123
  opinion of, as authority, 66
  picking up after, 60–1
  relatives of, as reference group, 64
  service to, 57–61
  traditional view of, upheld, 71
  world view, woman's dependence on, 67

ideological conceptions, importance of, 4
ideology, 47
  and family, 7–36
  and practice, 182–3
  contradiction with social practice, 29
  defined and discussed, 180
independence of women, 45

individualism
  and family, 33
industrial and family spheres, distinguished, 37, 71
industrial production, dependence of, on housework, 67, 71
Industrial Relations Act, 1971, 121
industrial sociology, male ethos of, 2
industrial workers, domestic commitments of, 3
inequality, basic, 41–2
ironing, 16–17, 45, 56, 114
isolation of women, 65–6, 79, 91

Jacobs, Jane, 90, 200
job
  marginality of wife's 112
  redistribution in family, 106, 112
jobs
  interfered with by domestic duties, 125
  men's and women's compared, 80, 108–9
  preferred by girls and boys, 21

Klein, Josephine, 200
Knight, Pat, 102, 161
Kohlberg, L., 7

labour market
  and sexual apartheid, 103
  obstacles to women in, 3
  position of women in, 83, 122
labour movement, 128–35
Labour Party, 93–4, 96, 98, 131–2
labour power
  as commodity in relation to housework, 114
Labour Research, 87, 122
Laing and Esterson, 15
Land, H., 116, 200
Lane and Roberts, 165–6, 200
Lawrence, D. H., 38
leisure, 49–52, 141
  as related to husband's work, 49
  women's home based, 49
Lenin, 167–8, 200
Lessing, D., 135, 200
Liberal Party, 94

Littlejohn, J., 168, 200
Lozovsky, A., 168, 200

Machie and Patullo, 3, 200
Mack, Joanna, 88
magazines, 24
male, *see* boy, husband, man, men
man
  as houseworker, 41
  significance of work, 27
Mann, Thomas, 77, 200
Marketing Magazine, 42
marriage
  as ending individual lifestyle, 80
  as making oppression appear private, 35
  as male benefit, 71–2
  as objective for girls, 24–6
  as turning point for women, 35
  tension in, arising from gender roles, 127
Marx, K., 166–7, 200
Marx, K. and Engels, F., 172, 200
maternal world, entry into, 81
maternity, significance of, 99
mealtimes, 49
men
  activities of, seen as more challenging, 13
  as active and assertive, 8
  as bosses in home, 18
  as controllers of pursestrings, 41–2
  as holders of authority, 27
  as supervisors, 19
  freedom to go out at will, 53
  household work by, 68, 123–4
  inadequacy as housekeepers, 62, 123–4
  jobs, at home, 108–9
  lacking anxiety about housework, 62, 123–4
  shopping, 42, 47
  tied to work treadmill, 45–6
  miners, 28
  attitudes to women of, 135
  mining, 143
Mitchell, Juliet, 155–6, 176, 200
money, 37–47
  as source of authority, 148ff

money (*contd*)
  considered more private than love, 37
  handling as an index of household relationships, 37
  'our', as myth, 149
  women's access to, 38
  women's use of their earned, 118, 149–50, 151, 156, 182
Morgan, D., 15, 35, 38, 168–9, 170, 200
Morning Star, 102, 120, 160–1
mother-daughter involvement, 66, 144
mother, respect for, generation not gender, 18
Myrdal and Klein, 3, 200

nappies, 19–20, 54, 56, 75, 148
National Assistance, 85–6
National Opinion Poll, 111, 116, 119
National Union of Mineworkers, 128, 158, 160, 162, 174
neighbours, 144
New Earnings Survey, 120
New Society, 88
Nichols, Theo and Peter Armstrong, 95, 130, 161, 166, 171–2, 179, 201
'non-careerist', 128
nursing, 25–6, 29

Oakley, Ann, 57, 201
occupational choice
  women's lack of, 124
Oren, Laura, 1, 201

parenthood
  contradictory aspects of, 175
Parksite Estate
  described, 90
  lack of public buildings in, 143
Parsons, Talcott, 8, 66
part-time work, 120–2, 124, 126, 162
perspectives on future
  lack of, 174
photographs, as reminders of better days, 58
picketing, 130, 163, 169
pin money, 118, 156

pocket money, 17, 18, 21, 42, 152, 153
  lack of, by women, 43, 46
political attitudes, 96
political parties, 93ff
politics, 27
  women's relative ignorance of, 97
pottery industry, 27, 88–9
poverty
  differential impact on men and women, 46
  effects of, 92
prams, 72, 92, 110, 148
pre-school childcare, 87–8
prices, 93
private life
  separate from public, 99
production
  impact on gender of industrial/domestic division, 6
  integration of domestic and industrial, 4
  of meals, 59
pub
  as man's world, 140
pushchairs
  attitudes of men to, 69–70
  problems of transport, 91–2

racism, 95, 96
Radio Solent, 91
Rapoport and Rapoport, 3, 201
Rathbone, Eleanor, 86
Redhead, Brian, 88
Redundancy Payment Act, 1965, 121
research, as consciousness raising experience, 192
retirement, 4
revolutionary party, need for, 177
role reversals, 83, 146–7, 181
romances, 35
Rowbotham, S., 1–2, 4, 70, 76–7, 91, 179, 201

Scargill, Arthur, 94
school, 54
Secombe, Wally, 60, 68, 201
self employment
  and domestic cooperation, 48
self help, 176

Sentinel, 136
Sex Discrimination Act, 161
sex role *see also* gender role, socialisation
    and gender identity, 8
sharing
    experiences with other women, 81
    genuine, 152
Sharpe, Sue, 13–14, 21–2, 24, 201
shiftwork, 132–3
shipyard workers as males, 2–3
shopping, 90–1, 113–14, 169
    as women's work, 21, 47–8, 108
    men and, 42–3, 47
shopwork, 124
Silverdale described, 90
single parents, 102
sissies, 11, 13–14
Skolnick, Arlene, 66, 201
Slater, W. S., 189
socialisation
    indirect, 20
    into adult work, 14–26
    into gender roles, 7
    process described, 9–14
social policy
    and women, 84ff
social security, 163
sociologists
    advantage over officials, 37
    as part of outside world, 38
son
    as extension of father, 13
Stacey, M., 21, 135, 201
state
    and domestic norms, 85–6
    and family life, 83–101
    surveillance over domestic capacity, 87
strikes, 94–6, 117, 129–30, 158–9, 162–8
structure
    of family in relation to other structures, 6
Sullerot, E., 8, 142, 170, 201
Sunday Times, 35, 42, 83, 111, 116, 119, 172
survey
    conducted by *Woman's Own*, 97–8
    general limitations of research by, 43

Tagney, Joy, 88
Terkel, Studs, 65–6, 201
theory
    importance of, to workers, 166–7, 182
The Times, 136
tomboys, 13–14
trades union, 33, 94–6, 98, 100
    and women, 155–68
    as career alternative, 129
Trades Union Congress, 158
trade union consciousness, 162–8
Transport and General Workers' Union, 174

unemployment, 41, 83, 120
Union of Post Office Workers
    male bias in, 161–2
Upper Clyde Shipbuilding, 2, 173, 177

Veevers, J. E., 32, 188, 201
Vincent, David, 86

wage, 68
    dependence of domestic workers on, 150
    how determined in Britain, 105
    labour, 1
    lack of, leading to being uninteresting, 81
    possessiveness of working women, 149–50, 151, 182
    secrecy about, 152
    system
        as reinforcement of ideology, 151
        ideological effects summarised, 82
        impact on family, 48
    women's as contribution to living standards, 118
work
    and domestic work, summarised, 82
walking out, difficulties of, 154–5
washing, as paid work, 16–17, 113
weekend, differential experience of men and women, 109
Weir, Angela, 1, 201
welfare
    agencies, arrogant enquiries, 37

welfare (*contd*)
  and class struggle, 167–8
  and humiliation, 163
Werneke, D., 121–2, 201
Whitehead, Ann, 141, 201
wife *see also* women
  as boss of household, 110
Williams, Gwyn A., 177, 201
Wilson, Elizabeth, 84–6, 201
window cleaning and gender roles, 19, 24
Wise, Audrey, 105, 160, 172, 201
Wollstonecraft, Mary, 1
woman's career abandoned, 23
Woman's Own, 97, 126, 138
women
  and advertising, 24
  and skilled employment, 52, 103
  and social policy, 84ff
  and trade unions, 155–68
  and work, seven compared, 89
  as militant unionists, 157
  as savers, 47
  as secondary work force, 83, 86
  as wage workers, 102–79
  dependence on husbands' world view, 67
  home based leisure of, 49
  isolated from decision taking, 99
  lack of individual identity, 47
  lack of knowledge of husbands' union, 97
  lack of knowledge of politics, 97
  loneliness of, 52–3, 65
  position in labour market, 103
  responsibility for children, 175
  responsibility for household cleanliness, 61

spending rights of, 38
under capitalism, 1
Women and Work, 121, 201
Women in Politics, 98
Women Under Attack, 103, 105, 113, 117, 121, 162, 202
Workers' humanistic approach, 171ff
workers, segregation of, 104
Women's Liberation Movement, 4, 13, 26, 30, 98
  seen as threatening, 31
Women's Studies Group, 44, 202
work
  and home, separateness of, 24
  as exempting *men* from housework, 20
  at home, 23
  attitudes of men and women to, 119
  expectations of men, 115–16
  experience of women seen as transitory, 99–100
  part-time, 120–2, 124, 126, 162
  role expectation by gender, 14
working-class childhood, historical differences, 15–19
working conditions, women's concern with, 171, 173
Working Women's Charter, 184
workload
  inequality of, 109

Young, M. and Willmott, P., 6, 144, 202
Yudkin, S. and Holme, Anthea, 102, 202

Zaretsky, E., 99, 202